Managing the Marketing Functions

Managing the Marketing Functions

The Challenge of Customer-Centered Enterprise

Stewart A. Washburn, CMC

Consultant to Sales and Marketing Management

McGraw-Hill Book Company

New York   St. Louis   San Francisco   Auckland
Bogotá   Hamburg   London   Madrid   Mexico
Milan   Montreal   New Delhi   Panama
Paris   São Paulo   Singapore
Sydney   Tokyo   Toronto

Library of Congress Cataloging in Publication Data

Washburn, Stewart A.
Managing the marketing functions: the challenge of customer-centered enterprise/
   by Stewart A. Washburn.
   Bibliography: p.
   Includes index.
   1. Marketing--Management. 2. Sales management. 3. New products-
Management. I. Title.
HF5415.13.W267 1988
658.8--dc19   88-14828
ISBN 0-07-068441-3   CIP

1234567890   DOC/DOC   8954321098

ISBN 0-07-068441-3

Portions of the volume have appeared in different form in the following copyrighted publications: *Business Marketing Magazine* and Dow
Jones–Irwin's *Sales Manager's Handbook* and the same publisher's *Marketing Handbook*. Their permission to reprint here is acknowledged with
thanks.

*The editors for this book were William A. Sabin, Jim Bessent, and Caroline
Levine, the designer was Naomi Auerbach, and the production supervisor was
Richard Ausburn. It was set in Baskerville by the McGraw-Hill Book Company
Professional and Reference Book Division composition unit.*

Printed and bound by R. R. Donnelley & Sons.

*For more information about other McGraw-Hill materials,
call 1-800-2-MCGRAW in the United States. In other
countries, call your nearest McGraw-Hill office.*

Contents

Preface   ix

1. The Challenges from the Environment
   in Which We Sell   1

Part 1   Markets and Marketing Organizations   23

   2. Seven Markets and How They Work   25
   3. Market Segments, Secret Dreams, and Market Niches   49
   4. The Functional Responsibilities of Marketing   63
   5. How Organizations Grow and Develop   83
   6. Advertising & Sales Promotion   95
   7. Developing an Effective Marketing Organization   111

Part 2   New Products—The Dimensions
          of the Challenge   125

   8. Developing Guidelines for New Product   129
   9. Finding New-Product Ideas in the Marketplace   145
  10. Conducting Market Audits and Market Research   157
  11. Selecting New Products for Development and
      Launching Them Successfully   165

Part 3   Successful Pricing   177

12. Market-Centered Pricing Challenges   181
13. Establishing Prices to Recover All the Costs   187
14. Trade Practices as Occasional Causes of Price
    and Profit Erosion   201
15. Pricing on Value: Nearly as Much as the Traffic
    Will Bear   205
16. Rational Responses to Competitive Pricing Situations   211

Part 4   About *Salesmen*   219

17. The Sales Force and Corporate Culture   221
18. What Salespeople Do   225
19. What Salespeople Don't Do   239
20. Converting Leads into Customers: Using the
    Telephone to Sell   255
21. Motivating the Sales Force Without Spending Money   273

Part 5   Measuring Marketing Effectiveness
            and Productivity   289

22. The Sales & Marketing Effort as a
    Measurable Process   293
23. Measuring Marketing Effectiveness to Establish
    Policy and Allocate Resources   301
24. Measuring Sales Effectiveness for Operational Control   309
25. Measuring the Performance of the 25 Functional
    Marketing Responsibilities   321

Part 6   Putting It All Together   331

26. Goodbye to Planning and All That   333
27. Improving Marketing Effectiveness   351

Index   357

Preface

It has become clear to me over the years that many of the people I meet and work with in the field of marketing share a rather surprising characteristic. They know a great deal more about effective marketing than they realize or than the results they achieve in the marketplace would suggest. It should not come as a surprise that people in marketing—in business in general—know more than they think. We are all active buyers in three markets. We buy consumer packaged goods, consumer durable goods, and services of all kinds. And in business, if we are not active buyers in the four industrial markets, we are at least keen observers of them since they affect our jobs.

In other words, we know from personal experience what it takes to move products and to make customers happy with what they have bought. Yet despite this sure knowledge and our very certain instincts, we adhere to traditional ways of doing business that don't work. We follow constrictive, academic precepts which also don't work and are even counterproductive in today's competitive markets.

The opportunities for improving this situation fall into six broad areas. How to manage these opportunity areas is what this book is about.

Markets and marketing organizations. Organizations have to match the markets they serve. The requirements of the seven common markets are all quite different and cannot be served by a one-size-fits-all organization. Furthermore, each market has its own pattern of growth and development. Marketing organizations must accommodate these differences too. This section, then, provides guidelines for adapting your organization to better serve your markets.

New product development. Here there are many concerns. Some new products help a firm grow and develop; others will cripple it. Since most new products grow out of the needs of the marketplace, it is essential to know which will succeed. How to distinguish the winners from the losers is the main objective of this section. Market research and launching procedures are really much simpler than they have been made to appear.

Pricing. The concerns in this area are for a simple system of pricing which makes it easy to ensure profits, control costs, and handle competitive situations. And it is important to know how pricing challenges vary from market to market and how trade practices can erode profits.

Sales and the sales force. Most sales forces are outside the corporate culture and are often in conflict with it. How to resolve this problem is one of the subjects of discussion here. In addition, many traditional concepts of sales need revision. All of the frontiers in sales have not been exhausted. This section will show you how to get better perfomance out of your sales force by introducing some new frontiers in the field of sales. For example, it is possible to motivate without money. It is also possible to sell high-ticket capital equipment by phone.

Measuring effectiveness. There is more to measurement than rewards and penalties. For many of the 25 marketing functions, there are no established ways of measuring performance. *Managing the Marketing Functions* helps solve the problem of measuring how well you're doing. You should also know about the three sets of measurement goals and how to keep them separate: measuring for operational control, measuring to set policy and allocate resources, and measuring to find out what is possible.

Planning and implementation. Traditional planning methods have become ineffective. Strategy has become a mere buzzword. Effective alternatives must be developed, and we must find a process for achieving continuous, incremental improvement. This section addresses these problems and offers realistic solutions. It helps you avoid overplanning, planning for the impossible, and helps overcome barriers in putting plans to work.

Finally, all of these marketing opportunities must be managed in an environment that continually presents new challenges. *Managing the Marketing Functions* sets out to create that environment, one that will stimulate your marketing creativity and put you on the road to improving your business's vitality.

This volume has been a long time in creation, and the ideas it contains have survived some rigorous analysis, both formal and informal. It's one thing to help clients solve problems in face-to-face consulting situations.

It's another thing entirely to try to accomplish such problem solving with a book.

The major sections of the book originated in a series of talks to the Industrial Marketing Group of the Boston Chapter of the American Marketing Association. Although not a supercritical group with which to work, in their gentle but clear-eyed and tough-minded way, they helped me clarify my thinking on many important issues covered in these pages. Many of these talks were reported in AMA's *Marketing News*, and this brought additional reaction and opportunities to refine my thinking.

Then there were the workshop-seminars, a series of early morning breakfasts at which I subjected the ideas expressed here to the practical scrutiny of several CEO friends and acquaintances.

Each section of the book has also been read and critiqued by a group of colleagues, other consultants like myself who specialize in the sales and marketing areas, as well as by a client group. Some portions have appeared in print, principally in *Business Marketing Magazine* and in chapters of the sales and marketing handbooks of one of the major business publishers. This exposure, of course, brought further comment.

The final manuscript was read by Nancy R. Cirillo of the College of Arts and Sciences, the University of Illinois, and by Richard J. Olsen of Applied Business Research. I very much appreciate their valuable comments.

Otherwise, it has been me and my typewriter, both working under the watchful eye of Marvin Raeburn, my partner in many enterprises, whose editorial questioning is the best around.

Stewart A. Washburn

Lakeville, Massachusetts

Tis impossible to save people against their own will; and we have been too much engaged in Patchwork already.

J. SWIFT

1

The Challenges from the Environment in Which We Sell

"Consumption is the sole end and purpose of all production; and the interest of the producer ought to be attended to, only so far as it may be necessary for promoting that of the consumer." ADAM SMITH

A good place to start is at the beginning, and any way you care to look at it, the beginning, 1776, was a great year.

In Quincy, Massachusetts, Abigail Adams brewed up her best batch of beer ever. Her husband, who would have been most able to appreciate the accomplishment, unfortunately, was in Philadelphia busy with other things.

In Philadelphia, Thomas Jefferson wrote the *Declaration of Independence*.

And in Kirkcaldy, Adam Smith finished the *Wealth of Nations* and with it wrote the charter for marketing people ever since.

It is now over two centuries later.

The Adams tradition of fine brewing continues through the efforts of the Koch family, themselves brewers for over 150 years. The irony is that in this era of women's liberation, the label on the bottle celebrates Samuel, merely an experienced tosspot, and not Abigail, the skilled brewer.

Jefferson's work still makes tyrants tremble and scares the hell out of a lot of others, too. However, his ideas, which used to be our greatest export with ever-expanding markets on all continents and among all peoples, are not being pushed much anymore. Our other products don't seem to do very well in overseas markets either.

And as for Adam Smith, well, that's what this book is all about.

Once again, this is what he wrote: *"Consumption is the sole end and purpose of all production; and the interest of the producer ought to be attended to, only so far as it may be necessary for promoting that of the consumer."* We seem to have lost sight of this admonition.

Frankly, these are very strange times. If Adam Smith were alive today, he'd be spinning in his grave.

The eternal verities don't seem to be so everlasting any more and not so true either.

Consider this.

The Davis Cup is in Sweden. The Stanley Cup is in Canada. And, the America's Cup was lost to Australia and barely rewon.

Five years after World War II, the United States had about 40 percent of the world's manufacturing capacity. In the mid-eighties, the figure stood at a little better than 20 percent. Separate national markets are coalescing into strong regional competitors. First came the European Common Market, and more recently a similar development got under way in South America involving Argentina, Bolivia, Brazil, Paraguay, and Uruguay. And the nationalistic producers of the Orient are just now beginning to cooperate in small areas.

During the same period, manufacturing dropped from 30 percent of our gross national product to a bit over 20 percent.

By design and default, we seem to have exported our manufacturing jobs and continue to do so. Our trade deficits run into the billions of dollars each month.

Caterpillar tractors are now put together with bits and pieces from Korea, West Germany, and Norway.

Stereo and hi-fi equipment, which used to be an American specialty—remember H. H. Scott, Harmon-Kardon, Fisher, to name just a few—now all comes in from overseas. Nothing is made in the States anymore.

Even tennis rackets have been taken over by offshore producers. In a very strange move, Wilson, Prince, and Spaulding subcontracted their manufacturing to the same Taiwanese firm, Kunnan Enterprises. After getting the hang of its customers' technologies, Kunnan moved ahead of them with a superior racket of its own, the Pro-Kennex, which is now a major seller in the U.S. tennis market.

Detroit, once the pride of each patriot's devotion, has become a distributorship for automobiles designed in California and either made in Japan by the Japanese or in the States under Japanese management. Recently, Korea, too, has become a supplier to Detroit.

Even that most American device of all, the computer, is assembled from bits and pieces manufactured in Korea, Taiwan, El Salvador, Portugal, the Philippines, Malaysia, Singapore, Indonesia, Japan, and Hong Kong.

Alarmists worry that we are becoming a service economy and, with no manufacturing base, will eventually become a banana republic, a vassal state to others with design and manufacturing capability. And there is much to support this view. For example, during the period from 1965 to 1985, the number of people involved in sales and marketing went from 25 percent of the work force to nearly 36 percent with *no* comparable growth in the gross national product.

There is another sign of the times which many find disconcerting. A growing, thriving middle class has always been the hallmark of a healthy economy and especially of the American economy. Yet for the past decade or so our middle class, however defined, has been decreasing and at an accelerating rate. At the same time, the number of the wealthy and of the poor is increasing.

There are many indicators of this change, but two in particular will amply illustrate this trend. A generation ago, only 14 percent of a middle-class family's income was required to support a mortgage for a typical American home. Now the cost has risen to 40 or 45 percent of income. Further, those working at the minimum wage can at best earn $6700 over the course of a year. The poverty level for a family of four in the United States is $10,990. The number of wage earners in this latter group is growing.

To some this is a temporary phase; they believe that the trend will reverse itself as we work our way into global markets. Others see this change as irreversible and a sign that we are converting into an old-fashioned banana republic with a two-class society, the very wealthy and a broad-based peonage.

Other observers, not quite on the edge of alarm, are merely concerned by the export of manufacturing jobs. They take some comfort from an annual real growth in manufacturing or blue-collar productivity of about 3 percent.

However, as blue-collar productivity and real output grow, white-collar productivity seems to decline by a percentage point or two each year even as the white-collar work force grows by 5 percent annually.

Thus, while we manage small increases in real growth or blue-collar productivity, we continue to export manufacturing jobs and accept the unproductive growth in white-collar employment.

It is a very curious situation for which a number of explanations have been offered, most of which are less than convincing.

Challenges and Distractions
in the Environment

There are serious challenges in the environment in which we design, manufacture, and bring products to market. All have a very real component which has become exaggerated to the point where challenge is all we see.

Take taxes for example; nobody likes to pay taxes and the effort to reduce taxes on industry is continuous. However, in the slow-growth mid-eighties, the tax burden on industry amounts to only 12 percent of the federal income. This is about half of what it was in the high-growth sixties when taxes on industry contributed a full quarter of federal income. Coincidentally perhaps, over that same period, confidence in American business leadership as expressed by an American Enterprise Institute Poll, dropped from 55 to 16 percent.

The prowess of the Japanese is enormous, but they are not invincible. Offshore labor is cheap, but more goes into a high-quality, marketable product than just labor.

It has been proposed that our current difficulties are due to the fact that our economy is in a state of transition. Indeed it is, but it always has been. Transition does not necessarily preclude growth and health; in fact, more often than not these factors are encouraged by transition.

Taxes, the Japanese, the state of the economy—these seem to be the big environmental factors. They get most of the attention and carry most of the blame for the fix we are in.

However, a number of other factors are at work in the environment, which may be less obvious but surely are more pernicious and subversive. A quick look at these challenges and distractions will provide a useful background for the discussion that follows.

Japanese Prowess

We marvel at the Japanese. We are astonished by quality control so exacting that vendors ship directly into customer's stock with no need for any inspection whatsoever. We marvel at production scheduling so finely tuned as to thrive on just-in-time delivery which reduces work-in-process inventories to a minimum and eliminates both materials buildup and machine downtime on the production floor.

Yet the techniques that permit these accomplishments are American. The quality assurance methods that make shipping to stock possible were outlined by W. Edwards Deming in the late twenties and early thirties, and the ideas were not exclusively his.

These techniques work for the Japanese. Maybe they don't work in this country. For example, on January 25, 1986, a Saturday, the business pages of the daily papers carried a notice that General Motors had recalled 400,000 1984 2.5-liter four-cylinder engines because the engine blocks could crack.

A simple measure of management's interest in quality is the use of consultants specializing in quality control and quality assurance. According to Rath & Strong, Inc., in the mid-seventies, the market for these services began to dry up. By '79, it was completely dead. It began to turn around in 1980 and now is quite vigorous.

Mr. Deming has said that quality is 85 percent a management problem and only 15 percent a labor problem. What do the Japanese know that General Motors doesn't?

Shipping to stock has been a requirement in many parts of our economy for nearly a century. The idea is commonplace for ready-to-wear clothing, grocery products, and consumer packaged goods. A defective light bulb is almost unheard of. What happened to the automotive industry?

Just-in-time delivery, the other Japanese marvel, is also an American commonplace. For example, in most major metropolitan markets, restaurants are supplied each morning and each afternoon with the required prepared vegetables and salad greens ready for cooking or tossing. Ready-mix concrete trucks provide an even more visible example.

Perhaps the supreme example of just-in-time delivery was the construction of the Empire State Building. For this effort, the next day's steel requirements were shaped in Pennsylvania, shipped at night to the New Jersey meadows, and delivered as needed the next day to the construction site. As a result, no traffic problems on New York City streets were caused by this effort.

The logistics genius responsible for this feat was James D. Farley who subsequently became Roosevelt's Postmaster General and after that ran Coca-Cola's export business.

Statistical quality control and just-in-time delivery are not the only American business techniques that the Japanese have adopted. Early in 1985 Japan's Sanko Steamship Company, the world's largest tanker operator declared bankruptcy.

Alcoholism, suicide, severe neuroses, and other stress-related ailments are common among Japanese managers.

The Japanese are not invincible.

But they are patient. They can wait several years for a payoff and seem to be satisfied with a lower rate of return than we.

And, Japan seems to understand the necessary relationships among manufacturing, technology, and product quality. We put Japan in the consumer electronics business by subcontracting manufacturing to them, by letting them master the technology and, eventually, by letting them establish quality standards. By subcontracting the manufacturing, we gave up mastery of the technology and with it the market.

But beyond these things, which the Japanese seem to understand better than we do, there is something else that sets them apart. Through their Ministry of International Trade and Industry, they have a strategy which guides their use of resources and a trade policy which mobilizes and subsidizes industrial potential to secure domination in overseas markets. It is the modern, trade equivalent of the Tanaka Memorial which directed its military expansion in the thirties and forties.

Japan's first target was steel production, which it came to dominate in the years immediately following World War II. Korea seems to have taken the play away from them on the basis of labor costs. Japan now exports technology and steel mills.

It next took consumer electronics away from us. It seized control of the technology and has dominated this market ever since.

Then came automobiles. After a couple of false starts Japan captured over 20 percent of the U.S. market. Now Korea is moving in on the market. So, Japan exports its manufacturing management know-how and operates plants in joint ventures with Detroit. And in Korea, Mitsubishi owns a large stake in the Hyundai auto works.

Similarly, Japan has taken strong positions in textiles, 35-mm cameras, machine tools, hand tools, and earth-moving equipment.

Now it is moving in on the microelectronics and semiconductor industries, and is buying market share.

A memo from Hitachi to its North American representatives is often quoted in the trade press. "Win with the ten percent rule. Find Advanced Micro Devices and Intel Sockets. Quote ten percent below their prices. If they requote, go ten percent again. Don't quit until you win."

The technique works both ways. And a number of U.S. firms with good understanding of their costs have been able to drop their prices and play Pearl Harbor with the Japanese.

Japan is certainly not invasion proof. A newly formed chain of American-style discounters called NIC's Supershops (NIC for newly industrialized countries) has upset Japan's traditional patterns of distribution. This chain makes TV sets, toys, cameras, and radios from Korea, Hong Kong, Singapore, and Taiwan available at bargain basement prices. And the O'Day 30-foot sloop, slightly modified to beat Japanese customs requirements, enjoys brisk sales to the Japanese upwardly mobile technocrats.

Even so, the Japanese are formidable competitors who appear to succeed by complete control of basic technology, mastery of production, and the provision of very high quality.

With all this, Japan has amassed enough capital to have purchased

New York City's Rockefeller Center and the Hotel Algonquin and to have become the low-cost lender of working cash to American municipalities. Indeed one firm, Nomura Securities, finances fully one-third of the entire U.S. national debt.

Having said all this, and in fairness, it should be pointed out that Japan's economic success is not entirely due to policy and to having won, by default, the use of American technology and our quality assurance and scheduling techniques. Less than 30 percent of Japan's industrial work force are the tenured employees of the big firms that get all the publicity. The balance, over 70 percent, work at barely subsistence wages for the vendors who ship to stock, provide just-in-time delivery, and maintain a large part of the inventory. Piecework and kitchen assembly are the rule.

It's a situation that brings to mind the conditions that prevailed in our garment industries before the great strikes of 1909 and 1910 and the Triangle Shirtwaist Fire of 1911.

Ultimately, Japan's strength seems to come from its helots. This was so as it went from Manchuria to Hiroshima. It seems to be so today. Incidentally, it is curious that the current division of work comes close to the time-honored military three-to-one (75 percent–25 percent) ratio— three civilian workers to support each soldier, three helots for every tenured employee.

There is a good chance, however, that Japan will be brought down by other economies with cheaper labor rates and more dedicated managers—by Korea, perhaps, or Taiwan.

Until then, perhaps our best long-term strategy against the Japanese is to foment an old-fashioned, American, we-hold-these-truths-to-be-self-evident revolution.

Cheap Offshore Labor

The General Agreement on Tariffs and Trade (GATT) which the United States signed just after World War II comes in for its share of credit or blame for the current situation. GATT generally supports free trade and discourages import restrictions. All other things being equal, goods made in areas where the labor rates are low have an advantage.

In 1961 Mexico began its Border Industrialization Program to let the United States open factories within its boundaries and take advantage of low Mexican wages. These *maquiladoras* now produce 40 percent of the products the United States imports. The attraction is obvious. Mexican wage rates are lower than those of either the Far East or of the Caribbean. They are bested only by the rates paid to the captive labor of the Japanese.

The advantages of low labor rates are clearest when commodities are involved. For example, common sheet steel fetches about $550 per ton in U.S. markets. Made in the States by U.S. Steel or Bethlehem Steel, the labor content is about $300 per ton. However, when made in Japan, the labor content is only about $70 per ton, and in Korea it is down to only $20 per ton.

This is the reason U.S. Steel gives for taking the money earmarked to improve its Geneva Mill just outside Provo, Utah, and investing it in Texas Oil and Gas.

Clearly, many United States firms see this as a no-win situation.

This view, however, is not shared by all.

Some minimills look at this situation as a challenge. Their position is simple. They are in the steel business and are going to remain in it. On this basis, they have revised the way they make steel so that now, while the Japanese require only 2.3 labor-hours per ton of steel, U.S. requirements are now down to 1.8 labor-hours per ton.

In the mid-sixties, Lionel Trains moved its production to Japan only to bring it back after just a few months. In 1983 it tried Mexico, and in 1985 came back. U.S. production was better and cheaper.

By following a "manufacture and sell where the imports ain't" policy, the American textile industry is working itself back into vigor and health.

Even the electric hand-tool market, so long the domain of imports, is beginning to yield to domestic products. For example, *Fine Woodworking* magazine reports that Porter-Cable's Orbital Sander is the equal of or better than any import and costs less than some and not much more than others. Domestically produced tools in other categories are getting the same ratings.

One more example.

When Victor Kiam acquired Remington Products, all its razor production was handled overseas. Only the finished product was assembled at Bridgeport. Now, there is no overseas production. Everything is made in the States. The razor does very well in the marketplace. Its market share was 20 percent when Kiam acquired the company; it's now 40 percent.

Whether it is steel or electric razors, it is clear that there is more to competitive offerings than just low labor rates, no pension liabilities, very slim benefits packages, and no EPA regulations.

A Transitional Economy

It is commonly believed that a major cause of our economic ills is the fact that our economy is in a transitional state. Although there is no apparent reason why an economy which is changing cannot also be healthy, in some eyes, it can't be so.

There is general agreement about what the economy is changing from. Some describe the economy we are abandoning as product- and production-oriented—an economy in which one can produce for inventory with some assurance that a continuing, stable demand will keep working that inventory down. Plants and equipment have been designed and scaled to support this kind of production. Operating philosophies have evolved to match, long runs of standard products where economies of scale come into play.

Over the past couple of decades, however, the demand has not proved as continuous and as stable as would be required to support such an economy. Yet old ideas die slowly. During the mid- and late eighties Detroit continued to build automobiles at a rate necessary to satisfy a market 20 to 25 percent larger than in fact it was. Layoffs became commonplace, payables increased, inventory carrying charges mounted, and prices began to deteriorate. General Motors, for example, managed to move inventory, but it had to underwrite sales with 2.9 percent financing, nine points below bank rates.

The change in the economy is not from a product- and production-based economy to one of two or three other possibilities. Rather, it is a change from a commodity-based economy to a specialty-based economy in which short runs and flexibility take the place of long runs and economies of scale. The emphasis has shifted from manufacturing to the customer. Many firms find it difficult to make the transition.

The concept of the change from a commodity to a specialty economy is a very difficult one to absorb. Petroleum products, wheat, steel, sorghums, and textiles have long since been recognized as commodities. Their specifications are well known, and it is a matter of indifference what their source may be.

The problem comes in also recognizing that automobiles, printed circuit boards, telephone equipment, and high-performance time pieces have also become commodities. It is a notion that is hard to accept.

Most vocal commentators on this change, therefore, fix on one or more of its significant aspects, ignoring the real underlying transformation. They discuss a change to a service economy, an information economy, or a marketing economy.

What is meant by a *service economy* is clear: an economy in which, round-robin fashion, each one takes in the next one's wash. Such an economy is perfectly satisfactory so long as—to continue the analogy—the manufacture of soap and scrubbing boards accounts for at least 25 percent of our gross national product and has a healthy export market.

What is meant by an *information economy* is less clear since there is no apparent agreement on the meaning of information. To some, information refers to all the bits and pieces of data which modern computer technology makes it possible to collect. However, odds and ends of data don't become information until someone puts them into a usefully organized form where they can guide understanding or action. Others take a more cosmic and idealistic view of information and envision an economy based on wisdom, experience, and knowledge.

The idea of a *market* or *marketing economy* should be a little clearer to most of us. It simply means an economy based on discovering and satisfying the needs of potential customers.

Let me cite three situations which may point up the differences between the three options: the service, the information, and the market economies.

In the few years that lawyers have been permitted to advertise, some have become quite adept at using the media. Their message is that, in addition to doing wills, divorces, and corporate mergers, they also have the knack of turning minor complaints into major lawsuits. The profession claims to be horrified at such commercialism.

However, consider this.

The 1981–1982 changes in federal tax laws were significant enough to require that from one-half to two-thirds of all unprobated wills be reviewed. Of these, probably half should be rewritten.

Yet to my knowledge and that of a dozen or so colleagues, no attorney that we know of—including our own—has contacted any clients to suggest such a review.

Is this a service problem, an information problem, or a marketing problem?

Then we have the telephone company, or what's left of it after six operating groups were spun off. It, AT&T Information Systems, owns the telephone companies' installed equipment. Some of this equipment is being phased out. The old-fashioned key-set equipment, the phones with the six light-up buttons along the base, are too expensive to maintain. Further, replacement parts are becoming more and more difficult to obtain.

The key-set equipment is being replaced by the new Merlin system, which is virtually maintenance-free, is readily expanded, and generates a much more satisfactory income at lower rental rates than does key-set equipment.

Yet, few customers know of Merlin's availability. I, for example, learned about Merlin during what had become a semiannual replace-the-circuit-boards visit by the friendly individual who services my telephones.

Once I knew about the equipment, it took five phone calls and a visit to the telephone company office to find out the details of the equipment. Then three more calls were required to get the new equipment installed. While this was going on, other vendors were offering me equipment quite similar to Merlin at what, at the time, seemed favorable rates. (I am curious to know how they found out that I was in the market for new equipment.)

The telephone company, with complete and detailed information on all its equipment by user and location, has made no effort to contact any of its key-set customers. Yet, curiously enough, the company representative, who eventually made the arrangements for my equipment, said they were all under great pressure to replace key-set equipment with Merlin.

The telephone company, apparently, lucks onto replacement business while its competitors aggressively seek it out.

Is this a problem of service, of information, or of marketing?

One more example.

Within 60 miles of my desk are seven national sales offices I know quite well. Each has a stack of unfollowed-up inquiry cards over 5 months old. The last pile I counted contained 43 leads. There were 12 bingo cards and 31 letters. The sales manager proudly gave me the stack to go through and told me how many millions in potential volume the stack represented. He said nothing about when these inquiries would be followed up.

Is this a problem of service, information, or marketing?

From all this, I conclude one thing: The economy is changing. Not many are doing much about it, and those who are doing something about it are doing quite well.

Misleading Measures—Biased Scorekeepers

The economy is news these days, and the press is full of stories about American business. Even the television networks and local stations now have business editors.

A firm cannot release its quarterly figures, announce changes in senior management, or field a new product without it becoming a news story. The bigger the firm, the bigger the story.

The drill is always the same.

The reporter gets the public relations release and telephones an analyst at a brokerage house for an opinion. The analyst, in turn, pontificates on—some would say, *speculates* about—the meaning of the announcement. The analyst discusses earnings per share, return on equity, and the possible effect of it all on the price-to-earnings ratio.

The importance of these numbers is confirmed by the fact that they wind up in *Business Week*'s annual Corporate Score Board.

A story will be written. People, including management, will read it or hear and see it on television. Share price on the market may change. People will buy, hold, or sell.

If everyone wants to buy, management are heroes. If the action is in the other direction, management are bums. There are other consequences, too. The value of its treasury stock goes up or down affecting an asset of the firm, occasionally a very sizable one. Management commences to think about the next announcement and how it will affect the behavior of its shares on the market.

The cycle is repeated with modifications. Eventually, the analyst's recommendation will change from sell to hold or from hold to buy or the recommendation will go in the other direction. After several cycles, the CEO will address the analyst's luncheon club to prove, demonstrate, and show why the CEO's firm should be the market's next favorite.

Before long, the focus is on the behavior of the firm's stock on the market rather than on the behavior of its products in the marketplace. Management is evaluated more for its ability to maintain or increase share value over the short term than for its ability to run a business profitably over the long term. Short-term feats of financial hocus-pocus draw enormous applause.

CEOs are encouraged in this by examples from on high. For over 20 years, even the Presidents of the United States seem to have been more concerned with a favorable image in specific situations than in overall, long-term accomplishments.

The name of the game has become, "make the numbers."

As a result, management is suckered in by commission agents and speculators—who will make it either way—and by the favorable write-ups in the press. On this basis, management fiddles with volume and/or cost figures just to keep the applause coming. Quality standards are relaxed just a little so that volume shipped can go up just a little. Service and warranty and guaranty support are also relaxed a little, too, so that costs can come down just a little.

Thus the numbers are made. And too many firms now float in the quiet backwaters of their industries, along with styrofoam, empty bottles, and other dead fish.

They are the wrong numbers.

I couldn't care less about return on equity, all by itself. I also want to know about return on total capital employed, debt as well as equity. It is a much more important number, which is why it is used by large firms to measure the performance of their subsidiaries.

Volume is a nice thing to know but I want to go beyond mere numbers. Market share may also be an interesting number, but other things are much more important.

What is the customer base like? It is easier and cheaper to keep an old customer happy than to find and develop a new one. We age receivables; why not customers as well?

The product base is another important aspect of volume. How much volume is generated from products that are more than 10 years old and how much from products less than 5 years old or, even, less than 3?

It would be nice to know how much was being invested in research and development and whether depreciation was actually a reserve for new equipment or merely a tax offset against income.

Who generates volume is another important consideration. How are sales divided between commission agents and salaried salespeople? How much by territory people and how much by inside telephone sales representatives?

I want to know something about the backorder situation and about how many new products are out for trial and testing with new customers.

Further, there are analogous aspects of the costs of producing goods and running a business that need exploration, to say nothing of such old-fashioned concerns as working capital and "quick" and "current" ratios.

Running a business for long-range health and profitability is enough of a challenge without adding to it the glitzy, show business task of keeping several classes of equities flying high over the exchanges. Circumstances, however, force some to play both games.

Contagious Hype

There is an old principle of economics which says that bad coinage will drive out good coinage. The principle is attributed to Thomas Gresham, a banker, textile magnate, and merchant who was England's fiscal agent on the Continent in the late 1500s. It means, simply, that if I have two silver dollars in my pocket, one fresh from the mint and the other worn, clipped, or plugged, I'll put the good one under the mattress and spend the other. Indeed, why not?

If a vendor will accept less than full weight of silver in payment for a purchase, why should I even think of offering full weight? Gresham used this idea to fill the Royal Treasury and to make himself rich.

The same kind of thing is happening in the way products are offered to customers. The advertising for most consumer products which most people are exposed to is pure hype. The reason given for buying most consumer products has very little to do with the quality or efficacy of the product being offered.

Pepsi moved ahead of Coke in market share—big news when it happened. Pepsi stole the march on Coke, not because of its advertising but because Coke made an egregious marketing blunder when it scrapped old Coke and introduced new Coke, thereby offending its established customers.

Blue jeans are sold through extremely suggestive advertisements featuring seminaked maids and striplings wearing, what else, only a pair of jeans.

For the past 2 or 3 years, patent medicine houses have sold their cold remedies on television through domestic dramas featuring all-knowing mothers and husbands who were cry babies or idiots, or both. As a result, my medicine chest contains Actifed or Sudafed—both seem to work—because an ex-astronaut said one of them worked for him in outer space.

It is proposed that middle-aged Americans buy certain production model American cars because that is the sure way to win the awe and respect of the young—Dad! You with a Pontiac whatever-the-hell?

Certain industrial products available through mill supply houses are sold with pictures of chesty blonds. And the telephone company encourages my patronage by offering discount prices on products for the home and office which I neither need nor want. I have accumulated over $3800 in credits which I can utilize only if I succeed in milking a ponderous bureaucratic cow. When I did, the payoff was in discount coupons good at local drugstores and national restaurant chains. Whatever happened to S&H Green Stamps?

There are other interesting trends in advertising. One of them involves not identifying either the product or its manufacturer. Thus, lavish television commercials go on for 45 or 50 seconds before a product or its manufacturer is identified. If one nods or turns away, that fleeting reference is missed. In a similar vein is a growing practice of referring to what's being advertised generically as a product as in the statement "It's a very fine product." Frozen dinners, hemorrhoid ointments, low-calorie beer, and headache remedies are described as "products" to such an extent that there is no referent for all the benefits that have been cited.

Recently, something else has been added to the hype mix: *patriotism.*

It has been said that patriotism is the last refuge of scoundrels. That may be so. But lately, however, many peculiar products come wrapped in the flag.

It is an old business.

At the turn of the century, Edison introduced his *Kinetograph*, an 1100-pound motion picture camera which could be moved only with great difficulty and then only for as far as its power cord would permit. The projector was called a *Vitascope*. At about the same time the Lumière Brothers of France introduced their *Cinematographe*, a 10-pound, combination, hand-held motion picture camera, developer, printer, and projector.

Imagine! A French camera which anyone could use to make, develop, and project French photographs that moved. The wizard and his friends got busy. Cameramen making a travelog in New York's Central Park were arrested and their French equipment confiscated. The Republican Party adopted the slogan *America for Americans*. And the Biograph Company, under contract to use the Edison equipment, adopted the same slogan.

Life is somewhat gentler these days.

Nevertheless, we have all been urged to drink Coke and buy film, zippers, beer, and Detroit-built cars and trucks for no other reason than that they are American.

So attractive is patriotism—*Made in the USA*—as a buying motive that the Sanyo Sewing Company now makes Bill Blass clothing and Burberry raincoats in Oneonta, N.Y.

There is no doubt that Americans prefer homemade and, other things being equal, that is the way they will buy. But things are not always equal.

For example, Detroit offers a car at $10,000 which is subject to recall because its engine block is liable to crack. Further, the manufacturer maintains a large legal staff to protect it from consumer complaints. Korea offers a comparable car at $5000 made by a firm whose policy seems to be to replace without question any lemons that get onto the market.

This contest between patriotism and pocketbook will be an interesting one to watch.

The point of all this is simple.

The advertisements to which we are exposed in the print media and which catch our attention on television, for the most part, have very little to do with the intrinsic qualities of the products being touted. To get fancy about it, "The benefits are associative, not attributive."

With a constant diet of such advertisements, some on behalf of quite superior products, we commence to see our own products in the same light. The hard benefits which should distinguish one product from another are replaced by frivolous hype. The way we view our own products suffers accordingly. "If others can sell products by wrapping them in the flag or by presenting them in production numbers that transform piano keyboards into swimming pools" the rationalization goes, "why should I struggle to establish and prove customer benefits?"

Fortunately, there are fashions in advertising which, like narrow ties, come and go. Art directors produce to astonish other art directors and copywriters write to terrorize other copywriters. And the reader or viewer is really never given a legitimate reason to buy. Flash and trash replace actual benefits. Production values replace product performance.

Clients pay the bills because they don't know any better. Besides, the advertising people are the "experts." Unfortunately, however, some clients begin to think this way too. Since hype is seen to succeed in selling almost everything, why struggle to make better products?

The situation isn't really hopeless, however. Once in a while some truly accurate advertising is done or a client happens to read David Ogilvy's *Confessions of an Advertising Man* and discovers that advertising works best when it touts the benefits of superior products. Then, of course, everyone benefits.

Imagine, "Only half the added sugar of the other leading brands!"

Make Nice and Other Distractions

We have discussed a few of the major environmental factors that influence the way firms are managed and products brought to market. Not all, just a few.

In addition, there are a number of small things. Each, like a loose tooth or athlete's foot, is bothersome and a continuing distraction. Sometimes, we don't even notice that we are being distracted. We take these things for granted. They are part of the landscape.

Make Nice

All of us have seen an angry toddler punch a sibling, twist the cat's tail, or squirt orange juice across the room and have heard the mother's plaintive, "No, no, baby, *make nice.*" If the child were older and the mother more self-assured, retribution would be swift and sure.

But they aren't and we aren't, and "make nice" conditions the atmosphere in which we buy, in which we sell, and in which we work.

We see it in action every day at the supermarket, in restaurants, in the office, on the production floor—almost everywhere we work. Continuous brutalizing is the other extreme. Make nice, however, seems to prevail.

We see its effects in the supermarket where baggers and checkers gossip while customers wait and in school where popularity and effort are more important than performance: knowledge, and right answers. In the office its effects are seen in too many personal telephone calls, in work from home being done at the desk, and in time lost visiting other desks. On the factory floor the results show up as unattended machines, long washup periods before punching out, and minor defects in parts or assemblies.

And always the supervisor is never to be found. When one finally locates a supervisor and asks "How come?" the supervisor makes nice with comments like "They are only kids," "We try to maintain a friendly work atmosphere," and "They have been under a lot of pressure lately."

Moving up a level, we who manage the supervisors, fall into the same trap. When we are not making nice, we have more important things to do.

Make nice and a dangerous incompetent becomes chief of cardiac surgery at Bethesda Naval Hospital. Eventually, he is found guilty of involuntary manslaughter, negligent homicide, and dereliction of duty.

Make nice and the man responsible for Time, Inc.'s TV-Cable Week fiasco—out-of-pocket losses of nearly $50 million and a $750-million loss in stock value—is still on the payroll earning better than $500,000 a year, with stock options.

Perhaps the saddest (or the funniest) example of the consequences of make nice is this situation: The Nuclear Regulatory Commission has refused to let the Philadelphia Electric Company restart its Peach Bottom reactor. The reason: Management cannot demonstrate its ability to prevent plant engineers from reading, playing cards, watching television, or sleeping when they should be monitoring operations.

Somewhere between making nice and brutalization there should be a demanding and productive atmosphere that remains fair, firm, and friendly. For many, this is a tall order.

Fads

These distractions arise from a combination of hope springing eternally and keeping up with the Joneses. For the most part, the search is for simple solutions to complex and vexing problems. Occasionally such solutions work, not through magic, but because a situation has been properly identified and the appropriate solution to it applied.

During the early fifties, for example, attitude conditioning was the rage. If only people had the right attitude, they wouldn't have accidents on the job, production would go up, salespeople would make more sales, and on and on. This was certainly a reasonable observation. Soon, attitude conditioning programs were laid on like maple syrup on pancakes.

Experienced supervisors sighed and said, "This too shall pass." And it did, except that some folks said if our people have unproductive attitudes, it is because we are hiring the wrong people or are mistreating those we have. Changes were made in the way things were done, and accidents did go down, production went up, and sales increased.

Then came MBO (management by objective). Here, too, the idea was simple. If everyone agrees on goals, perhaps even helps to set them, and understands what is necessary to achieve them, then everything will go forward smoothly and productively. A lot of chickens were plucked over this one, and for a long while the air was thick with feathers. There were training meetings and planning meetings and implementation meetings. Then came a crunch, and the decision was made: "We can't afford to do this any more."

Some firms weren't so quick to keep up with the Joneses. They found places in their operations where MBO could be applied with great effect. MBO was quietly folded into the way in which they did things.

Toward the end of the MBO craze, a client came back from a friendly visit with a competitor, a competitor who held a little better position in the markets they shared. The client was astonished to discover that his competitor had a human resources manager on the payroll. He resolved to have one too. He soon had one, and a very good one indeed, but the fellow lasted only 6 months. He was found to be disruptive.

Other corporate crazes have met with a similar fate, including long-range or strategic corporate planning, quality circles, the management of strategies, product positioning, and other new ways of looking at common problems. Always they have come packaged in two ways. One way is as a cure-all, complete with instructions, guaranteed to sweeten the breath, strengthen the libido, and increase return on investment. The other way, they come as a simple idea, a concept to be adapted and tailored and fitted to the organization where, after a while, it will make a contribution.

Lately, with sales costs continuing to rise, markets continually expanding—over 600,000 new businesses formed each year—and the telephone company looking for volume, telemarketing has come on the scene. One result is that, on average, I receive 16 telephone calls per week from dial-up machines with recorded messages describing offers I cannot refuse. Another result, and a very beneficial one at that, is that people are now well aware once more that the telephone properly used is still a very powerful sales tool.

Back to Basics, but the Basics Have Changed

The challenges from the environment in which we produce and sell products are severe. We've reviewed a few—the range is from the economic machine of the Japanese to the latest distracting fads and fancies—and the list was not exhaustive.

It is a difficult situation which has been at least 20 years in the making. Reestablishing the healthy position our economy held in the fifties and sixties cannot be accomplished overnight. And the solutions proposed boil down to a simple injunction: *back to basics.*

The trouble is that the basics have *changed.*

Once, long runs of standard products, permitting economies of scale, was the manufacturing basic. Now the need is for short runs, extreme flexibility, and products tailored to the needs of single customers. This is a quite different basic.

The basics of finance are changing too. Currently, the major value of an equity is as a speculation—buy cheap, qualify for a gain, and sell dear. Those firms overstuffed with lazy assets become targets for the takeover extortionists. There may be a new basic shaping up here especially after October 19th, one that will, once more, permit equities to be income-producing investments, not mere speculations.

And the basics of marketing and sales are no longer what they were. In almost every market the number of competitors has increased, the number of product offerings has increased, and, what's more, the number of markets has increased. These changes put a special burden on firms where sales & marketing is an assumed function—less well understood than manufacturing, finance, or engineering—and where the CEO and the firm's directors are apt to come from a background of finance, law, manufacturing, or engineering, or to have an MBA.

In addition to the constraints from the environment, there are a couple of other contributing factors.

One, quite simply, is the seeming inability of managers to relate their own experience as customers and buyers and their knowledge of the markets in which they participate individually to the conduct of their own businesses.

A friend, quite legitimately, is one of the most complaining people I know. Slow delivery of goods and services drives him up the wall. He'll be patient for a while with his car dealer, Burger King, Brooks Brothers, or Osco; then he will demand to see the manager and raise hell. Yet this same person runs a company with possibly the *worst* customer service operation in his industry.

Similarly, there are people who hoot derisively at pointless advertisements and run equally meaningless ones of their own, who are angered and offended by late-night telemarketing efforts and never wonder about what their own sales force is doing.

This seeming inability to project or empathize on the part of managers causes many firms to lose their customer franchise.

Another contributing factor is the unwillingness of senior managers to ask what others might consider to be stupid questions and to persist with them until they are answered. There is an undue deference to the presumed expertise of others. One result is that at higher management levels and especially at board levels, subjects are not explored as thoroughly as they should be. Half-baked schemes get approval, and potentially sound ideas are abandoned. This is especially true of marketing.

High-tech has been defined as the situation in which today's knowledge is inadequate to solve tomorrow's problems or is made obsolete by tomorrow's developments. With new markets, new competitors, and new competitive offerings appearing almost daily, marketing is, of all the management disciplines, the most high-tech. Senior managers must be able to understand its problems and to speak its language.

The pages that follow address the critical areas of marketing where new basics must be established to ensure both happy customers and healthy vendors:

Markets and marketing organizations. A single, monolithic marketing organization no longer works. Here the requirement is for flexibility to match the special requirements of each served market.

New products. Breakthroughs are a will-o'-the-wisp. The reality is a careful modification of existing products through an accurate assessment of the needs of the served markets.

Pricing. Formula pricing, based on outmoded absorption accounting methods, should be replaced by direct-cost techniques. Pricing and profits should be based on total capital employed, not on stockholders' equity.

Sales and the art of selling. Since few senior managers have ever carried the bag, they need to understand how and why sales personnel are different and do not ordinarily share what has come to be called the *corporate culture.*

Measuring sales and marketing productivity. There are two concerns here. One involves a confusion of two kinds of measure: measuring for operational control and measuring long-term cumulative effects. The other concern arises from the fact that many of the traditional marketing and sales functions have never been subject to measurement and there is no agreement as to how this should be done.

Planning and implementation of improvements. Short-range planning is a very useful device for management. Long-range planning, however, is less useful than is generally thought. There are more useful substitutes which simplify rather than complicate management's work.

When senior managers do not understand these subjects, two things seem to follow. Either they meddle with the work of subordinates, or they fail to provide support, help, and counsel when it is needed.

Since most people, including CEOs, directors, and other senior managers participate in and share in only two markets—the consumer packaged-goods market and the consumer durable-goods market—most of the examples used in what follows will be drawn from those markets. I can't help but feel that, for good or bad, the way we are treated and hustled as customers in these consumer markets has a large influence on the way we, as managers, run our own businesses.

Further, many of the examples used here have been drawn from the press, principally *The New York Times, Business Week,* and *The Boston Globe.* Other examples have been based on my own experience as a consultant.

In some of these situations the participants have been identified. In others they have not. That's because, quite simply, when General Motors recalls 400,000 cars, that's not confidential information. Lots of people are bound to hear of it. But when General Somebodyelse whispers in my ear that he has corporate chilblains, nobody else has to know.

Our own experience as buyers in two markets and at least as observers of the others, should add a personal dimension to the discussions which follow. When that's done, we will explore a few new ideas and outline a simple procedure for ensuring continued business growth and improved marketing effectiveness. And that will be enough for a while.

PART 1

Markets and Marketing Organizations

"How do I love thee? Let me count the ways."   E. B. BROWNING

What I mean by a *market* is simply the smallest group of user-buyers with similar wants and needs that can be served profitably. A *marketing organization* is the group that fills those needs. As a logical extension of these two definitions, one should conclude that the entire business enterprise is the marketing organization.

This conclusion is certainly correct. However, for the purposes of this discussion, I'll take a more focused view and leave manufacturing, personnel, and finance to others. As subjects, markets and marketing organizations are complicated enough. In fact, they have become too complicated, unnecessarily complicated. They don't need to become more so.

Fortunately, these complications really are unnecessary. For we all know quite a bit about markets and marketing organizations, perhaps much more than we think.

We know about markets because we are active in several of them as buyers and in several others—again on the buying side—as very interested observers. It is the knowledge we have of these markets as buyers which should enable us to bring our own products and services to market more effectively and profitably.

We understand three of these markets quite well—the consumer packaged-goods market, the consumer durable-goods market, and various service markets—because we are active buyers in them. They consume most of our income.

We may, perhaps, be a little less familiar with four other markets—three industrial consumables markets and the capital goods market—but if we don't participate actively in them as buyers, we at least see them at work. And we are careful, interested observers of them because they affect our jobs.

After reviewing these seven markets, we'll take a look at ways to segment them, ways to make them smaller, easier to manage, and more secure.

Then we'll take a look at the principal functional responsibilities of marketing. There are 25 of them, and many are frequently overlooked. Their relative importance, also, changes from served market to served market.

Our own experience as buyers should give us insight into each of them and show us how to enhance our own sales and marketing effectiveness.

Next, we'll review briefly how marketing organizations grow and how each of the common functional responsibilities has a different role to play depending upon the stage of growth we are in and the way we want to grow.

Then we will take a look at those closely related subjects lumped together under the title, *advertising & sales promotion*. We will see how they help shape markets and define products.

Finally, we'll take a look at what's required to develop an effective marketing organization.

There is nothing new in the next six chapters, just stuff some of us may have overlooked or forgotten we knew. All of this may, however, be viewed from a perspective we are not used to.

2
Seven Markets
and How They Work

In what follows, we'll be taking a close look at seven markets: two consumer markets, four industrial markets, and one market which both
consumers and industry share. There are a few similarities between
these markets, but there are more differences.

What these three general categories of markets have in common is
people. And people tend to act in predictable ways, depending upon
the situation in which they find themselves.

When a person buys for his or her own account, that is, buys as a consumer, the buying decision tends to be based on *subjective* criteria.

In contrast, when a person buys for someone else's account, as is the
case with most business or industrial purchasing, or when a person buys
in consultation with another, as when a husband and wife buy a TV set,
the buying decision tends to be based on more or less *objective* criteria.
This is not to say that subjectivity is absent from these joint or agency
purchases. However, where it does exist, it is cloaked by the appearance
of objectivity.

The way buying decisions are made establishes the major differences
between all served markets.

As we move in closer to consumer and industrial markets, other differences become apparent. Paradoxically, with consumer products, the
primary sale is made to the reseller, not the consumer. In contrast, in
industrial selling, the primary sale is made to the user. There are a
number of other significant differences, but this is the most important
one. Not only does it influence the way products are developed, advertised, and sold, but it has a profound influence on the way market research is gathered and on the way new products are brought to market.

The greatest influence this difference may have, however, is in the
way the marketing functions are themselves managed.

The individual consumer is of little interest to the manufacturer of consumer goods. Once his or her profile has been drawn, attention shifts from that individual to large masses of people who match that profile. This group of consumers is separated from other people by the most practical means—zip codes, neighborhoods, magazine subscriber lists, and affinity groups of all kinds.

Just the opposite is true in industrial selling. The identification of customers begins with a large mass of firms with similar wants and needs who have been grouped together under a single Standard Industrial Classification (SIC) grouping. However, it is the individual firms that make up the SIC grouping who become important, not the group itself. And, going further, it is the people within each firm who make the actual buying decisions who must be identified.

Thus in consumer selling, it is large aggregates of people who are important, whereas in industrial selling it is the individual. This difference, as we shall see, dictates both the way consumer and industrial markets work and what's required to succeed in them as well.

There is yet one more significant difference. New products are rare in consumer markets. A phonograph, a radio, a television, a home computer—something that is really new and different—comes along once every 20 years or so. Consumers, therefore, think they know everything about anything that is offered to them. (Maybe this is why they hardly ever read labels or instruction books.)

Industrial markets, in contrast, are continually being asked to evaluate new products or, if not new products, at least products which have been significantly modified. In industrial markets the purchasing decision generally involves at least two people, the ultimate user of the product and the purchasing agent. In cases where purchased products will be incorporated into the goods designed and built by a company, three people would be involved—typically representatives of engineering, manufacturing, and purchasing. Each person brings a unique set of concerns to the buying decision and the interests of each must be satisfied.

It is characteristic of both markets, consumer and industrial, that the more people who become involved in a buying decision, the more expressed concern there is with value and, often, with the mere appearance of value.

There are, however, not only two markets here: consumer and industrial. There are at least seven that are readily identifiable and many many more if market segments are included (see Fig. 2.1).

It is the way that markets work and the manner in which products behave in these markets that will give us the clues we need to meet the

CONSUMER
   Packaged goods
   Durable goods
INDUSTRIAL
   Support consumables
   Process consummables (commodities)
   Make-or-buy consumables
   Capital goods
COMMON SERVICE MARKETS

Figure 2.1. Seven commonly served markets.

challenges that are continually with us, challenges which must be overcome if we are to sell successfully in those markets.

Consumer Packaged Goods

When we talk about *consumer packaged goods*, we are referring to food products, soaps, paper goods, soft drinks, health and beauty aids, candy, tobacco products, laundry and cleaning supplies, and similarly packaged merchandise.

These are all standard products, and everyone who buys them knows, or pretends to know, what functions they serve and how to use them.

Such products are rarely, if ever, sold by the manufacturer directly to the consumer.

The primary sale is made at the executive level to a departmental buyer or to the buying committee of a department store; a discounter; a specialty store; or a supermarket, drugstore, or convenience store chain. Purchases are made at this level on the basis of anticipated performance; e.g., stock turns and contribution measured in terms of sales per square foot. The vendor's claims are supported by test-market results, details of performance elsewhere, and the particulars of the advertising and promotional efforts which will support the product and build traffic for the reseller.

The vendor may also be required to pay the reseller a *slotting allowance* to get shelf or freezer space for new products or upgraded space for established products. The name comes from the custom of buying a row in a cigarette machine and paying extra for the center slot. The practice itself is merely a formalized kind of spiff or bribe.

Costs to the reseller are not as important as considerations of stock turns and contributions. Optimizing the productivity of available floor and shelf space is the major concern.

Sales at this level are sweetened by devices which effectively lower the cost of the merchandise but not its invoice price: things like twofers, superpacs, and one case extra with every ten. Major advertising allowances are uncommon although co-op programs are a requirement. The advertising costs of such resellers is typically under 3 percent of sales, and this must support thousands of inventory line items.

Once accepted, a product is assigned a specific shelf and display space and is expected to produce. It is up to the vendor to see to it that the product produces at least as well as claimed during the sell-in. The reseller, in effect, becomes a landlord and the product a concessionaire. If the rent isn't paid—OUT!

With consumer packaged goods, there is little if any opportunity to exercise the art of selling at the point of sale. The consumer's buying decision is made on the basis of what the consumer knows about the product. What the consumer knows is the combined result of past experience and advertising, and what the consumer knows may be nothing more than that the stuff comes in a yellow box and fixes headaches.

Thereafter, it is a combination of packaging and posted shelf price. At this level, purchasing is made on the basis of the appearance of value, not true value itself.

For example, there are at least three kinds of acetaminophen on the market: Tylenol, the hospital's choice; Datril, which costs less; and Panadol, the European secret. For doses of equal efficacy, the costs of these products at a local cut-rate drugstore compare like this:

	Customer Price	Store Price
Panadol	$0.112	$0.095
Tylenol	0.063	0.053
Datril	0.053	0.045

The retail spread is from $0.053 to $0.112, or better than 110 percent, for the same quantity and quality of headache relief. This price difference is supported by advertising for which the manufacturer will spend from one-quarter to one-third of sales income. Each of these brands has its loyal following.

Another example is even more illustrative of this kind of consumer buying.

For years, cotton percale has been used for the finest bed linen and M. Lowenstein's Wamsutta Supercale, 200 threads to the inch, has been the standard of excellence. (To be sure, pure linen is available but at a two-digit multiple of the cost of percale). At a recent white sale, Wamsutta Supercale, double-bed top sheets were barely moving at $20 each, while the same sheet made by J. P. Stevens and carrying the Ralph Lauren label was moving along nicely at $28.

With consumer packaged goods, the price on the package is less critical than the deal with the reseller. It is the price the reseller pays that covers everything including the producer's profits. The consumer's perception of value can be shaped by packaging and advertising. Hence these are critical elements in the total cost of the product.

The price the consumer pays is of secondary consideration. Most consumers will go to another store or will do without rather than downscale their purchases. Fig. 2.2 summarizes major characteristics of this market.

- Little opportunity for selling at the point of purchase.
- Bargaining or price negotiations between consumer and reseller very rare.
- Wide price spreads between similar or identical products tolerated at the point of purchase.
- Buying decisions based on *apparent* value.
- Movement at the point of purchase responds to advertising more than to pricing.
- Consumers will do without rather than downscale the purchase.
- Primary sale is to reseller, with cost less important than performance.

Figure 2.2. Characteristics of the consumer packaged goods market.

There are four major sales and marketing challenges for these products.

Distribution and Authorization

The *first* challenge involves distribution, increasing the number of outlets for them and increasing the number of shelf facings and displays authorized at each outlet.

The basic sale of these products is made on the basis of anticipated throughput or stock turns and, as we have said, is supported by details of product tests and the advertising and promotions which will both ensure customer purchases and build store traffic. Resales and increased shelf and display authorizations are secured on the basis of new promotions and proof of past performance, generally, in a business review which shows that store movement of the product has been as great or even greater than anticipated.

In judging the movement of a product relative to competitive products, great reliance is placed on information supplied by third-party research organizations. This information is prized by manufacturer and reseller alike. A. C. Nielsen keeps track of the shelf space allotted to products and store out-of-stocks. Towne-Oller keeps track of warehouse withdrawals and movements into store inventory. Mejors's keeps track of the newspaper advertising supporting products in major markets.

Lately, with the advent of universal price codes and optical scanners at the checkout counter, several other organizations have begun to offer data on what actually goes through the checkout counter, how much and when. Thus store movement can be related to advertising and promotion almost on an hourly basis. All this data is combined in various ways to guide the reseller and the manufacturer in the sales and marketing of packaged goods.

A major goal at this selling level is to secure authorization for shelf positions at or above eye level and to place freestanding floor displays.

Displays and Shelf Stock

The *second* major challenge occurs at the field sales level in individual stores. Here the goal is to make sure that store managers and department managers actually maintain shelf stocks according to authorizations, provide space for special displays, and utilize the point-of-sale materials provided.

Accomplishing all this often requires that the field representative stock the shelves personally, set up displays and place point-of-purchase materials, check and rotate store inventory, initiate transfer orders and warehouse withdrawals, and persuade stocking clerks to favor his or her products. Stock-outs—nothing on the shelf and nothing in the back room—are to be prevented at almost any cost.

Product Differentiation

The *third* challenge takes place at the consumer level. Here, the aim is to differentiate one product from many essentially similar products. The challenge for advertising becomes enormous and with established products or brands is often solved with pure hype. For these products, the kind of cost effective benefit selling that gets a product authorized by headquarters is impossible.

Advertising, therefore, revolves around new packages, new labels, new sizes, new flavors, and new formulations; it offers "new and improved," "sugar-free," "caffein-free," "pine-scented," "lemon-freshened," a "hint of mint," and so on. Nutra-Sweet becomes a benefit. Often the only thing that can be advertised is a promotion for the product, not the product itself: sweepstakes; buy one, get one free; cents-off coupons; premium offers; tie-in promotions ("you buy the ham, we'll give you the eggs"), and on and on.

A few advertisers have been able to create a preference for their products without such gimmickry. Frank Perdue's efforts come to mind, the "Let's get Mikey" commercial for Life Cereal, the late great "It isn't just for breakfast anymore" campaign for the Florida Citrus Commission, and Nestles' "Singin' in the Rain" commercial for Quik Instant Cocoa.

Line Additions

The *fourth* challenge involves new products or, more properly, changes in or additions to established and accepted products or product lines. (A new product in this market would involve securing shelf space in another part of the store and, perhaps, calling on another buyer at headquarters.) Here, the goal is increased shelf space and more brand visibility. The terms *flankers* and *extenders* are often used in this connection.

However, display and shelf space is limited in any store. And even with computers and optical scanners to facilitate stock taking and inventory control, there is continued pressure from resellers to limit the number of stockkeeping units and inventory line items. There are, for example, at this writing more than 23 different kinds of cola drinks on the market, many more than any right-minded merchant would handle. Altogether, supermarkets contend with over 17,000 line items or stockkeeping units.

New sizes, new flavors, etc., are introduced at the expense of existing shelf items. The hope is that a competitor's package will be displaced. Often it is one of the marketer's own sizes or flavors that suffers. *Cannibalism* is the term used. For example, when Coca-Cola introduced its Diet Coke, it took space from other Coke flavors, and their sales fell by 30 or 35 percent. What happened when Coke introduced its new-old and its old-new Cokes is anybody's guess.

Finally, in the sale of consumer packaged goods, direct contact with the ultimate consumer is a rare thing. Most typically, such contacts result from a product complaint. Occasionally, they may occur during a market research project of one kind or another. However, consumer contacts are most frequently made by an outsider, a third-party research agency. Once in a while, a marketer may meet consumers at focus group interviews.

The principle contacts are with the key figures who control distribution, the buyers, store managers, and department managers. Their concerns are vastly different from those of the consumer. In moving consumer goods the goal is to optimize shelf facings and product movement for both the reseller and the vendor. This is the joint goal the reseller has with every other supplier whose products are authorized and displayed.

Consumer Durables

Durable goods range upward from small appliances like coffee brewers and popcorn machines, through the midpriced appliances like TV sets and refrigerators, to the high-cost durables like automobiles, homes, and, lately, college educations. However, for reasons which we will cover only briefly, we will not discuss high-cost durables.

The events of the past few years have brought about a drastic change in the traditional ways cars are brought to market and in the ways in which people buy them. No longer are all new models introduced in the fall creating a new car fever throughout the country. No longer do people trade in every 3 or 4 years. New models are now introduced as significant changes occur or when lagging sales need a boost. Chrysler, for example, claims it will introduce a new model every other month.

The new home market also is undergoing major changes. Few homes are being built on speculation. New home starts, even tract homes, are made only in response to a firm commitment from a buyer and then only with money up front.

With college educations no longer ensuring good jobs, marketing here is also being reappraised. Obsolete curricula and overproduction in once-fashionable specialties are just two of the problems to be solved.

But, even though these large segments of the consumer durables market are reshaping themselves, there still remains a sizable market for large and small appliances, some undreamed of just a few years ago. It is a market that behaves pretty much as it always has.

Resellers in this market have the same concerns as resellers in the packaged goods market, that is, turnover and productivity: turnovers of

3× to 4×, productivity of \$200 per square foot, and 40 to 50 percent markups are goals. Fig. 2.3 highlights this market.

- The function and purpose served by the items are well known to prospective buyers.
- Product differences (feature and benefits) justify personal selling at the point of purchase.
- The market has a good sense of what the items should cost.
- Buyers believe they can sort out the features and benefits and reach an enlightened buying decision.
- Product movement responds equally to features-benefits advertising and to pricing.
- Bargaining and price negotiation are an accepted part of the process by which a customer buys.
- The prime sale is to the reseller, not the consumer.

Figure 2.3. Characteristics of the consumer durable-goods market.

Low-End Durables

At the low end of the market are a host of small, no-name appliances made and priced for use as promotional items and traffic builders—appliances like pulsating shower heads, lawn edgers, crockpots, and coffee brewers. These are all of modest quality, with limited warranties, and they merely ape the higher-quality appliances of known manufacturers. Generally, these are sold to retailers through brokers who specialize in promotional goods.

The next tier of durables includes the same kind of appliances. These are from name manufacturers, have workable warranties or guaranties, are supported by national advertising, and receive nationwide service and warranty support.

Here there are a number of marketing challenges. They stem from the fact that these appliances, too, are sold on price like packaged goods. These appliances are extremely sensitive to competitive forces—either lower prices or new features.

Since there are real differences between appliances of the same kind—different features mean different benefits—personal selling may become a factor. The economics of retailing, however, do not permit much of it.

Because these appliances are relatively low in cost and do not require a large inventory investment on the part of the reseller, even the smallest outlets can carry them. Thus, wide distribution can be and is a primary marketing goal. Further, since these items also carry a name associated with other appliances, the reputation, quality, service and satisfaction of warranty and guaranty claims are all substantial requirements. Failure in any of these areas may adversely affect the sale of other, high-ticketed appliances carrying the same name.

Finally, because these appliances all have competitors and all have real features and benefits, advertising can differentiate one make and model from another. There are in fact two advertising and promotional challenges. One aims at establishing that differentiation. The other aims at providing a reason to buy now. The product movement generated by traditional gift-giving occasions (except, occasionally, Christmas) or by the creation of new housekeeping units is, usually, not large enough to support high-volume, economical production. Special promotions are therefore required. Advertising allowances supporting price promotions are a common device. However, since these appliances carry a slim markup, there is danger that price promotions will erode further the retailer's already narrow margins. Manufacturer's rebates to the consumer are the common promotional device in this market. Recently, it has been adopted by the automobile industry.

As with most consumer packaged goods, the basic sale is made to the chain or store buyer. The buyer's major concerns are stock turns and store traffic. If necessary, these appliances—no matter how high their quality—may become self-liquidating traffic builders.

Finally, these low-end items are well within the means of a single purse. One person can make the buying decision which will be based on availability, of course, plus a combination of price and advertising.

Midrange Durables

As consumer durables increase in price, their purchase becomes less and less an impulse item affecting just one person's pocketbook and more the result of consultation and deliberation. Buying becomes a joint activity of two or more people. Although the deliberation may be shallow and the consultation casual, when it comes time to decide which to buy, the customer will ask questions. This provides the retail clerk with an opportunity to sell. The options are limited: trade up to a different model or switch to a different make, but not much more.

In the days before discounting became common, it was possible to demonstrate that a skilled salesperson made a difference in trading-up buyers and in converting *shoppers* into buyers. Now, slim markups prevent most retailers from being able to afford either skill or product training. Only manufacturers who control their own distribution like Sears, Singer, Radio Shack, or Curtis Mathes are able to provide sales training to retail people. Even their success is, however, limited.

Resellers, therefore, frequently swap price negotiations for sales prowess, causing a serious deterioration of margins.

Most retail clerks are trained only in in-house procedures: how to write up a sale, how to read a stock sheet, how to place a special order, and how to arrange financing. Since reliance cannot be placed on the sales clerk to create a preference at the point of sale, manufacturers continually look for other ways to accomplish this.

Point-of-sale promotional material which restates and reinforces the advertised benefit story is one means. Restricting the choice offered to the customer, thus making decisions easier, is another. This usually involves limiting models, colors, and special options. Reducing delivery time and increasing the availability of special orders are others. This means keeping distribution channels full and simplifying procedures so that the customer can get what has been ordered in a matter of days, not weeks. Failure here increases the risk that the order will be cancelled or that the customer will switch to another make and model or even to another retailer.

And, of course, prices must be competitive.

The key price in this market is that offered to the reseller. There must be enough of a spread between it and the ticket to allow considerable negotiations with the buyer and still leave a reasonable markup for the reseller.

Withal, this market requires that price differences between makes and models be justified by observable differences between them. Further, consumers in this market have a general idea of what a freezer or television set should cost. For years, a large segment of this market consulted the Sears Roebuck catalog to find out how much something should cost. This method of establishing value is less common than it once was. These days, it is the price advertising of discounters that establishes what something should cost. This market will accept a modest increase above these preconceptions of price but requires that sizable increases be justified.

Most consumer durables, large or small, are not new to the market or to the people who buy and use them. Their functions and the purpose they serve for the user-buyer are well known.

Rightly or wrongly, people think that they can ask a few questions, sort out the features and benefits, and come to an enlightened buying decision.

Industrial Support-Consumables

The products grouped as industrial support-consumables range from paperclips and paper towels to welding gasses and janitorial supplies. The need, purpose, and use of these items are well known to everyone. Orders and reorders are nearly automatic. They may be placed by a purchasing agent but more usually are placed by the users themselves: secretaries, shop supervisors, and maintenance supervisors.

The buying patterns here correspond closely to those for consumer packaged goods. Compared with the cost of other consumables purchased by businesses, the amount spent for these supplies is low. Price, therefore, is rarely a consideration. Further, since the level of these purchases rises or falls with general business activity, these are not budgeted items. (The characteristics of the industrial support-consumables market are summarized in Fig. 2.4.)

- Purchases are unbudgeted: Dollar volume is low compared to process-consumables
- Not a price-sensitive market
- Purchases are usually made from a stocking distributor
- Ordered when needed by the user: secretary, maintenance supervisor, or shop supervisor
- Consumption can be encouraged by special industrial packages which promote waste or pilferage
- Product movement responds more to sales promotion than to price or advertising
- Buying decisions are based on familiarity, availability, and price—in that order

---

Figure 2.4. Characteristics of the industrial support-consumables market.

Purchases are usually made from a stocking distributor or supply house on the basis of availability and familiarity with the brand. Catalogs play a big role in this market. With prudent firms, orders are not placed until the cupboard is nearly empty.

Buyers can be induced to buy more than they need through special industrial packages which encourage waste or pilferage. Purchases can be guided or stimulated by sales promotional devices, giveaways which range from coffee machines for the office to TV sets for the home. The spread between the list or package price and that charged the distributor must be large enough to accommodate specials, markdowns, and giveaways. Products in this category can be sold effectively by mail or by phone.

New products—such as correcting ribbons for typewriters, special mopping compounds, or newly formulated cutting oils—are generally introduced during joint sales calls by the manufacturer and the distributor.

Industrial Process-Consumables (Commodities)

The products we are talking about here include wire, sheet steel, nuts and bolts, paint, and other material actually consumed in the manufacturing processes. Such material is often of a commodity nature. Purchasing from approved sources is usually automatic, triggered by projected materials requirements. Availability is the first consideration, then price. Since production cannot be shut down for lack of material, it is usual for there to be both a primary and a secondary supplier. As long as it meets established specifications, which often include price, its source is a matter of indifference. The general characteristics of the industrial process-consumables market are listed in Fig. 2.5.

- Complete indifference as to source so long as specifications, which may include price and availability, are met
- Purchasing is automatic from suppliers whose offerings have been approved jointly by engineering, purchasing, and manufacturing
- The market is potentially unstable if a supplier wants to buy volume
- Second sourcing at a higher price is often the preferred position for a supplier to hold
- Success and the higher price go to the supplier who can differentiate the product from competitive offerings

---

Figure 2.5. Characteristics of the industrial process-consumables commodities market.

Under some circumstances, the secondary source may be able to command a slightly higher price than the primary source. Where long-term requirements can be established, supply contracts are frequently signed at a price advantage to the buyer.

Purchasing agents typically shop around to keep established suppliers honest.

The buying decision takes on a different form with this kind of material. It is primarily a joint decision involving engineering, production, and purchasing.

Selling-in a new product or the product of a new supplier requires demonstrated superiority in quality and availability at or near the established prices. Becoming a second source is often the easy way to introduce a superior product at a superior price.

Commodity markets, however, can become quite unstable. A new supplier with a lower price can be very unsettling. Established prices can become a football to be furiously kicked around, as first one supplier then another drops the price to preserve share or volume.

This situation can often be prevented through the establishment of industrywide specifications which some suppliers can meet handily, and others only with difficulty. Many military specifications, for example, are in place more to stabilize a market than to ensure quality.

Often a single supplier can upgrade a product and remove it from commodity consideration by enhancing the packaging or the product surrounds or by having it incorporate one or more steps of the customer's production process. Sheet steel, for example, is often given a first coat of paint, treated to make forming easier, or perforated in special ways.

Close familiarity with the customer's personnel and processes are required to accomplish this. Often what the supplier thinks is obvious and of no value is of immense value to the customer. The dotted line on the outside of corrugated boxes to show how they should be opened to make a display is a case in point. Successful selling of commodity products often depends upon finding ways to make them something else: specialty or differentiated products.

The notion of a system is often used here. The stock and equipment to assemble and fill cardboard milk and juice containers is referred to as a *packaging system*. Favorable sale or lease terms for the equipment helps ensure the continued sale of the knocked-down containers.

Industrial Make-or-Buy Consumables

This class of industrial consumables is made up of items which the purchaser has decided it is cheaper to buy elsewhere than to make. Some call this the OEM (original equipment manufacturer) business.

These consumables include ready-formed electrical contacts, special castings and forgings, cabinet hardware, microprocessors, motors and, even, ready-to-plug-in major components. Often these are stock items with the vendor. But, as frequently, they are specially made to the plans and specifications of the buyer.

Since this is a make-or-buy proposition, the initial competition is the customer's in-house capability, or presumed capability, to make the item instead of buying it elsewhere.

Initial sales are difficult to make. Manufacturing people must be convinced that the item will work well in their manufacturing processes. The designer or specifying engineer must be assured that the item will work well when the end product is being used by the customer. And, of course, the purchasing agent must be certain that the cost is reasonable and, more important, that the item will be available whenever it is needed.

Once a supplier for these products has been selected, a certain amount of inertia sets in. A new supplier is unlikely to be considered unless and until there is a seriously adverse change in the quality, availability, or price of the item being supplied. Despite this inertia, and even under the most favorable circumstances, conscientious purchasing agents will try to identify potential second sources.

Standard items are often sold through distributors to provide local inventories and so to meet the requirements of availability. But there is a hazard. Because of the deep discounts afforded to stocking distributors, they are able to undercut factory prices and, on occasion, will do so. Established supply relationships are thus upset. Controlling this situation without reducing factory margins is difficult. (The characteristics of the industrial make-or-buy consumables market are summarized in Fig. 2.6.)

- Basic conflict 1—Selling a standard product at the price of a special versus buying a special product at the price of a standard.
- Basic conflict 2—Long-term supply contracts which guarantee price but not volume versus long-term contracts which guarantee volume but not price.
- Standard products in distribution may upset carefully arranged supply relationship.
- The major competition is the customer's presumed in-house capability.
- The buying decision jointly made by engineering, manufacturing, and purchasing.
- The major challenge is ensuring margin over the life of the supply agreement.

Figure 2.6. Characteristics of the industrial make-or-buy consumables market.

The sale of an existing product or of a manufacturing capability to a new account is most easily done during the initial stages of the account's product design and development process.

To illustrate: The automobile industry is tending away from steel bodies and the use of metals in other automotive parts. Specially engineered plastics are the most likely replacements. Du Pont, already a large supplier to the industry, has consolidated all its automotive products—finished and fabricated products—regardless of which division makes them into a single automotive products department located in Michigan. By doing this, Du Pont hopes to be better able to guide the industry in the selection of new materials and to lock itself in as the prime supplier.

Once a vendor's product is built into the specifications and manufacturing processes, a competitor will have trouble displacing it. And if the vendor can also help its customer sell a particular product or provide other valuable services as well, the relationship will be that much stronger.

Selling a new or improved product to a nonbuying account requires replacing an existing vendor. If the demonstrated cost effectiveness of the new product is overwhelming, this is easily done. Usually, however, the differences between a new and an existing product are not that significant. Therefore, supplanting another vendor's product or manufacturing capability is most readily done when there is some fault with the current supplier's quality or service. Moreover, if the product to be supplanted is specially manufactured to the customer's specifications, all other sales problems increase in seriousness.

As always, when customers buy a ready-made component from a vendor, they need the assurance that the component will continue to be available. They are concerned with their own manufacturing processes and, as importantly, with their ability to repair and maintain their own products once these products have been sold and are in use by their customers.

There is a basic tension here between vendor and buyer. One aims to sell a standard product at a special price, whereas the other aims to buy a special product at a standard product price. Further, the buyer wants a low price guaranteed for a long time with no volume commitment, whereas the vendor wants the volume commitment with no guarantee on price. This creates another kind of tension between vendor and buyer.

Prudent marketing of such items requires that vendors expand the product "surrounds" to include many engineering and marketing services which buyers cannot afford to provide for themselves. These surrounds then become part of the product and its cost, just as advertising and packaging are part of the cost of consumer packaged goods.

Effective sales of this class of product depends upon continued, close liaison between the vendor's management and sales force and the customer's buyers, development engineers, manufacturing people, and, more often than not, with the customer's senior management.

Industrial Capital Goods

Here the reference is to big ticket items—new plants, a fork-lift truck, executive jets, a new milling machine. The bigness of the ticket is relative to the size of the firm. This market behaves very much like the consumer durable-goods market. Other industrial purchases cannot be postponed. Typewriter ribbons are needed. So is rolled steel and cabinet hardware. The business cannot go ahead without them. However, the purchase of capital equipment can be postponed indefinitely, and unless there is an emergency or some clear economic or competitive advantage to be gained, the buying decision will be put off.

In contrast to industrial consumables, where the evaluations, selections, and buying decisions are made by line operating people, senior management is normally involved in the purchase of capital equipment. Technical inputs may be supplied by engineering and operating people, but the final evaluations, selections, and decisions to buy will be made at higher management levels.

Selling capital equipment, therefore, has to take place at two levels. One level is the technical-engineering level at which engineers, manufacturing, purchasing, and the sales force hammer out technical recommendations and cost justifications. These contacts must be maintained until the sale is consummated. However, selling is also required at the executive, decision-making level. These contacts also, must be maintained until the decision to buy is finally made.

Further, while the decision to buy industrial consumables is predictable and arises naturally from the needs of an ongoing manufacturing operation, the decision to buy capital equipment is neither predictable nor necessary. Occasionally, an essential machine breaks down and cannot be repaired. A plant may burn down or be destroyed by an earthquake. These situations are quite rare however.

More usually, in-house analysis points up a need, a potential benefit, or a competitive advantage requiring new capital expenditures. Occasionally, the idea that a benefit or an advantage may exist is planted by other means: Advertising, adroit product public relations, an exhibit at a trade show, or a well-respected salesperson—any of these may start the deliberative process that leads to the eventual purchase of capital equipment.

Once this deliberative process has been started, it can be helped along its way by a salesperson who has established a consultative relationship with the management of the potential purchaser and who has maintained a good working relationship with manufacturing, engineering, and purchasing.

The likelihood of a sale is greatly increased if someone can be found within the prospect organization who has a legitimate business interest in seeing that the purchase is made. Such a person can provide valuable guidance in bringing the sale to a successful conclusion.

As a rule, the closer to the beginning of the process vendors enter the picture, the easier it is for them to "cook the specs" in their own favor. This again points to the need for a supplier to have effective contacts established within the organizations of both buying and potential customers.

Not all firms, however, follow such a deliberative process in the purchase of capital equipment. Indeed, even the most well-regulated firms may set aside the process or telescope it in the face of an emergency or a clear competitive or economic advantage.

The big challenges this market presents to a vendor are the availability of funds to finance a customer's purchase and the length of time the decision-making process takes. Unless reserve or contingency funds are available for unexpected capital purchases or unless lease purchase plans are available, a complete budgeting cycle or even several may be required from concept to purchase order and installation.

Further, if new technologies are involved—technologies which require changes in established methods and procedures—an even longer period may be required. For example, both the new dry-painting techniques in which electrostatic forces provide the initial bond and the Sanborn cutting-oil and coolant recovery system ensure enormous savings. But each requires a rejiggering of established methods, procedures, and work flow. Unless management has maintained good records on the cost of paint and cleanup or on the costs of metalworking fluids and their disposal, it cannot immediately determine the magnitude of its potential savings. In such situations, if vendors want to cut the time between idea and installation, they must be able to provide convincing cost-reduction data from established installations.

However, without questioning the validity of the foregoing, it should also be pointed out that senior managers, CEOs, and boards of directors are human. They, too, want "to be the first on their block," or at the very least, "to keep up with the Joneses." Thus, utilities start nuclear plants with no idea of costs or of evacuation plan requirements, refineries are built with no markets to serve, executive jets are purchased when commercial carriers are both more cost-effective and more convenient, and new casinos are built in Atlantic City even though the market cannot support what's already there.

Vendors in the capital equipment market require enormous staying power. Sustaining a sales effort over several years is not easily accomplished by the underfinanced. The big challenges in this market are (1) shortening the time between recognition of need and the purchase order and (2) maintaining contact at both levels at a reasonable cost. It is for this reason that many vendors rely on manufacturers' representatives to handle their field sales. Anyone with a well-balanced line card can maintain the necessary contacts while selling other products or services. Fig. 2.7 summarizes the important characteristics of the industrial capital goods market.

- Purchases are rarely made on an impulse or emergency basis.
- Purchases can be and often are postponed through several budgeting cycles. The vendor requires enormous staying power.
- The acquisition is usually planned and budgeted according to this process:

    1. Need or benefit/advantage identified
    2. Potential suppliers identified
    3. Anticipated benefits and costs quantified
    4. Budget line item scaled and approved
    5. RFQs/RFPs issued
    6. Bids and quotes evaluated
    7. Expenditure authorized
    8. Contract or purchase order negotiated, signed, and issued

- Senior management makes the buying decision
- The buying decision is subject to "consultative" influences.
- The buying decision may be influenced by "status" considerations
- The big challenge is to reduce the number of budgeting cycles between recognition of need and purchase order

---

Figure 2.7. Characteristics of the industrial capital goods market.

Common Service Markets

These markets are quite unlike any of the others we discuss here. Two major reasons account for this difference. The first is, quite simply, that the *product* doesn't exist until it is delivered. The *product* is created as the service is performed.

This makes it impossible to compare the offerings of two vendors. Even where the product seems to be identical—as, for example, two insurance policies—the variations, the differences show up only after a claim has been made and is being processed. The offerings in other markets can be placed side by side and compared in various ways. They can even be subjected to various kinds of destructive and nondestructive testing. This is not the case with services. All one can do is compare benefit claims and past performance and, from these, try to calculate the likelihood of future success.

The second reason service markets are different from other markets lies in the fact that providers of services claim special knowledge and skills not shared by their customers and, for the most part, not even understood by their customers. This high quotient of mystery places the customer at an extreme disadvantage and in some may produce feelings of resentment and suspicion. Television and automatic transmission repair technicians share this general opprobrium and in some jurisdictions must demonstrate qualifications and obtain licenses.

These characteristics apply across the board in all service markets. They apply as equally to the auto mechanic recommending replacement of the microprocessor that runs ignition and fuel injection as to the surgeon recommending radical mastectomy, to the insurance agent suggesting special riders and floaters as to the attorney preparing a foolproof major contract, to the investment counselor advising the best way to manage family funds as to a management consultant advising on the best way to ensure corporate health 5 years hence.

There is one further difference between service markets and others. In service markets, the *product* has no scrap or resale value. Fig. 2.8 presents a fair summary of these markets. They are even more complex than the capital equipment market.

Identifying qualified suppliers is the major difficulty buyers face in service markets. And the people to whom one can turn for advice and recommendation are frequently as nonplussed as the seeker, the prospective customer. Some efforts have been made to relieve this situation. Thus there are certified public accountants, certified management consultants, and board-certified physicians and surgeons.

At other levels there are licensed technicians and mechanics of all kinds and even yellow cards for street hostesses.

However, these diplomas are only negative endorsements. They merely state that at one particular time the holder was not known to be incompetent or dishonest (or diseased). They provide no assurance of the quality of future performance. For this reason, buyers once in a ser-

- A high quotient of mystery or of technological expertise in service offerings puts the buyer at a disadvantage.
- Since the product is created as it is delivered, evaluation of a single offering or direct comparison of competitive offerings is impossible.
- Identifying qualified suppliers is a major difficulty for the buyer.
- Inertia is a major factor in ensuring contract renewals.
- Maintaining frequent contact with decision makers is difficult, permitting competition to move in undetected.
- The captive nature of the customer makes cost runups and other flimflams possible.
- A basic conflict exists between buyer and seller over guaranteed price and guaranteed service. The customers' inability to measure quality usually leads to disappointment.
- A basic problem for the buyer is demanding and getting high-level performance versus the member-of-the-family feeling which encourages the forgiveness of sins.
- Quality control and over- or under-delivery are equally serious problems for the supplier.
- The assurances or reassurances provided during the sell-in and performance may be more important to customer satisfaction than the quality of the service provided.

Figure 2.8. Characteristics of common service markets.

vice market, whether individual or corporate, tend to remain with a single supplier—my attorney, my plumber, my insurance agent, etc. Inertia builds up. It works for the provider where contracts and renewals are concerned. Insurance policies, for example, tend to be renewed each year by the same broker, barring incidents of extreme incompetence; maintenance contracts are renewed automatically; and retainer agreements are extended without too much discussion.

This customer inertia works for the benefit of the vendor in other ways as well. After a while, a certain amount of noncritical acceptance sets in. Small sins on the part of the vendor are tolerated. They are even forgiven if they are noticed. It becomes increasingly difficult for buyers to demand and get high-quality performance even if they could recognize it. (The critical situations which really demonstrate the quality of service are extremely rare.)

There are other ways in which this situation seems to work to the advantage of the vendor. Because of the captive nature of the customer, vendors may be tempted to inflate costs, overcharge for services performed, bill for services not actually performed, and, in other ways, underdeliver.

However, this inertia has its negative side. It causes service vendors to take customers for granted, with unfortunate results. Maintaining contact with customers in a natural and effective way can be extremely difficult. For example, most casualty insurance policies are renewed annually, and 12 months is a long time between contacts. Competition can move in undetected, and come renewal time, the business is lost. Shrewd agents recognize this situation and try to sell several kinds of coverage with renewal dates spread throughout the year. Thus the frequent and desired contacts are ensured. Others add products, financial services, and real estate, not only to have something more to sell but to have additional reasons to call. However, this ploy often backfires because someone creditable as an insurance agent may not have sufficient presence to be a financial advisor especially for customers who have known him for a long time.

Finally, since service products are created as they are delivered, there is the risk of either overdelivery or underdelivery. In one situation the supplier invests more time and effort than can be covered by fees and other charges. Often, this is justified by the supplier as good public relations—good customer relations. More often than not, however, the customer is unaware of the overproduction since he or she is unable to measure or otherwise distinguish exceptional from adequate performance. Frequently though, overdelivery becomes a burden to the customer and is viewed with resentment. Oversolicitous undertakers and head waiters are prime exemplars of this.

Underdelivery, too, has its hazards. In time, customers will catch on, and the supplier will develop a reputation for sloppy or incomplete work or even, perhaps, dishonesty. An attorney who fails to proofread an important document or a mechanic who fails to refill a crankcase are typical examples of underdeliverers.

The more serious consequences of underdelivery, however, are to the supplier, not to the customer. With continued sloppy or incomplete work, the command of the special knowledge and skills begins to atrophy and soon the basis for the practice or the business ceases to exist.

Control of overproduction or underproduction can be achieved in many ways. The techniques that have proved most effective duplicate those common to manufacturing and, indeed, aim at converting a hard-to-bound service to a packaged product.

Thus, procedures are established for checking the quality and quantity of effort at various stages of a project. These procedures range from an architect's final punch-test to the step-by-step, troubleshooting procedures a service representative follows. Occasionally, a service can actually be converted into a standard product—for example, the workshops which some management consultants run to help groups of clients identify and solve their own problems or the natural childbirth clinics obstetricians run for prospective parents.

Paradoxically, in all service businesses, the assurances and reassurances provided during the sell-in and the performance may be more important to customer satisfaction than the quality of the service actually provided.

Summary

By understanding the way markets work, the way products behave within them, and the leverage points they offer to a supplier, management should be able to determine what resources should be applied against markets to make them optimally productive. Management should also be able to determine how to divide markets into segments which are then even more productive.

3
Market Segments, Secret Dreams, and Market Niches

Most of us involved in the management of the sales and marketing functions have secret dreams. The dreams may vary from time to time as our circumstances change, and the shape they take will depend upon our backgrounds and experience. Nevertheless, the dreams are there.

For some, the dream is of a product with a name and package so special that they, the package and the name, solve the marketing problems and enable the product to dominate its market.

L'eggs, for example, was such a product.

For others, the dream is of a unique product with an ever-expanding market and little or no competition. A product which has only two problems: optimizing distribution and optimizing package size.

This would be a product like WD-40.

A few of us dream of a business where there is no salesforce to keep track of and no dealers or distributors to supervise.

A business, perhaps, like Book-of-the-Month Club would fulfill such a dream.

Still others dream of a product that will create its own market, generate profits which are all new, and just grow and grow.

Self-developing film did this for a small manufacturer of sunglasses and polarizing film.

And some of us, overwhelmed by circumstances (or with very little experience), dream of a niche somewhere in the marketplace into which we can retreat with our products, our prices, and our market shares and where we will be safe from the raw winds of competition.

Something, for example, like....

Well, perhaps this one really *is* a dream.

It seems that for us in sales and marketing, there are no niches offering long-term protection and security for our products, our prices, and our market shares. Rather, it appears that there are only groups of customers with common needs, common preferences, or other shared characteristics—a segment of a larger market that is not well served by current offerings or whose characteristics we can take advantage of for our own purposes.

Such market segments, however, do not come into being by themselves. They need to be helped along.

A vendor, for example, recognizes the possibility of such a market segment and designs the product or service or the advertising program or sales approach that brings that segment into being as a special market. Occasionally, the product or service or idea comes first, and the market segment coalesces around it. More usually, though, they all grow and develop together.

Once in a while a market segment appears, attracts lots of attention and then—poof!—disappears in an instant. Advertisers spend pots of money to attract members of the segment, advertising agencies produce clever campaigns, and a few individuals from the edges of the presumed segment buy a little of what they would not otherwise have purchased. But the segment itself is a myth. During the eighties the Yuppies were such a phenomenon. Lots of attention, lots of noise, but no substance.

The vision was of a market made up of thousands of young, urban, upwardly mobile professionals in their late twenties or early thirties, living in apartments that rent for $2,000 or $3,000 per month, at the top of high rises, driving BMWs, drinking French champagne, outfitted by Gucci and Dunhill, and dining at only the tonier establishments. The mere thought of such people in any number is enough to make merchants and manufacturers looney with greed. A Hollywood dream, circa 1936—"My man Godfrey", and all that.

The reality is quite a bit different. In each of the 20-odd major metropolitan markets there may be around a hundred or a hundred and fifty such souls—hardly a market. Actually, a close careful reading of the demographics would hang these characteristics not on the young, upwardly mobile, but on the over-50 crowd who have already arrived—a much larger group by a factor of thousands and a quite different proposition entirely.

We can dream about yuppies and about market niches. The reality, however, is an imperfect market segment, a segment whose longevity and composition are at the mercy of customer self-interest and the competitive activities of others.

If the fit between product and customer is a good one, the market segment develops and grows. Often it grows way beyond any original projections for it. Eventually, it stabilizes, and it lasts until customers decide they no longer need whatever it was (the desire to own a pet rock is not perpetual) or, more usually, until someone else finds a better way to satisfy that need. The better way may be merely comparable quality at a better price.

Market Segments Are Not Forever

Make no mistake, the goal here is to dominate or, better yet, to monopolize a market segment for as long as it can be done profitably. However, the more visible the segment, the more quickly it will attract competition and the more difficult it will be to maintain even dominance.

To illustrate, rocket launching is big business. Rockets are used to explore space. They are used for military purposes. They are used to launch defense satellites. And, lately, they are being used to launch commercial communications satellites.

This latter segment, launching commercial communications satellites, has very high visibility and for a long, long time was the monopoly of our National Aeronautics & Space Administration (NASA) and its shuttles. NASA had a good thing going, monopoly of what has grown to be a half-billion-dollar business. NASA would loft almost anyone's communications satellites at $80 million for a full payload.

Lots of television and lots of publicity were bound to attract competition and, indeed, it did. The European Space Agency with its Ariane rocket entered the market with a lower price and a smaller payload. By the mid-eighties it had 43 percent of the market and was way ahead in bookings and backorders.

And, while NASA was busy figuring out new, lower prices, the Russians and their Proton rocket entered the market and began buying share with real bargain basement prices.

Then an executive order took NASA out of the commercial launching business. The *Challenger* disaster demonstrated the inferiority of our equipment. And, finally, the Japanese announced that it had moved into the launching business and would have separate vehicles for passengers and cargo in operation by the beginning of the nineties. However, U.S. industry can not wait that long. So in February of 1988, agreements were signed to take advantage of the space stations and rocket launching capabilities of the USSR.

Thus NASA has gone from a monopoly position to that of an also-ran in a market segment which it created.

Market segments are not forever, even those in which a vendor has a monopoly position. Monopoly seems to dull the senses. Segment size and visibility attract competition. Often, it is more profitable and less work to control a small segment.

Segments Need Not Be Large

For example, the open market for girlie magazines seems always to have been with us. It is, as they say, old as the hills and twice as lively.

At one time, it was served by the *Police Gazette*, the *Lucky Tiger Girls*, and the *Sunshine & Health* magazines. Not-quite-respectable barbershop stuff—the kind of thing men did, like keeping a bottle of whiskey in the barn.

Then came repeal and *Esquire*. The whiskey moved from the barn to the sideboard, and, thanks to the pastels of Petty and Vargas, girlie magazines moved from the barbershop to the den if not all the way to the living room.

Next, World War II, pinups, and added respectability.

Then Korea, improved photography and inexpensive process color printing, Heffner's *Playboy* and that glorified pinup, the centerfold. *Girlies* became *nudies* but innocent nudies in the tradition of Petty and Vargas. Respectability was challenged once more but the nudies and the news dealers won.

With a respectable girlie magazine market finally established, others found their own opportunities to serve it. They moved in and made that market grow.

According to the *N. W. Ayer Directory*, as of the mid-eighties, *Playboy* guaranteed its advertisers 4 million copies monthly, *Penthouse* guaranteed its advertisers 3 million copies (about the same as *Newsweek*), and *Hustler* 1 million copies monthly. An interesting situation.

From one point of view, this could be seen as one market's evaluation of three competitive products. Accordingly, *Playboy* is the clear winner, *Penthouse* is a close second, and *Hustler* is the clear loser.

However, that is just one point of view.

From another perspective, there are three quite distinctive magazines each serving its own market segment and the preferences of its own readers.

Playboy, for example, serves up the girl-next-door in *tableau vivante* poses—nubile, innocent, well-scrubbed, and cleanly shaven.

With *Penthouse*, it is no longer the girl-next-door. The innocence is gone, so is the razor, and action shots are common.

And with *Hustler*, everything is gone—innocence, the scrubbing brush, and the razor. It's secondhand goods all the way, photographed as they landed.

While figures are not available for this situation, it is hard to believe that *Hustler* is the "clear loser" in this field of three. It could be, in fact, the money-maker in the crowd.

These, then, are the two major characteristics of profitable market segments.

- First, market segments do not last forever. They are vulnerable to the changing offerings of competitors, vulnerable to the changing needs of customers, and vulnerable to external forces which may stamp them out.

- The second characteristic of market segments is that profitability is not necessarily related to segment size or market share.

Procter & Gamble's Ivory soap may be the largest seller in the bath soap market. It has high visibility and is the soap to beat in a battle for market share. And no doubt, it turns a pretty penny. In contrast, Elf-Aquitaine's Roger & Gallet, a fine, nicely perfumed, french-milled soap, has a loyal following, although it is barely visible in the marketplace; it is rarely threatened by competition. It contributes its small numbers to that category called *other* in share studies of the bath soap market. However, it would not remain on the market if it did not provide a nice return on investment for its French *proprieteurs*.

If these two characteristics are understood—the impermanence of market segments and their occasionally low market share—market segmentation or the pursuit of identifiable chunks of a larger market can be very profitable indeed. It becomes important, then, to know how to segment a market, how to find small, profitable hunks of a larger activity.

Markets, like the Empire State Building, appear from a distance to be monoliths. They are not. Anything which separates one group of customers from another has the potential for being the basis of a market segment.

Eight Common Ways of Segmenting Markets

There are a number of ways in which markets have been segmented. Eight considerations which have influenced market segmentation are presented in Fig. 3.1. They suggest the many possibilities. We'll take a look at each of them.

- Buyer sophistication: the way the buying decision is reached
- Reseller pricing practices
- Purchased volume
- Product line growth
- Unfulfilled or imperfectly fulfilled customer needs
- Distinctive funding practices
- Product use requirements
- Status—perceptions of value

Figure 3.1. Eight considerations which influence market segmentation.

Buyer Sophistication: The Way Buying Decisions Are Reached

Here the basis of segmentation is not the product or service and its features and benefits as they relate to customer need. Rather it is the process by which the buying decision is made and the sophistication of the decision makers. Here segmentation is based on the vendor's needs and the most effective way to reach buyers at different levels of sophistication.

An easy example of this can be found in the automotive market. At one level of sophistication are those who merely kick tires and ask how much. At another level, there are those concerned with expected value and who discuss warranty protection, EPA ratings, and the like. Then there are others who are concerned with MacPherson Struts, Zero Scrub Radii, compression and displacement, and other such arcana. Watching television for a week will show how manufacturers and dealers address these three primitive market segments.

The same type of segmentation can be seen in industry where, for example, a process plant or machine tools are the products being sold. It is a typical four-tier mix of capital equipment buyers.

The *first tier* is made up of the big boys. There aren't many of them, but there are enough to make a market. These are the Exxons and the General Motors who have the scratch to buy anything they care to buy and who can afford to take their time in doing so. And they do. These firms have engineering departments who can and will do cost-benefit analyses on all proposals submitted. This process often requires two or three or even four budgeting cycles to complete.

To write current business with one of these firms means either short-circuiting established buying patterns or being smart enough to have submitted the winning proposal two or three or even four budgeting cycles earlier.

This market segment is profitable for those with staying power whose proposals can withstand nitpicking and for those who have the ability to short-circuit established procurement procedures.

The *second tier* market is just as well off as the first tier, but operating units tend to be smaller and staffing a bit leaner. Management is quite able to evaluate a proposal on its own merits, to ask for more information if it is necessary, and to make a buying decision within one buying cycle or even sooner if some competitive or financial benefit is there.

Here it is possible to sell, book, and bill within a reasonable period. This is a market segment exploited by hungry vendors who have good products and good people able to make good presentations and answer tough questions. The second tier may be 10 times larger than the first tier.

The *third tier* may be 8 or 10 times larger than the second. It is made up of firms who can use financial help in making a purchase but, more significantly, who do not have the depth, the experience, or the sophistication in their management to evaluate proposals on their own merits. Management may even hire a consultant for advice before making its buying decision.

Success in this market segment requires providing all kinds of assurances that the buyer is indeed making the correct buying decision. Showcase installations, case histories, congruent or compatible references, and people to call will all be important parts of the sales efforts, as will be easy-payment plans. This segment requires a quite different sales approach than the other two.

The *fourth tier* is by far the most numerous: small establishments made up of mom-and-pops, startups, doubtful credit risks—establishments with hard-to-predict needs and hard-to-identify buyers. It is a sizable segment to be sure, but not focused enough to warrant a special advertising or sales effort. It can be safely ignored. Word of mouth and rub-off from advertisements and sales efforts aimed at the other three segments will provoke inquiries from these establishments.

Reseller Pricing Practices

Some markets readily segment themselves on the basis of the way resellers price and sell their goods. This is especially true of consumer markets where pricing norms are more apt to be established by the advertisements of discounters than by the suggested retail prices of the manufacturers.

Health and beauty aids, appliances, especially white goods, and clothing regularly segment into regular price and discount operations. In some parts of the country a third, lower-priced promotional segment may be added to the clothing and appliance markets.

Here, it is the merchant, not the manufacturer, who is the driving force in market segmentation. It is the high-turnover, middle-market discounters who set the pace. The demand for promotional goods, factory rejects, seconds, and name-brand goods to be marked down is virtually insatiable. A special group of manufacturers of no-name goods serves this market. Their stock in trade consists of low prices achieved through imitative or knockoff styling and shortcut manufacturing techniques. Such manufacturers rarely, if ever, are able to establish a brand name of their own and to achieve any kind of position in the regular-priced market. However, some manufacturers from Korea, Taiwan, Hong Kong, and Singapore seem to be having some success in this effort.

There are hazards to producers of brand-name goods who seek to serve this off-price market. That hazard is the loss of the brand-name cachet which made them attractive to this segment in the first place.

Purchased Volume and Packaging

Here the basis of market segmentation is the size of a typical purchase and the packaging which makes that purchase possible.

A simple example of this is acetone. It is sold in bulk as a process feedstock or as a compounding ingredient. And it is perfumed and sold by the ounce in fancy flacons as nail polish remover.

In situations like this, the product is usually a commodity sold competitively with very tight margins. Profitability for the producer seems to be in inverse ratio to the amount of handling and packaging the product requires to move in the marketplace. Frequently, the original producer will not sell to all the market segments that use that particular product.

Portland Cement is a good example of this. Some market segments are served by the producer, some by distribution, and some by repackagers and by compounders of other materials.

Typically, a manufacturer will sell in bulk to large manufacturers of concrete products: pipe and block. He will sell in bulk to transit mixers who deliver ready mix to construction sites. He will make bulk sales to compounders of dry cement-based products. Finally, he will sell packaged cement to distributors who supply the building and construction trades, the home centers, and the building materials yards.

Since all commodities come close to meeting or actually do meet the same specifications, there is little on which to choose a supplier. Buying decisions, therefore, are made on the basis of price and delivery. Dominance or leadership in any one of these market segments requires something way beyond the offerings of other manufacturers. Technical support, special formulations and promotional support are typical of the product add-ons used here.

Product Line Growth

Occasionally the demand for a product or product line which historically was profitable only if sold along with other lines suddenly begins to grow. Growth is sufficient to warrant separate distribution and sales efforts. For example, a recent analysis of the active lines at F. W. Woolworth variety stores disclosed that many were active enough to support separate specialty store operations. Thus, in addition to its separate Kinney Shoe and Richman Brothers men's clothing chains, Woolworth has added specialty chains selling stationery and office supplies, picture framing and posters, children's clothing, and athletic shoes. Freed from the low-price Woolworth stigma, each supports higher prices. All began as line items or small departments at old-fashioned five-and-ten-cent stores.

Unfulfilled or Imperfectly Fulfilled Customer Needs

The health care needs of the public have traditionally been met by the private physician, by hospitals, and by special-purpose clinics. However, over time, this configuration of services has too often proved incapable of providing emergency or other on-demand services. Private physicians are unreliably available in emergency or other on-demand situations. Hospitals are overpriced, and in emergency situations become an ordeal of waiting. Further, access to special clinics has become overly bureaucratic.

In such situations, enterprising physicians have seen an opportunity and have established 24-hour, walk-in treatment centers. Typically, such operations are located in areas of easy access and high visibility.

They attract customers who use cash or credit cards to pay standardized and slightly higher-than-usual fees for services. By providing services around the clock when needed, the centers which make up this segment of the health care market syphon off cash business from public hospitals and private physicians. Although this trend is only a few years old, by the mid-eighties, there were already over 2500 centers operating nationally. Their owners are already well off and well on their way to becoming rich. Even department stores have entered this market offering primary health care services during regular store hours.

Hospitals are beginning to strike back. For example, the Mission Oaks Hospital of Los Gatos, California, has faced up to the long-wait problem common to most emergency rooms. If the wait is more than five minutes for emergency care, the accounting department grants a 25 percent discount on the bill.

Distinctive Funding Patterns

The market for fire apparatus would seem to be a rather straightforward one. A fire truck is, after all, just a fire truck. However, this market, too, may not be as monolithic as it would seem.

There are, of course, the usual governmental, municipal, and industrial situations where it is "bid against specifications" and more-or-less standard capital goods selling practices apply.

However, there is also a large, volunteer fire department market, where pride in equipment is nearly as important as its utility. Here, fund raising is the critical activity. The proceeds from raffles, carnivals, suppers, and barbecues take the place of budget line items. This is clearly a special market, and those who are able to cater to it—help with the fund raising and provide good basic equipment to which more bells and whistles can be added later—have a very good thing.

Product Use Requirements

A good but historical example of segmentation through product use is provided by the offset duplicator market. Here the need is for a press with a greater capacity than a Xerox machine but smaller than a large, commercial webfed press—something with a capacity of roughly 100 to 5000 impressions. This is not just one market but four: office, small commercial, in-plant, and instant printing.

The instant printing market, the fastest-growing segment of the total, is characterized by many short runs of reasonable quality, typically runs of 100 to 500 copies. It requires a press that takes up very little floor space (these are mostly storefront operations), one that is easy to maintain and simple to set up and wash up (these are minimum-wage businesses). Further, this market needs plate-making equipment that, too, is quick and uncomplicated to operate.

AB Dick has developed the press that helped bring this market into being, and ITEK has provided the required plate-making equipment. Together, they seem to have this market segment locked up.

A similar situation is developing in the EDP (electronic data processing), or computer market. Once this market was viewed as a monolith, built of mainframes accessed by one or more terminals which could only ask questions and print out answers. Now the market has split into three discrete segments, with a fourth gradually forming. All involve extremely sophisticated equipment.

At the bottom is the home computer market, an offshoot of the video game craze. These machines can store and manipulate data and display it as useful information on a screen. Such machines can balance a checkbook and teach children their math. Commodore may dominate this market, a market which reflects a need for status more than for computing capability.

At the next level is the personal computer. It too can store and manipulate data and bring forth useful information on a printer or a screen. Personal computers (PCs) can talk to one another, access mainframe data if properly programmed, and manipulate and store vast amounts of data. IBM appears to have about 60 percent of this market segment.

At the top is new and vastly more sophisticated equipment in the old mainframe configuration. IBM may have about 70 percent of this market.

In between mainframes and personal computers is a large amorphous middle market which needs more flexibility than mainframes permit but which also requires more power than PCs can deliver. This middle market may turn out to be several separate market segments which will become apparent as their requirements are defined and special equipment is developed to satisfy them.

Status—Perceptions of Value

Finally, there are market segments based upon the buyer's desire for status and various perceptions of value.

Examples here abound.

Writing instruments provide a very good example. Among the name brands for this market, the range is from the Bic ballpoint at a cost of pennies to the Mont Blanc at a cost of thousands of dollars—with a vast midrange made up of Scriptos, Papermates, Pentels, Shaeffers, Crosses, Parkers, etc. With any product family from automobiles to writing instruments there are marketing opportunities at either end of the price range. At the low end, it is the price-performance combination that is critical. A Bic, for example, is just as effective a writing instrument as the Mont Blanc. A Yugo or Hyundai provides as adequate transportation as a Rolls Royce.

At the high end, status is really what is important. The quality of performance, so long as it is adequate, is less important than the simple fact of ownership.

The hazards of trying to exploit either the low-end segment or the high-end segment of any market are sizable. However, if Bic and Gucci can be used as examples, both segments can be exploited successfully.

Finding a Basis for Segmentation

From the foregoing, it is possible to draw a few conclusions to guide a vendor in finding ways to carve off a more profitable chunk of a served market. One of these conclusions may be a bit surprising. The traditional view has it that the driving force in market segmentation is a difference in the needs of two groups of customers who make up a market. Often, one or both of these groups can in turn be segmented. To illustrate: the telephone company publishes and distributes a directory of its subscribers: name, address, and phone number. R. R. Donnelley went one step further and developed the *Yellow Pages* in which it could sell advertising—a directory by major category of product or service, a directory of who sells what, including name, address, and phone number.

Then came the *Business to Business Yellow Pages*, a listing of who sells what that would be of interest to businesses and, of course, another opportunity to sell advertising.

More recently, another hunk of the *Yellow Pages* has been sliced off, *The Silver Pages*, an appropriately named listing of who sells what products and services that might be of interest to senior citizens.

This is the way most markets are segmented: by a division of the customer base and the development of new products or the modification of existing products for that segment of the larger base. And this is the way that most markets will continue to be segmented.

However, there is another basis for segmentation as well, a basis that has more to do with the needs of the vendor than the needs of the customer. In this situation, what gets modified is not so much the product, as the way the product is brought to market—the advertising and promotional and sales efforts required to sell it.

We have seen, for example, a situation in which the vendor needs customers who can pay cash for what they buy and who also can come to a buying decision quickly. The vendor then segments the market to identify those who meet these requirements and focuses all advertising promotional and sales efforts on them. The other potential customers, the other markets segments, become over-the-transom business.

Here is another example of the same kind of thing.

There are manufacturers and providers of service who have neither the staff nor the facilities to furnish specially engineered products or services to all comers. They must sell standard products or services in which the creative and engineering content of each sales unit is standard and well established.

To illustrate: with some industrial process equipment, the engineering content of each standard unit may be only 3 percent of costs, whereas for a "special," the engineering content may exceed 40 percent of costs. The problem becomes this. With limited facilities and staff, if only specials are sold it will be difficult to keep a manufacturing crew together while engineers fuss over the details of special equipment which are rarely, if ever, critically important.

The requirement here is to identify that segment of the market which will be happy with standard equipment and then advertise, promote, and sell to it.

Ultimately, successful segmentation of any market depends upon:

1. Knowing the market and the way it works
2. Knowing the customers it serves and their needs
3. Knowing the competitive offerings to that market (The view of competition must not be restricted: Gypsum board, Sheetrock, can be held in place by nails, by dry wall screws, or by construction adhesive; these products are competitive with one another)
4. Knowing one's own products, capabilities, and needs

Summary

Market segments may not be forever, and they may turn out to represent a small market share. However, if they are properly selected and served with imagination, they can be long-lived as well as profitable.

4

The Functional
Responsibilities of Marketing

The key to the development and management of a successful marketing effort lies in understanding three things:

1. The nature of the market to be served
2. The behavior of products within that market
3. The specific functional marketing responsibilities that must be controlled for any marketing effort to succeed

We have taken a close look (Chap. 2) at the way seven kinds of markets work: two consumer markets, four industrial markets, and the service market. As we did this, we also got an idea of how products behave in those markets.

Now we'll take a look at 25 activities—functional marketing responsibilities—which any marketing effort must control if it is to be successful. How they apply will differ from situation to situation, but *all* must be accounted for.

Before we get started, however, it might be a good idea to restate a definition of marketing. By *marketing*, I simply mean all those things which help define a product and bring it to market profitably and do so in such a way that whoever buys and uses the product (or service) is glad to have done so.

Twenty-Five Responsibilities
of Marketing

There is no ready-built, one-size-fits-all structure for a marketing organization that applies equally to the sale of insurance, chewing gum, automobiles, investment services, copper tubing, grass-roots chemical plants, or any other product or service which people buy. Similarly, one cannot pick up an organization chart from another organization and expect it to fit like a shirt with standard neck size and sleeve length.

What is possible, however, is to monitor product and market behavior to identify the few relevant variables that control product profitability and productivity. What results is not a static assignment of duties, responsibilities, and reporting relationships that can be depicted by a two-dimensional organization chart.

Rather, what results requires a continuing adjustment in the assignment of duties, of responsibilities, and of reporting relationships as products, markets, and competitive activities change. What's required is management, active management.

Marketers may and do share a number of problems. To a greater or lesser degree, a department store shares all the marketing problems of a paper mill, a restaurant, or a manufacturer of minicomputers. However, the form in which these problems appear and the means used for solving them will be unique to each marketing situation.

Among the major functional responsibilities that commonly fall under the heading of marketing or that have a profound effect on marketing's success, 25 come readily to mind. These are listed in Fig. 4.1 and seem to be common to all organizations with products or services to sell.

Some are clearly the province of marketing, some may be shared with other traditional functional groups—manufacturing or finance, for example—and some, unfortunately in too many organizations, are orphans without status or an agreed-upon place in the structure. Yet, all are part and parcel of the business' contacts with customers and potential customers and are, therefore, vital to continued marketing success. Some may be combined, and some clearly stand alone. All are important, however, and none can be neglected.

This is not to say that other functions are not also important in ensuring success in the marketplace. Quality assurance is certainly a function, but even though the standards by which quality is measured may be based in large part upon information supplied by marketing, the measuring and control functions by which quality is ensured are clearly the responsibility of manufacturing.

We'll review each of these marketing responsibilities briefly. But as we do, keep in mind that these responsibilities are never seen in a vacuum but always in a continuing and changing relationship with overall firm capabilities, the needs and wants of the markets it serves, and, of course, the activities and offerings of competition.

1. Product design and development
2. Market identification and development
3. Product strategy, positioning, and surrounds
4. Packaging
5. Pricing
6. Advertising: Creating a preference
7. Promoting sales
8. Generating and following up leads
9. Physical distribution
10. Outside sales
11. Inside sales
12. Direct response sales: telephone, television, and direct mail
13. Key account management and sales
14. Controlling product mix
15. Applications engineering: Label instructions
16. Customer service
17. Order entry
18. Fulfillment: Installation and startup
19. Warranty and guaranty: Maintenance and repair
20. Tracking competition
21. Market research
22. Training
23. Forecasting
24. Planning
25. Managing all of the above

Figure 4.1. Twenty-five functional responsibilities of marketing.

The first two items on the list, products and markets, represent a chicken-and-egg situation. I don't wish to prejudice things by the order in which they are discussed. In most ongoing business situations, the products already exist. In that sense, therefore, products come first. In other situations, however, especially startups, all that may exist at first is a well-defined market with a clear need. The product will come later. Here, clearly, the market comes first. With this as our only hedge, let's review the list.

1. Product Design and Development

Quite simply, this means determining (1) what a firm can produce and sell profitably, (2) something that will have a long market life, and (3) a product that will give the producer a competitive edge. For a new firm, this is the initial product offering. For an established organization, it concerns what else can be developed and sold that meets these three requirements.

For a restaurant, this means menu planning. For attorneys, accountants, and management consultants it means defining areas of specialization and the services to be offered. For department stores, it might mean finding suitable promotional merchandise to build traffic. The analogous concerns of manufacturers are, perhaps, better known.

Always, product design and development involve dialogue with the marketplace. For manufacturers of consumer goods with millions of potential buyers, this requires shrewd observation or carefully structured and statistically valid research projects. For fast-food chains, it means the continued testing of menu items. For the manufacturer of industrial goods, it means the continued liaison with the decision makers and buying influences at key accounts.

2. Market Identification and Development

Conventional wisdom holds with Ralph Waldo Emerson that "If a man can write a better book, preach a better sermon or make a better mouse trap than his neighbor, though he builds his house in the woods, the world will make a beaten path to his door." Unfortunately, it doesn't always work like that. Road maps must be printed and distributed to those who are or might be interested in the better book, sermon, or mouse trap. Put another way, the market for each must first be identified and defined. Often it must be created.

To illustrate with a single example, generations of young people have become habituated to chewing gum, a practice which, for many, continues into adulthood. At some point, however, dentures become common. The presumption is that some will stop chewing lest their cuds stick to their plates. With nonsticking Freedent, William Wrigley has found, or created, a profitable new market. Similarly, new markets were created with body lotions that have no bitter aftertaste, special offset presses for the instant printing market, home video games that duplicate all the on-screen activity of arcade games, and Cabbage Patch dolls and all that goes with them for children who want to play at being parents without having to pay the bills.

Consumer markets are made up of enormous numbers of individuals who share one or more common characteristics. Thus, markets may be made up of denture wearers, people with fixed incomes, women whose hair has split ends, sexual swingers, home owners with cinch-bug problems, etc. Once a market has been identified and its demographics established, the importance of the individual disappears.

In contrast, industrial markets are made up of firms that share common characteristics, firms that require overnight delivery of small parcels or firms that pressure-treat wood, process fresh fruits and vegetables, or mold plastics. However, once an industrial market has been identified, the units that make it up become very important. Further, the identification of the individuals within each organization who make or influence buying decisions becomes critical.

Paradoxically, industrial markets are made up of people identified by name and title, whereas consumer markets are made up of great gobs of people identified only by zip code, neighborhood, or affinity group.

3. Product Strategy, Positioning, and Product Surrounds

Once the product and the market have been identified, the next step is to establish how the product is to be presented to the market. This is a matter of strategy, positioning, and surrounds. There are three challenges here.

The first is this. The product, especially a new product, ought to fit the manufacturer's reputation and be compatible with its other products and with the way it does business. It must be seen by the market as an appropriate offering. For example, 3M Company has recently introduced a new product for home owners—a caulking compound to go around door and window frames to seal out wind and water and seal in heat. In contrast to the very messy cartridge applicator, the 3M product is a bead of compound mounted on tape. It can be cut to length and pressed into place with no muss or fuss. It fits nicely in with other 3M products for the consumer. It is the kind of thing consumers expect from 3M.

In contrast, GE's and RCA's attempts to enter the mainframe computer market failed in large part because their potential customers never perceived either GE or RCA as having the same qualifications as IBM, Univac, or Burroughs. Only "Japan, Inc.," has a sufficiently broad reputation to be able to offer a new product in almost any area and have the market-producer relationship viewed favorably.

The second challenge has to do with deciding against whom you are going to compete—if against anyone at all. When Volkswagen first appeared, it was presented as a small, inexpensive, funny-looking car that provided reliable, fuel-efficient transportation. Doyle-Dane's advertising did this job brilliantly. Volks ignored competition, did its own thing, and prospered. Detroit wasn't even aware that the market was interested in such small cars. By the time Detroit caught on, Volks, under a new management, switched its approach and began to offer, "Different Volks for Different Folks." In doing so, it took on the entire automobile industry and lost whatever advantage it had gained.

Occasionally, one encounters a product that is so versatile as to be almost unbelievable. The minicomputer is such a product. A more common example is sodium bicarbonate—baking soda—a perfectly marvelous and infinitely versatile substance. Baking soda is, for example, a baking essential, a refrigerator deodorant, a swimming pool clarifier, a laundering agent, and a palliative for insect bites and sunburn. Church & Dwight's initial efforts to make the product more believable was to market it under two brand names, Arm & Hammer and Cow, and to ascribe a different set of attributes to each.

Lately, the same firm has begun packaging baking soda in liquid form and offering it as a laundry detergent. Thus, it has positioned itself, picked its competition, and given a single focus to some of its advertising and promotional efforts. Whether the market will perceive Church & Dwight to be a believable manufacturer of a laundry detergent along with Procter & Gamble, Lever Brothers, and Colgate-Palmolive remains to be seen.

Ammonia and trisodium phosphate are other equally versatile substances with similar positioning and strategic challenges. And, of course, there is Chase Bag Balm, which is even more marvelous than baking soda.

The third challenge has to do with the way the product is presented—what surrounds it as it is offered to buyers.

One might, for example, quite legitimately be offered a flawless diamond at a bargain price by a Times Square bum. Only the very knowledgable could consider such a deal. This prospect may strike you as being very farfetched perhaps, but businesses do things equally foolish. For example, product surrounds are critical in the banking and financial services industries. Yet banks continue to put kids and trainees on the platform to handle the initial screening of commercial loans, and financial service houses try to sell investment programs through failing insurance agents and chrome-plated used-car salesmen.

Most of the 25 functional responsibilities discussed here help make up the product surrounds and help determine the way a product is perceived.

4. Packaging

There are several possibilities here, some for the benefit of the customer, more than a few for the benefit of the producer, and some in which the package appears to be more important than its content.

Packaging can even create markets. For example, the miniature metering pumps and valves for nasal sprays and inhalents which dispense very accurate dosages have created a market for a new kind of prescription pharmaceutical.

Occasionally, the package can be used to make the product easier to acquire, easier to use, and less costly to buy. For example, Portland Cement comes in bulk in 94-pound paper sacks and in smaller quantities ready-mixed with sand. Liquid lawn fertilizers, delivered by and applied from tank wagons, are another illustration of ease-of-use packaging. Mortgage insurance is available as declining term so that only the mortgage balance is covered and needs to be paid for. Occasionally, the package itself is designed for special usefulness; the specially embossed Skippy peanut butter jar can serve as a fine measuring cup.

As often, the package is designed to increase shelf visibility. For example, sterile eye pads seem to be all the same size, 2 × 2½ inches. Most come in a box with a 3½ × 3½ inch face to allow room for the sealed wrappers that protect each pad. However, Johnson & Johnson's box, which offers the same quality and same-sized pad as other firms, has a face that measures 4¾ × 4½ inches, thus assuring itself more shelf visibility. The J&J package costs more, as it should since it takes up more display space.

Package size can also be used to introduce or reintroduce potential users to a product. Specially sized samples are commonplace. Changes in chewing gum packaging provide an interesting example of this use of packaging. Over the past few years, the standard package for stick chewing gum grew to 15 or 17 sticks per pack, quite a sizable bundle to carry about. In the belief that this large package size prevented a number of people from buying gum, William Wrigley has reintroduced the five-stick pack for a quarter. For years the five-stick pack at a nickel was the industry standard.

Occasionally, the package is designed to increase consumption. The 11-oz bottle of Prell shampoo in my bathroom has an opening under the screw cap that has a 1-inch inside diameter. When used in the shower, it delivers over a tablespoon of shampoo when a half teaspoon will do. Cigarette manufacturers are now pushing soft packs with 25 cigarettes rather than the usual 20. This increases the number of bent and broken cigarettes at the end of the pack. Similarly, Kodak 35-mm film in 12-exposure rolls is nearly impossible to find during summer months. One can more readily find the 24- or 36-exposure package.

And, of course, there is the notorious case of the little grey cardboard box that paper clips come in. Fewer than half the secretaries I've ever known can move one of these boxes from stockroom to desk without having the box come apart and its contents go all over the floor. Consider what happens to consumption when these little boxes get into the hands of people who are *klutzes!*

Finally, there is the situation in which the package seems to be more important than its content. Before World War II, a liquor purporting to come from France and called Forbidden Fruit was commonly available. It tasted like Ann Page apricot preserves and came in a bottle that was a cross between a royal orb and an anarchist's bomb. Its look appealed to growing children and others with low and undiscriminating taste. It disappeared during the war. Now the bottle is back, this time called Chambord, with the color and flavor of over-sugared raspberry Kool-Aid. Its appeal is still to the same undiscriminating crowd.

Packaging is surely an important part of sales and marketing.

5. Pricing

Here the problem is one of balancing real costs and the need for a profit against perceived value and customer expectations and ability to pay. No one could afford to buy the original Xerox machines. Leased out at a nickel a copy, however, they moved well and were both cheaper and more convenient than carbons or hectographed and mimeographed copies.

The possibilities range from a retailer's large markdown from an even larger markup to the value billings of certain professionals in which the worth of the services provided is directly proportional to the size of the fees charged. The goal here is to cover costs and overhead and make a substantial contribution to profits; but one has to be fairly clear about both costs and profits. If the product cannot be packaged and presented to achieve this goal, then perhaps it should not be brought to market.

But, however carefully prices are calculated, they are always subject to deterioration from unexpected causes. Cumulative discounts, volume rebates, and even shipping practices and sales terms can reduce otherwise satisfactory margins (see Chap. 14).

6. Advertising: Creating a Preference

Too frequently, advertising is confused with sales promotion or direct response selling or with lead generation. Although they all use the same media, they have entirely separate goals. With advertising, the aim is to create recognition of and preference for a specific product, service, brand, or firm. "With a name like Smuckers, it has to be good."

Successful advertising requires that the medium, the market, and the message be appropriate for one another. Creativity consists in selecting the most effective combination of message and media for the market to be reached. Thus spot radio advertising during prime drive time has been highly effective in selling ocean freight services, lumber and plywood, high-priced foreign cars, and electronic devices.

Effectiveness is ensured when advertising is continuous and repetitive.

All too frequently, advertising aims exclusively at the ultimate decision maker overlooking completely those who can influence a buying decision. Thus the advertising of technical industrial products addresses the specifying engineer and often overlooks purchasing agents and manufacturing supervisors or the people responsible for selling the finished product. (Of course, the exact opposite is true when it comes to advertising toys at Christmastime. Then, advertisements seem directed exclusively at kids who may not have money or decision-making ability but who know how to drop hints and otherwise pester those who do.)

Finally, with industrial products, especially well-placed product public relations is often more effective than many bought-and-paid-for advertisements.

7. Promoting Sales

In contrast to advertising, which seeks to create recognition and preferment, the aim of sales promotion is to get people to do it now—sell it now, buy it now, move it now.

Sales promotion takes many forms. On a formal institutionalized level, we see it in advertisements which offer reward for buying now, such as a premium, entry into a sweepstakes, a two-for-the-price-of-one deal, or a cents-off coupons. We see it also at the point of purchase: counter cards, shelf talkers, table tents, and display racks at the cash register. All these promotions prompt impulse buying: "You saw it on TV, here it is." Other forms of sales promotion aim at retail and checkout clerks, distributors, dealers, and salespersons.

On a more personal, less formal level, other kinds of reward are offered for selling or buying. Thus, retail clerks may be "spiffed" or offered tickets to a ballgame. And buyers may be offered a night on the town with a prepaid playmate or a week at the company hunting lodge.

Effective advertising is continuous and repetitive, but effective sales promotion is novel and infrequent. Continuous sales promotion forces the promoter into a constant search for a bigger bang for the buck or, even, more bucks for the bang. It shifts the attention of the market from the product to the next promotion.

8. Generating and Following Up Leads

Generation of leads must be considered separately from advertising and sales promotion, although it employs the techniques of both. Here, the goal is to induce prospective customers to identify themselves and to express interest in the offered product or service. Typically, these offerings are complex and will involve some consultation with the prospect before a sale is made; this is the case, for example, with insurance, financial services, and new or high-tech industrial products. All the conventional media are useful in generating leads as are seminars and workshops, technical papers, and exhibits at fairs and trade shows.

Lead generation is costly. The big challenge here is to make sure that the leads generated are adequately screened and that the live ones are followed up (see Chap. 20). Too frequently, postcards and coupons languish in a corner and eventually go out with the trash. The tendency always seems to be to wait for next month's bingo cards. Next month, of course, is forever and old leads are *dead* leads.

9. Physical Distribution

For many products, industrial as well as consumer, availability—often instant availability—is the key to market success. The Hershey Chocolate Bar may be the supreme example of this. For years, Hershey dominated its market without spending a nickel for advertising. Rather than advertise, Hershey went for universal distribution and nearly achieved it. At almost every location where one could expect to buy a chocolate bar, there was a display of Hersheys.

Not all products require universal distribution and instant availability. Some buyers, especially of industrial products, build in lead time in their ordering processes and seem to tolerate delay between the placing of an order and actual delivery. Some products, such as tailored clothing, even require such a delay as sleeves are shortened and hems and cuffs turned.

The goal of wide, if not universal, distribution and of full pipelines to the user is to prevent another supplier from getting between the producer and the producer's customers when they are ready to buy. The objective, of course, is to prevent a customer from gaining experience with a substitute. Availability is a serious problem with established products for which there is a continuing demand. It becomes critical with new products when the customer responds to an advertisement or to a sales presentation and is ready to buy. But beyond ensuring the availability of a product to its market, the physical distribution function has other roles to play in marketing.

Back in the early twenties when refrigerated transportation of frozen foods was rare, the manufacture of Popsicles was licensed to dairies in major markets. The dairies also handled local distribution. Eventually one hundred or so were under license. Under these circumstances quality was difficult to supervise and, as time went on, deteriorated badly. Now Popsicle has reduced the number of licensees to about twenty-five and handles its own distribution. Quality and sales volume have improved considerably.

The solution of distribution problems has other benefits as well. Back in the early fifties when Mike Todd was planning the almost-3-D production of "Around the World in Eighty Days," wraparound wide-screen effects were achieved with three synchronized projectors. The number of movie houses that could show wide-screen productions was limited. Saturation bookings, commonplace today, were therefore impossible. This meant that the repayment of funds used to finance the film would be slow and interest charges would accumulate rapidly.

One of Todd's objectives was to find a way of increasing the number of houses that could show the film and thus shorten the payback period. To achieve this he needed an optical system that would achieve the wide-screen effect without the need for three synchronous projectors. He turned to American Optical and commissioned them to design a system so that, in his words, "It should all come out one hole." The single lens Todd-AO process that resulted enabled him to achieve the near-saturation bookings needed.

It is important to determine the mode of physical distribution which will ensure each product's market success. With the progressive deregulation of the transportation industries, traditional modes of moving goods to market can be reexamined. Often there are savings which are enormous. These can be passed on to customers in various ways or added to the marketer's own profits.

10. Outside Sales

Sales are made in many different ways and only one involves salespersons who call on customers to sell products and write orders. Indeed, with the cost of a single sales call now over $230 and nearly six calls being required to develop an order, few firms can afford to rely exclusively on field salespeople to develop business. Whenever possible, other sales techniques are used.

Selling at the executive-to-executive level can be extremely cost-effective. The practice is commonplace in consumer packaged-goods selling where a product manager, brand manager, or regional sales manager handles selling at chain headquarters. Selling at the executive level is also effective in industrial sales when the objective is to get a new product accepted, to negotiate a supply contract, or to sell capital equipment.

The use of field sales representatives is justified when the size of the potential order is large, when special, nonstandard products are involved, or when the call objectives include developing information about the account as well as writing orders.

So if "salesman" conjures up visions of someone in polyester double-knit, a white-on-white shirt, pastel plastic loafers, and a tie that would blind a gorgon or of a retail clerk too busy gossiping to pay attention even though money is burning a hole in the customer's pocket, remember that the reality is vastly different.

11. Inside Sales

It is not always necessary for a sales representative to call in person on an account to write business. A number of capital equipment firms serving well-defined markets with equipment whose use is well-understood sell quite nicely by telephone, even though an order may run into six or seven figures. Typically, the process begins when incoming inquiries are followed up to determine the level of response required. The process continues on through developing specifications and application data, preparing and issuing quotes and proposals, on to the receipt of purchase orders. Thus two or three people can cover the entire country without spending a dime for travel (see Chap. 20).

This long-distance selling is unusual. More typically, when standard products are involved—products whose use and purpose are well-understood—field sales efforts are supplemented by telephone sales efforts to solicit add-on or fill-in business from established accounts. The telephone company calls this *telemarketing* and suggests that it is a new idea. However, stock and commodity brokers have been using this technique since their first telephones were installed at the turn of the century.

12. Direct-Response Sales—Telephone, Television, and Direct Mail

When purely standard products are involved and the creditworthiness of potential customers is assured, personal selling may be replaced by impersonal direct mail, television, or telephone solicitation.

The widespread possession of bank credit cards makes it safe to use direct-response marketing techniques with individual consumers. Thus, orders for standard domestic products are solicited by telephone. "Call or write" orders for phonograph records and tapes, costume jewelry, kitchen gadgets, etc., are solicited on television, and nearly anything can be sold by direct mail.

13. Key Account Management & Sales

All customers are equal—as far as product performance and the satisfaction of warranty and guaranty claims are concerned. However, for a variety of reasons and in a number of special ways, some customers are more equal than others.

A key account, for example, may be a volume buyer whose large purchases at a modest markup make possible many small sales to others at high markup. Other key accounts may be trend setters in their industries or social groups, and sales to them—especially of new products—helps ensure product acceptance by others.

Another class of key accounts is made up of the technological leaders in their industries. These accounts can and often do lead their suppliers into the development of profitable new products or the identification of profitable new markets.

Failure to pay attention to key accounts may lead to disaster. For example, a large national service organization derived 20 percent of its multimillion dollar income from only 23 volume buyers of its published material. The buying patterns of these accounts had been stable for decades. Budget allocations for the next year were scaled in midsummer, approved and authorized in the fall, and the purchase orders issued in March. Disaster came when the vendor doubled its prices in May, failed to inform these accounts in time to influence the summertime budgeting process, and delayed announcing the price increase until January after everyone had allocated the usual funds for traditional purchases. The result? Anticipated income was halved, buying habits were broken, and the key accounts found that they could do nicely with smaller quantities.

A firm may have several different kinds of key accounts, and a single key account may be important in several different ways. All must be identified and close liaison maintained with them. Further, except in rare cases, that liaison will have to be maintained by management personnel, not the sales force. Sales representatives, after all, are under great pressure to sell existing products. That imperative colors the relationships they have with key account personnel. Developing useful information is not so easily done when the underlying motive is a sale.

14. Controlling Product Mix

The mix of products actually sold can be an important factor in the success of a marketing effort. Sometimes it is merely a matter of product availability, there being no point in selling something that cannot be delivered.

Occasionally, the situation may be more serious. For example, a manufacturer of process equipment for the electronics industry had, after much effort, standardized its product line. Standard items, with 30 percent of the price as up-front money, required very little engineering time—only 3 percent of the total cost. Standard products satisfied nearly 80 percent of the market. By selling standard products, engineering would have time to develop new standard products and pay attention to the occasional special. Manufacturing, for its part, would be able to develop and maintain a cadre of skilled people.

Without supervision, however, sales continued to sell specials (even though standards would do) in which the engineering content averaged 40 percent of costs. Up-front money dried up, and manufacturing had to let people go.

Controlling product mix is often overlooked as a major marketing responsibility.

15. Applications Engineering: Label Instructions

Applications engineering, as a term, is most commonly associated with technical industrial products. The idea is simple, however, and its significance goes beyond this single class of product. Customers must know how to use whatever they have bought.

The importance of this notion can be illustrated simply and directly by the following: The sale of oysters and cherrystone clams at a nearby fish market nearly doubled when the clerks began routinely asking all customers "May I show you an easy way to open them?" In a similar vein, *plain boiled* in the shell is the simplest and most profitable way for a restaurant to fix and serve lobster; and most restaurants that serve whole lobsters also provide detailed instructions, via napkins or place mats, for getting the meat out of the shell with minimum mess.

The need to know how to use and how to enjoy a product exists at all levels of sophistication. Satisfying that need generates customer loyalty. It also suggests ideas for product improvements and even new products themselves.

16. Customer Service

Customer service people are the sales correspondents, the voices on the other end of the telephones, the people who staff service desks and follow through on warranty and guaranty claims. Customer service supplies literature; answers questions; explains procedures; tries to correct inaccurate or strange-looking bills and invoices; handles returns, credits, and exchanges; tracks down lost orders; and expedites the shipment of orders that have been delayed. Customer service may also qualify leads for the sales force, separating the literature collectors from real prospects.

Next, after verifying the quality and the performance of the product itself, customer service is most responsible for customer loyalty. For example, it is not merely the quality of the magazine alone that accounts for the continued growth of *National Geographic*. Its customer service, special-order people are a joy to work with. Similarly, for years, J. Willard Marriott, Sr., as befits an innkeeper, was his own customer service manager with considerable benefit for the growth of his organization and his loyal clientele. In contrast, Sears Roebuck, once renowned for its customer service, seems recently to have become a bureaucratic nightmare, its customer service a form of guerrilla warfare. It has only recently begun to correct itself.

In some firms, indeed, the customer service function is barely tolerated—a poor orphan assigned to whatever functional group has excess supervisory capacity, such as sales, manufacturing, shipping, finance, or whatever. But, since customer service is the only place within an organization where all aspects of a firm's performance in the market place come together—product performance, pricing, packing, shipping, service, etc.—some firms have this function report directly to the CEO. Actually, customer service is a critical marketing function and belongs there.

17. Order Entry

This is often a shared function since it is equally important to sales & marketing and to manufacturing. In the bookkeeping sense, it is a double-entry process. Each order becomes a credit to sales & marketing and a debt to inventory. It tells both sales & marketing and manufacturing what has been ordered or sold, the rates at which orders are being received, how much inventory remains to be sold, and where the orders have come from. This data enables sales & marketing to evaluate the sale efforts and the changes in the product mix available to sell. From the same data, manufacturing determines what it should order, what to make, and when it will be needed.

However, beyond entering orders into the system and triggering all that follows from that, order entry performs several other important functions. It edits orders to make sure that product identification codes are correct, and it issues order acknowledgments and acceptances. It also furnishes delivery dates and may recommend substitutions for out-of-stock or discontinued products.

Finally, order entry has an important role in verifying the creditworthiness of a customer before an order is accepted.

18. Fulfillment, Installation, and Startup

A predictable episode in any on-going TV situation comedy is the assembly of a complicated Christmas toy or the installation of an intricate mechanical device like a garage door opener. Mislabeled parts and things that don't fit are common. Customer expectations in this area are quite simple. They want to be able to use what they have bought within a reasonable time after it is delivered. A T & T's new phone system for the U.S. House of Representatives still didn't work after weeks and months of tinkering and fine tuning. Product design can do much to enhance the simple plug-in-and-use capabilities of products.

Most faults, however, are of a more immediate human origin. A single illustration from a service market will suffice. One September Tuesday, not long ago, British Airways Flight 329 left the Arabian Gulf for London. One passenger was aboard and only one piece of luggage had been checked in. Yet when the flight reached Heathrow, the suitcase was nowhere to be found.

19. Warranty and Guaranty Support: Maintenance and Repair

Consumables and disposables apart, people expect the things they buy to give good service for a long time. They expect maintenance to be easy and repairs, when needed, to be convenient to arrange.

Corning Glass replaces certain of its tableware without question if it breaks. Wang Labs drastically cut back its European sales activity until its service capability was able to support the units already sold. Pella and Andersen, highly competitive manufacturers of superior quality windows and sliding glass doors, seem to have higher expectations for their products than most of their customers. Both provided maintenance and repair assistance long after the expiration of normal warranties or guaranties. Unfortunately, Andersen seems to have lost its zeal for satisfied customers.

These and the practices of many other manufacturers contrast with the Detroit experience which is so bad that many states have been constrained to enact *Lemon laws*.

20. Tracking Competition

No product is ever sold in a vacuum but always in relationship with other competitive products which perform the same functions for the customer, often with different technologies: Amtrack and Eastern Airlines, for example. What's required, therefore, is a continuing audit of all competitive activity. In planning and carrying out such an audit, keep in mind that price alone is not the only competitive factor. Other considerations may be and often are more important than mere price. The audit, therefore, must cover the entire spectrum of products serving the same purpose for the customer, regardless of price. Audits should include packaging, physical specifications, performance, availability, service, and anything else that could be made to seem an advantage or a benefit to a prospective purchaser.

Product samples should be tested in appropriate ways, and advertising, promotions, literature, and warranty and guaranty terms all analyzed. Occasionally, it may be necessary to have a competent third-party interview users and prospective users to establish the perceived strengths and weaknesses of competitive products and their manufacturers.

21. Market Research

The term *market research* has nearly as many meanings as there are people with projects to propose. However, most market research aims at accomplishing one or both of two major goals. One goal is to define or quantify the market for an existing product or for a product in development. The other aim is to explore the wants and needs of a market or market segment with a view toward identifying new product opportunities.

Consumer product marketers with their tenuous contracts with consumers must rely heavily on research conducted by third parties. Industrial marketers with more continuous and personal contacts with customers and prospects have much less need for third-party research. In fact, management contact with the personnel of key accounts should provide the basic market research.

Research techniques are many and varied. Telephone and mail surveys are common, as are sidewalk (intercept) interviews and home or office interviews. Product tests and comparative samplings are also useful. Focus group interviews, in which several people explore a well-defined subject, can be very powerful. Polaroid, for example, conducted over 1000 focus group interviews in developing its new 35-mm slide processor. Most focus groups, however, only *seem* to be productive.

Depending upon project design and goals, each of these techniques can work equally well for industrial and consumer products.

Formal research works best when it is used to confirm or modify conclusions reached by less rigorous, in-house efforts, and when the respondents are truly interested in the subject being explored, when they are competent enough to answer the questions asked, and when they have the time to pay attention to the process. In the ideal situation the researcher knows enough about the subject to set the clipboard aside and go beyond mere checkoff questions.

22. Training

The slogan says "If training seems expensive, wait until you have tried ignorance." There are 24 other essential marketing functions listed and discussed here. Each of these may be divided into several subfunctions. All of them have their own skill requirements, skills which must be performed at a very high level.

Additionally, each of them shares a common need for a general understanding of the firm's products and services as well as of relevant policies and procedures. These needs extend beyond the firm's own personnel to that of its resellers, especially wholesale distributors and retailers of consumer durables.

Training is, therefore, a critical marketing function.

23. Forecasting

Accurately forecasting sales by quarter for each and every product or product group is acknowledged to be one of the most difficult tasks that face sales & marketing (accurate forecasting over a longer range is nearly impossible). Yet the importance of forecasting for planning and scheduling production, procuring materials, hiring personnel, and anticipating the generation of income cannot be overestimated.

To illustrate: During the introductory period for its new disc camera, Kodak shipped 4.5 million units but sold only 3.8 million. This shortfall of 17 percent becomes significant when it is noted that the shortfall in Kodak's earnings before taxes during that period was also in the 17 to 18 percent range. Was this an error of forecasting, a gamble that failed, a planned investment in future earnings, or a systematic error?

There is no question about this example. One of the reasons for the Texas Instruments home computer disaster was its very optimistic forecasts. It predicted a 6.7-million-unit market for 1983 and built inventory to cover what it imagined its share would be. Others predicted a 5-million-unit market. One forcaster, the most accurate, predicted only a 2.5-million-unit market.

Inputs for accurate forecasting are of three kinds. The initial inputs are supplied by the sales force. Data originates with each field representative. This is combined with inputs from other field people and modified at each level of sales management until all inputs are gathered.

Another set of inputs come from key accounts who are asked to anticipate their requirements for the forecast period. Although such figures will represent only a fraction of the anticipated totals, they will serve as useful check on the figures provided by sales.

The third set of inputs comes from marketing management itself and should reflect such things as changes in product mix, advertising, sales promotion, distribution, deployment of the sales force, and training.

Taken together and with the addition of a great deal of judgment, these three sets of inputs provide the basis for a reasonable sales forecast. This forecast, in turn, must be compared with the requirements of management and reviewed by manufacturing and finance.

Necessary adjustments are then made and specific goals and targets are established for the forecast period.

There is a caution, however. The initial forecasting inputs originate with salespeople who are notoriously poor at this kind of effort. Most are overly optimistic and tend to overstate what will sell. A few tend in the other direction. The accuracy of these inputs will be considerably enhanced if forecasts specify how much of each product will be purchased by each account. This requirement has the further benefit of making it easy to compare the estimates provided by sales with those provided by key accounts.

24 and 25. Planning and Managing All of the Above

These two related functions are somewhat different from the others. They are what this whole volume is about. How they are handled depends upon a number of considerations, not the least of which is the stage a firm has reached in its growth and development.

A Footnote

Most management inquiries into sales and marketing usually focus on the first five or six functions listed here. However, it is the remaining nineteen or twenty that really make the difference.

5
How Organizations Grow and Develop

Once a firm passes through the initial stages of development and becomes something more than a handful of people working in a garage, the separate functional responsibilities of marketing become easy to see and begin to sort themselves out.

Typically, a pattern like the following evolves:

- The functions of sales, key account sales and management, tracking competition, applications engineering, and forecasting become associated under a single manager. Generally, the person responsible becomes the sales manager and was a member of the original team.

- The functions of advertising, sales promotion, lead generation, packaging, and market research clump together under someone who is usually young, from the outside, and comes cheap.

- Customer service, order entry, fulfillment and warranty and guaranty support become associated in a limbo somewhere between sales marketing and manufacturing.

- The functions of product and market definition, pricing, training, and planning remain with management.

This seems to be the common organizational pattern regardless of whether the firm makes consumer packaged goods, consumer durables, industrial consumables, or industrial capital goods or whether it provides services. Sales grow under this type of organization until, eventually, they become stalled on a plateau and competition becomes difficult to manage.

At this stage, a reorganization and a reassignment of functional responsibilities is necessary. It is often painful to accomplish. It is often the first real attempt at organization.

The goals of this reorganization (or initial organization) are twofold:

(1) to move sales up, off the plateau and start them growing once more and (2) to provide a more flexible and profitable response to competitive activities. Thereafter, change becomes almost continuous. Managing change is the prime responsibility of marketing management.

During this reorganization, the similarities between the various types of firms should begin to melt away. The next kind of organizational pattern to evolve will depend upon the kind of product offered, the markets being served, and the way management perceives its opportunities and competitive challenges. The same functional responsibilities remain, but they get sorted out differently for each situation and, of course, take on a more specific and specialized form.

Consumer Packaged Goods

Growth is a relatively straightforward proposition for the manufacturer of consumer packaged goods. There are three opportunities for growth. First, the basic market for established products can be expanded. If, for example, purely regional distribution has been achieved, the existing product line can be rolled out nationally. A second growth opportunity comes from increasing the number of products offered. Thus, a manufacturer of regional or ethnic specialty foods who offers, say, tortillas, enchiladas, and chili might add refried beans to the line. Finally, the third opportunity would be to find new markets for existing products. If food products are involved which, for example, are sold through the usual retail channels, then institutions might be a new market: restaurants, hotels, prisons, school cafeterias, college dining halls, etc.

Each of these three opportunities—expanding the basic market, adding new products, or finding new markets—requires a separate marketing effort with its own management, goals and targets, and separate set of marketing responsibilities.

Expanded Distribution

If a decision were made to achieve growth through expanded distribution of the existing product line—expanding regional to national distribution—the management of the effort would have to control and be responsible for the items checked in Fig. 5.1.

The products, their packaging and pricing would be the key givens as would be all the marketing support activities. The major challenges would be achieving expanded physical distribution, managing sales and key account activity in the new territories, tracking competition, and providing whatever training would be required for new salespeople and

	Expanded Distribution	Additions to Line	Developing a New Market
1. Product design and development	X	XX	X
2. Market identification and development	XX	X	XX
3. Product strategy, positioning, and surrounds		XX	XX
4. Packaging		XX	XX
5. Pricing		XX	XX
6. Advertising: Creating a preference	X	X	XX
7. Promoting sales	X	X	XX
8. Generating and following up leads	X		XX
9. Physical distribution	XX	X	X
10. Outside sales	XX	X	XX
11. Inside sales	XX	X	XX
12. Direct response sales: Telephone, television, direct mail			
13. Key account management and sales	XX	XX	XX
14. Controlling product mix			
15. Applications engineering: Label instructions			
16. Customer service			X
17. Order entry	X	X	X
18. Fulfillment: Installation and startup			
19. Warranty and Guaranty: Maintenance and repair			
20. Tracking competition	XX	XX	XX
21. Market research		X	X
22. Training	XX	XX	XX
23. Forecasting	X	X	X
24. Planning	X	X	X
25. Managing all of the above	X	X	X

X = Necessary   XX = Critical

Figure 5.1. Importance of the functional responsibilities of marketing: consumer packaged goods.

reseller personnel. The basic functions of forecasting, planning, and managing are always with us.

Additions to the Line

If a decision is made to achieve growth through addition to the line, management of the effort must be to control and be responsible for all the items checked in Fig. 5.1.

Since the new product would be for an established market, the key givens would be the market itself, existing physical distribution, established selling activities, and all the marketing support functions. The major challenges would be product definition, packaging, strategy, pricing, key account sales tracking competition, and training sales and reseller personnel.

Developing New Markets

If the decision were made to achieve growth by taking the existing product line into a new market, management of the effort would require control of and responsibility for the items also checked Fig. 5.1.

In this case, the key givens would be the existing products (but not necessarily their pricing or packaging) along with all the existing marketing support activities. The main challenges would be market definition, market research, packaging, pricing, strategy, advertising, promotion, lead generation, selling activities, and tracking competition. Depending upon the nature of the new market to be served, special physical distribution may have to be established and training provided.

The size of these three challenges—expanded distribution, additions to the line, and developing new markets—and the magnitude of the potential rewards will determine whether these efforts become the part-time or full-time responsibility of a manager or of a small staff.

Once a consumer packaged-goods product line has achieved national distribution, the significant growth opportunities become limited to two: (1) adding to the line or (2) finding new markets to serve. These opportunities and challenges become permanent, and marketing efforts and organizations can be structured to meet them.

Expansions into overseas markets are, of course, special situations.

Consumer Durables

These products, as we have seen, fall into one or the other of two categories: standard established products which most people understand, and really new products which are not very well understood.

Standard established products are all the me-too items like radios, lawnmowers, kitchen ranges, and electric blankets. In some ways, as we have seen, these products behave much as consumer packaged goods. The big difference, of course, is cost. There are, however, exceptions. A frozen turkey or a roast beef may cost more than a coffee brewer, although the decision to buy involves less deliberation.

For the manufacturer, however, there is another significant difference as shown in Fig. 5.2. With consumer durables, there are only two

	Expanded Distribution	Additions to Line
1. Product design and development	X	XX
2. Market identification and development	XX	X
3. Product strategy, positioning, and surrounds		XX
4. Packaging		XX
5. Pricing		XX
6. Advertising: Creating a preference	X	XX
7. Promoting sales—Now	X	
8. Generating and following up leads		
9. Physical distribution	XX	X
10. Outside sales	X	X
11. Inside sales	X	X
12. Direct response sales: Telephone, television, and direct mail		
13. Key account management and sales	XX	XX
14. Controlling product mix		X
15. Applications engineering: Label instructions		X
16. Customer service	X	X
17. Order entry	X	X
18. Fulfillment: Installation and startup	X	XX
19. Warranty and guaranty: Maintenance and repair	XX	XX
20. Tracking competition	XX	XX
21. Market research	X	X
22. Training	X	XX
23. Forecasting	X	X
24. Planning	X	X
25. Managing all of the above	X	X

X = Necessary   XX = Critical

Figure 5.2. Importance of the functional responsibilities of marketing: consumer durables.

growth opportunities: (1) Distribution may be expanded. The existing market may be expanded from regional distribution to national distribution or the number of outlets increased within the territories covered. (2) A new model or a new item may be added to the established line.

Finding a new market for existing products is highly unlikely. There are possibilities for segmenting established markets, but not for finding entirely new markets. Most consumer durables are, after all, adaptations of existing products which serve other markets (see Chap. 9). There are, therefore, only two options for achieving growth with standard consumer durables.

Expanded Distribution

If a decision is made to achieve growth through the expansion of the existing market, management of the effort would have pretty much the same set of challenges as for rolling out packaged goods. But there would be a few significant additions. The capabilities for providing customer service, maintenance and repair, and warranty and guaranty support would have to be expanded. Further, training new people to provide those services would become critical (see Fig. 5.2).

Additions to the Line

If growth is to be achieved by adding to the existing product line, the major challenge beyond developing the product itself and establishing its packaging and pricing would be to adapt existing sales and marketing support activities to accommodate the addition. Spare parts, for example, and special tools would have to be distributed to the service organization, and existing personnel would have to be trained to sell and service the addition. (See Fig. 5.2).

Really New Products

If, however, the manufacturer adds a really new product to the line—home computers, for example—then all 25 functional marketing responsibilities become important (see Fig. 5.3). A few become critical: pricing, advertising, promotion, physical distribution, key account sales, handling competition, and all the service warranty and fulfillment functions.

However, as the new product succeeds and its market matures, a further development must be considered. Often the new product and the market it has created provide an opportunity for, or actually requires, the formation of a separate operating division. Some firms, 3M for example, routinely use a new product as the nucleus of a new operating division.

Once in a while, the new product may even change the nature of the organization. Polaroid, after all, began as the manufacturer of polarizing film·and sunglasses. The Land camera, introduced in 1948, changed all that.

Industrial Consumables

Industrial consumables, as we have seen, fall into one of three general categories: support-consumables like paperclips and welding gases; commodity consumables like sheet steel or insulated wire; and make-or-

1. Product design and development	XX
2. Market identification and development	XX
3. Product strategy, positioning, and surrounds	X
4. Packaging	X
5. Pricing	XX
6. Advertising: Creating a preference	XX
7. Promoting sales—Now	XX
8. Generating and following up leads	XX
9. Physical distribution	XX
10. Outside sales	X
11. Inside sales	X
12. Direct response sales: Telephone, television, and direct mail	X
13. Key account management and sales	XX
14. Controlling product mix	X
15. Applications engineering: Label instructions	X
16. Customer service	XX
17. Order entry	X
18. Fulfillment: Installation and startup	XX
19. Warranty and guaranty: Maintenance and repair	XX
20. Tracking competition	XX
21. Market research	X
22. Training	XX
23. Forecasting	X
24. Planning	X
25. Managing all of the above	X
X = Necessary XX = Critical	

Figure 5.3. Importance of the functional responsibilities of marketing: really new products, industrial or consumer.

buy consumables like motors and cabinet hardware. Since the volume of purchases rises or falls with the general level of business activity, their purchases are usually not budgeted.

Industrial Support-Consumables

These are nearly always established products and, of the three categories, behave the most like consumer packaged goods. These are ordered, for the most part, directly by the user on the basis of familiarity ("I have heard of that") and availability ("So and so has it in stock"). The purchasing department is rarely involved and, except for times of austerity, price is usually not a consideration.

The functional responsibilities to be controlled in marketing this kind of product are checked in Fig. 5.4.

Here, the products themselves are the key givens along with the mar-

	Support-Consumables	Process-Consumables	Make-or-buy Consumables
1. Product design and development	X	X	X
2. Market identification and development	XX	X	XX
3. Product strategy, positioning, and surrounds	X	XX	X
4. Packaging	XX	XX	X
5. Pricing	X	XX	X
6. Advertising: Creating a preference	XX	X	X
7. Promoting sales	XX		
8. Generating and following up leads	XX	X	XX
9. Physical distribution	XX	XX	X
10. Outside sales	X	X	X
11. Inside sales	X	X	X
12. Direct response sales: Telephone, television, direct mail	XX		
13. Key account management and sales	X	XX	XX
14. Controlling product mix		X	X
15. Applications engineering: Label instructions	X	X	XX
16. Customer service	X	X	X
17. Order entry	X	X	X
18. Fulfillment: Installation and startup	X	X	X
19. Warranty and Guaranty: Maintenance and repair	X	X	X
20. Tracking competition	X	XX	XX
21. Market research	X	X	X
22. Training	XX	X	X
23. Forecasting	X	X	X
24. Planning	X	X	X
25. Managing all of the above	X	X	X

X = Necessary   XX = Critical

Figure 5.4. Importance of the functional responsibilities of marketing: industrial consumable.

keting support activities. The major challenges are physical distribution, which ensures same-day or overnight delivery; packaging, which reflects the special requirements of business or industrial users; lead generation, which identifies the many likely sources or points of origin for orders; and advertising and promotional efforts, which reaches the consumer. Training reseller personnel may also be critical.

Process-Consumables
(Commodities)

Although process-consumables are also standard products, they bear little resemblance to consumer packaged goods in their behavior. These are purchased, usually on price, after some deliberation among purchasing, engineering, and manufacturing to make sure that the interests of all are protected.

Successful marketing of these products requires control of the responsibilities checked off in Fig. 5.4. Here the key givens are the products themselves and the marketing support activities. And there are three major challenges.

The first challenge is to make the product somehow distinguishable from other essentially similar products. The goal is to make selling easier and to justify a higher price. This, of course, involves packaging and adding to the product itself.

Distribution is another critical challenge. Instant availability may not be required, but short lead times are.

However, the biggest challenge, here, lies in the management of key accounts and in the maintenance of a close liaison with key account personnel, for they will be the ones who will provide the clues as to how to modify a commodity product and make it a specialty that is clearly distinguishable from all other similar products.

Make-or-Buy Consumables

These products behave least like consumer goods. The sale is made on the basis of manufacturing capability and on-time delivery. Here, the basic interests of buyer and seller are different. The buyer looks for a special product at the price of a standard catalog item, whereas the seller wants to sell a catalog item at the price of a special item. Most specials require extraordinary support activities which, in turn, lead to eroded margins. If, of course, competition is weak or if proprietary processes are involved (as for example, with electronic welding or the ability to machine high-performance alloys), then special items may be very profitable indeed.

The key givens here are the general catalog and established manufacturing capabilities, plus the usual support activities. Marketing success requires control of the functional responsibilities checked in Fig. 5.4.

There are several critical challenges including market definition, lead generation, applications engineering, key account management, and keeping track of competition. Of these, identifying the decision makers

1. Product design and development	X
2. Market identification and development	XX
3. Product strategy, positioning, and surrounds	XX
4. Packaging	XX
5. Pricing	XX
6. Advertising: Creating a preference	X
7. Promoting sales	X
8. Generating and following up leads	XX
9. Physical distribution	X
10. Outside sales	X
11. Inside sales	X
12. Direct response sales: Telephone, television, and direct mail	
13. Key account management and sales	XX
14. Controlling product mix	XX
15. Applications engineering: Label instructions	XX
16. Customer service	X
17. Order entry	X
18. Fulfillment: Installation and startup	XX
19. Warranty and guaranty: Maintenance & repair	X
20. Tracking competition	XX
21. Market research	XX
22. Training	X
23. Forecasting	X
24. Planning	X
25. Managing all of the above	X
X = Necessary XX = Critical	

Figure 5.5. Importance of the functional responsibilities of marketing: industrial capital goods.

and buying influences within each account, managing contact with them, and maintaining the quality of applications engineering are the most important.

Industrial Capital Goods

There is a substantial difference between industrial consumables and industrial capital goods, and that difference is this: The cost of consumables is handed on to customers in the price of the products sold. Capital equipment, in contrast, is paid for from accumulated funds or through special financing. Its acquisition affects both taxes and capital structure. Only public utilities can hand on the cost of new non-nuclear plants and equipment to their rate payers without a thought. This difference places a premium on the vendor's ability to offer creative financing, especially when money is tight.

To illustrate: Part of Xerox Corporation's early success resulted from the realization, early on, that few customers could afford the price of a Xerox machine and that those who could afford one would probably not spend the money to replace a mimeograph or a hectograph machine. Its sales policy, therefore, was to install and maintain its machines and to charge its customers only a nickel a copy. The money just rolled in.

Successful marketing of capital goods requires that management of the effort control and be responsible for the items checked in Fig. 5.5. (See opposite.)

The givens, here, are established products, the vendor's design and manufacturing or construction capabilities, and the usual support functions.

There are several critical challenges. Foremost among them are market definition and development; packaging, especially as it involves financing; lead generation; key account management; controlling the product mix; applications engineering; installation and startup; and keeping track of competition. This last element in the mix is of special importance, for once a competitor has made a sale, that opportunity is off the market for a long, long time.

Finally, since capital goods are sold at the executive level, the vendor's senior management must be involved in each sale and must be involved in a more active role than merely showing the company flag.

Footnote

A major characteristic of healthy marketing organizations is that circumstances are forever changing. Guiding that change along productive lines and not resisting it is the prime task of marketing management.

6

Advertising & Sales Promotion

There is one curious and important aspect to advertising & sales promotion that is too frequently overlooked. What management says about the products and services it sells is a very deep reflection of the way it thinks about those products and services and about the customers it hopes will buy. Advertising & sales promotion is a critical factor in establishing product quality and in defining markets. These may be the important roles.

Properly managed, advertising & sales promotion can provide powerful, if uncertain, support for the entire sales & marketing effort. For example, with advertising & sales promotion it is possible to

- *Create a buyer preference among products that are virtually identical—*What, pray tell, is the essential difference among raisin bran cereals beyond the box and, perhaps, the amount of sugar on the raisins?

- *Create a product and a market for it almost overnight—*The notion of collectability, supported by television spots and full-page advertisements in *Parade* magazine and similar publications, creates almost overnight a market for the wares of the Franklin Mint and its imitators.

- *Keep products afloat which are known to be deadly or criminally dishonest—*The Dalcon Shield and the offerings of First Jersey Securities were kept afloat long after their dangerous inferiority had been demonstrated.

- *Provide guidance for those who design and develop new or improved products—*Honda says of its lawnmowers, "Buy ours, we got it started at the factory." Toro says, "Buy ours. You can get it started at home, or we'll fix it." If advertising reflects its product, Honda's designers better get busy.

- *Provide guessing game entertainment for television audiences*—Recent TV advertisements for IBM's PC featured the cast of M*A*S*H. The audience's reaction was to try to identify who was missing from the lineup, not to remember the information about the IBM PC.

Properly managed, advertising & sales promotion can have enormous power. However, they are also services, sold by very skillful people, and they have all the characteristics of other services described in Chap. 2. They are games played according to rules written by those who sell space and time. These rules, which mostly concern money, distract from essential considerations of goals, available media, market needs and characteristics, and the quality of the product itself.

How Much Should We Spend?

Consider this example of their rules: A common question which management frequently asks itself and others is "Are we spending enough (or too much) to promote the sale of our products?" A reasonable answer would revolve around another consideration: "What do we want to accomplish? What are our goals?" The discussion should then turn to the achievement of goals and the removal of obstacles in various product-market combinations.

Too frequently this is not what happens.

Usually, when the question is asked, "Are we spending enough?" an answer is given in almost knee-jerk fashion in terms of what others spend. Knowing what others in the same industry spend can be important to a firm whose performance in the marketplace lags behind that of the competition or to a firm that suspects that its expenditures are higher than they need to be. Usually, though, knowing what others spend leads to an unproductive keeping-up-with-the-Jones's attitude. For, when it comes to determining what others spend, there are several sources, and they all appear a bit biased.

Some trade associations are able to supply this information in several seemingly helpful categories. Occasionally the data is quite accurate and sophisticated. Usually it is not because it fails to distinguish expenditures for creating a preference, promoting sales from each other.

Another common source is the annual mid-September issue of *Advertising Age* which tells what industries spend according to four-digit SICs. The data is presented with a brief apology; it may not be pure. When *Advertising Age* talks about *advertising dollars as a percent of sales*, it means money spent just for print and broadcast, production plus time and space. Since the source of the information is the K-10 forms filed with the Securities Exchange Commission (SEC), the information may be contaminated with data on expenditures for literature, direct mail, catalogs, and point-of-purchase materials.

An even more sophisticated source for this information is the Profit Impact of Market Strategy (PIMS) data gathered from the members of the Strategic Planning Institute. This data, presented by size and type of business, separates expenditures for advertising from expenditures for sales promotion. Money spent for advertising is, as above, defined as money spent for radio, television, and print. Sales promotion is defined as everything else from direct mail and trade shows to "spiffs" and the costs of special discounts.

Thus in these two well-known sources for information on how much marketers spend to promote the sale of their products, advertising is focused narrowly on print and broadcast. Sales promotion is everything else including, it seems, the label on the kitchen sink.

McGraw-Hill Research's *Laboratory of Advertising Performance* is another source of such information, very useful but not very well known, and it is derived exclusively from industrial marketers.

There are a few other significant differences. McGraw-Hill, for example, uses the term *marketing communication* when others say advertising & sales promotion; the term includes everything. It provides nice figures on what industrial marketers spend for market research and for each of eight separate categories of marketing communications—print advertisements, exhibits, catalogs, broadcast, direct mail, etc. For industrial marketers these are useful points for comparison.

However, all of this tends to keep the discussion focused on money and away from the problems and opportunities facing each product-market combination. These are the real issues, and broadcast and print may not be the best means for handling them. Other media may be more effective if less commissionable.

Product Differentiation

Here, too, there is another influence at work. Its effects on the way advertising & sales promotion is perceived by those who pay the bills may be even more pernicious.

Most of the advertising & sales promotion to which we are exposed is on behalf of undifferentiated or commodity consumer products. Some people use the terms *me-toos* or *parity products*, or so it would seem. There is little to differentiate one product from its competitors, or so it would seem to those preparing the advertisements.

With no differences and no benefits to tout, the efforts focus on presentation of the product, on exotic locations, dramatic situations, family affairs, suggestive situations, etc. Sometimes the results are astonishingly effective. Usually they are not. The challenge, after all, is formidable.

Too many advertising agencies seem unable to rise to this challenge. This in turn has led to the development of houses specializing in the differentiation of essentially similar products.

Sedelmaier Productions in Chicago has developed a kind of surrealistic humor to achieve this goal. "Where's the beef?" for example.

Cardon & Cherry of Nashville achieve this goal with the picaresque adventures of Ernest P. Warrell and his friend Vern. The tone of these efforts may be suggested by the fact that the creative force behind them, John Cherry, is known to all as "Buster." "Know what I mean, Vern?"

Occasionally, a product will be made promotable and salable through the selection of its name. There are probably dozens of *natural* breakfast cereals on the markets, but none are as advertisable as "Nut n' Honey." It will be several years before all the changes are rung on the question, "What are you having for breakfast?"

However, most creative or clever solutions to the problem of differentiating me-too products are not very effective.

For example, when Chicago's Michael Reese Hospital and Medical Center wanted to differentiate itself from other Chicago area hospitals, its agency used a photograph of a nouvelle cuisine presentation of French lamb chops, broccoli, and baby carrots. In contrast, Massachusetts General avoids advertising and gets publicity about its new research facilities and new discoveries.

When Young and Rubicam sought to differentiate Colgate Tarter Control Formula toothpaste from the brand that talked about tarter first, it showed workers climbing about on a 17-foot wall of teeth and plastering the teeth with tarter. Then they showed a tidal wave of Colgate whooshing the workers and their ladders away.

The difficulty in developing effective commercials in such situations may explain why the William Wrigley firm has used its "Double your pleasure, double your fun" twins commercial since the mid-fifties.

Thus, discussions of advertising & sales promotion revolve around the cost of broadcast and print or around efforts that stress production values, and not around product benefits. Such competition as there is shifts from products in the marketplace to advertising & sales promotion in the media.

In what follows, therefore, we will try to bring the discussion and the focus back where it belongs on the performance of individual product-market combinations.

We'll look at:

- A few common goals for advertising & sales promotion—There are quite a few that are possible, and they are quite specific.
- A few of the media available for advertising & sales promotion—There is a lot more available than most people think, and, on occasion, much of it is more effective than print or broadcast.
- A brief review of markets and customers and what makes them buy—Those advertising & sales promotional efforts in support of products that offer real benefits have an advantage over those which do not.
- A few comments on products themselves—This is where all the problems begin and where the solutions to them lie.

Goals for Advertising & Sales Promotion

In Chap. 4, we discussed three common goals for most advertising & sales promotion. Each goal requires its own effort. But there are more, many more. A few of them, presented in Fig. 6.1, are discussed below.

1. Ensure Recognition

The major goal here is to get the product and the benefits associated with it recognized by potential customers. That is the primary goal. A

---

1. Ensure recognition of the product and its benefits by both the prospective purchaser and the people who sell it.
2. Create and maintain a preference for the product over competitive offerings.
3. Encourage prospective buyers to identify themselves by asking questions about the product.
4. Let prospects know where and how to acquire the product.
5. Encourage prospects to buy, hopefully now.
6. Make the sales force's job easier and help it write orders.
7. Encourage distributors and warehouse and stock clerks to favor the product.
8. Temper the prospect's expectations, especially where new products are involved, so that there are no surprises or disappointments.

Figure 6.1. Common tasks of advertising & sales promotion.

secondary goal would be to make the people who sell the product aware of product benefits also.

2. Creating and Maintaining a Preference

Although recognition is a legitimate goal (brand-name recognition tests are a popular research activity), preference over competitive products as reflected at the cash register or by market-share figures is the real goal. Creating a preference is an obvious goal with new products. Maintaining that preference once the newness is gone is often forgotten.

3. Encouraging Prospects to Identify Themselves

This is very important when the product cannot be picked from a display or asked for across a counter. Careful attention to the source of inquiries (who is making them) is important; changes often signal the development of a new market or shrinkage of an established market. Prompt follow-up of leads is important to prevent the alienation of prospects.

4. Letting the Prospect Know Where and How to Buy

Advertisements with no name, address, or phone number are a commonplace of neighborhood newspapers. However, careful attention to the television advertisements of major car manufacturers shows that they too can forget to tell folks what is being sold and by whom.

5. Encourage Buying Now

Three separate goals are common here: bringing a new product up to speed quickly, increasing volume during slow periods, and loading up a customer or reseller in anticipation of a soon-to-be-released competitive product. The typical device is a price reduction or a tie-in sale with cut-off dates for both. Coupons are a commonplace with consumer packaged goods. Some firms, Proctor & Gamble for example, issue coupons with no expiration dates, thus placing a permanent lien against sales income but not encouraging sales now. Dating programs are a common practice with resellers…"We ship in March. You sell in April and May, and pay us in June."

6. Making It Easier to Write Orders

Most retail salespeople do not know their products well enough to guide prospects to a purchase. Most industrial salespeople make over five calls for each order they write. Reasonable goals for advertising & sales promotion would be to reduce the selling task at the point of sale for both.

7. Encourage Stock Clerks to Favor the Product

Another goal of advertising & sales promotion is to create a demand for the product and, thus, pull it through the channels of distribution. Distributors and warehouse and stock clerks must help make it happen. They must not be overlooked in advertising & sales promotion activities.

8. Condition the Prospect's Expectations

This is especially important with new or substantially altered products—new Coke, for example. There should be no surprises or disappointments. This concern takes many forms. On occasion, it is merely a notice in large type to "allow 6 or 8 weeks for delivery." Sometimes it is the whole thrust of the effort. When Schweppes first introduced its tonic water to the States, it did so with the slogan, "Curiously refreshing." It certainly was that, but the slogan also alerted the market to the fact that the stuff *tasted funny*.

These are all legitimate goals for advertising & sales promotion. Further, these goals may not just reflect the problems and opportunities of the national market. Localized regional or district situations may be more critical. These problems and opportunities may be unique to one or more channels of distribution, or they may be associated with just one product or with several.

Identifying proper goals and objectives for advertising & sales promotion activities requires a detailed knowledge of the problems and opportunities at all sales levels, in all markets, with all products, and in all channels of distribution. Those responsible for carrying out the advertising & sales promotion functions must work closely with all levels and functions within the marketing organization. Chapter 4 discusses twenty-five such functions. Efforts which focus purely on national campaigns and ignore these nuts-and-bolts issues, will be less than effective.

Media

Just as the number of goals and objectives for advertising & sales promotion is much greater than many think, so the number of components of the media mix is much larger too. Some sizable markets are still best-reached by palmetto fans for churches and funeral parlors or by signs on bus-stop benches, whereas other markets are best-reached through exclusive seminar workshops.

Figure 6.2 lists a little of the media that is available. Ingenious minds are always adding to the list.

Here we begin to see a basic problem with advertising & sales promotion. Perhaps we begin to see why the emphasis is on national campaigns with a single theme run in the high-cost media—print and broadcast. It is easier. Even IBM and Wang go along.

The alternatives include at least 8 separate goals and 15 different me-

---

- Word of mouth, personal recommendation
- Billboards, subway cards, etc.
- Periodicals: magazines and newspapers
- Exhibits at trade shows and elsewhere
- Flyers, broadsides, and rack literature
- Seminars and workshops
- Television
- Speeches and papers
- Radio
- Shelf talkers and other points of sale
- Trailers for motion picture theaters
- Blimps and skywriting
- Programs, matchbook covers, bus stop benches, etc.
- *Yellow Pages*
- Direct mail

Figure 6.2. Available media for advertising & sales promotion.

dia: 120 different combinations to consider for each product-market combination. That's not so easy.

However, the problems of product movement are rarely uniform across all markets, and opportunities are never uniform across anything. The evidence seems to support the notion that a fragmented effort directed against each of the big-problem and big-opportunity product-market combinations will pay off better than a single one-size-fits-all campaign. But, it is very tough to manage.

Customers—Markets

In Chap. 2 we reviewed seven markets: two consumer markets, four industrial markets, and the common market for services. We saw what drives them, reviewed how decisions are made, and briefly discussed the kind of sales approaches each seems to require. These insights, however useful, are broad generalizations. When it comes to planning a sales call or developing an advertising & sales promotion program, we need to know a great deal more.

We need to know as specifically as we can the wants and needs of the people and the firms that make up a market or a market segment. We need to know what their expectations are and how well they are being served by competitive offerings. The goal is to identify the hot buttons of our prospective buyers, to determine what benefits or combination of benefits will lead to a sale. The possibilities are more limited than most would suppose.

Industrial Markets

In business or industrial markets, two kinds of benefits are possible, those which accrue to the business and those which accrue to the people making the buying decision. Business benefits are generally quantifiable and boil down to money: either the generation of more revenue or the reduction of costs. These days, increased revenue seems to be more important as an overriding benefit than the reduction of costs.

On the personal side of business, the benefits are harder to identify and nearly impossible to quantify. Here the benefits include such things as convenience, making the buyer's job simpler or easier, making the buyer a hero by solving problems that have frustrated others, or, especially, removing anxiety and providing reassurances that the buying decision is correct.

Other things being equal, the personal benefits are often the deciding factor in the buying decision. The history of IBM provides a good example of this. For years IBM dominated its market although the equipment of other firms was more powerful, easier to maintain and reprogram, and cheaper to buy and own. IBM provided enough business benefits so that owning IBM equipment was better than owning no computing equipment at all; in that sense IBM was competitive. What made the difference in IBM's favor was not superior equipment but a superior reputation which allayed the fear, uncertainty, and doubt that most buyers of computing equipment share. It is even possible that IBM encouraged these feelings of *fear*, *uncertainty*, and *doubt*—the *FUD* strategy, as competitors called it. IBM could paraphrase the Hallmark slogan: "When you're scared enough, you'll buy the best!"

Personal benefits can be quite powerful.

Because of the relatively few people involved in serving an industrial market—from product designer to sales engineer—it is possible for them all to have a rather fair picture of which benefits are important to their customers and which are less so. This understanding can be readily shared by the people who design and develop new products, by the people who plan and develop the supporting advertising & sales promotion, by the people who actually sell these products, and even by the buyers themselves. For this reason, industrial advertising can and should be more effective than consumer advertising; often it actually is.

The buying motivators in each market are similar enough so that one summary will do for both (see Fig. 6.3). The difference between the two markets lies elsewhere.

Consumer Markets

When it comes to consumer markets, the possible benefits are a little less structured and a little less focused. To be sure, in consumer markets,

```
ECONOMIC
    Increased income or revenue
    Increased savings or reduced costs
PERSONAL
    Convenience
    Reassurance
    Status in others' eyes
    Pleasure
    Efficacy
    Enhanced self-image
```

Figure 6.3. Common buying motivators.

there are analogues to business benefits discussed above, however, they are generally much less compelling.

The benefits that seem to appeal most to consumers are more analogous to the less quantifiable personal benefits for business buyers: convenience, reassurance, efficacy, durability, etc. There is even a large element of status guiding most consumer purchases. The typical consumer seems to prefer branded or nationally advertised merchandise to store labels or generics, even though an economic decision would favor house brands and generics. Consumers are not adverse to saving money but prefer not to make purchases that would cause them to lose face. The higher up in the economic order and the more confident the buyer is, the less dependence there seems to be on national brands.

There is also an element of faddishness guiding consumer purchases. After years of slow movement in the marketplace, an item will suddenly be discovered. Thus in the early seventies, crockpots were all the rage; in the early eighties it was PCs, and in the mid-eighties, the urge was on to own a microwave oven.

Because of the broad and variable nature of consumer buying motivations, advertisers search for the psychological foundation of motivation and spend vast sums for motivational research.

Right after World War II, Ernest Dichter proposed to the advertising community that everyone suffered from a primordial sense of guilt and was yearning to get rid of it. "Feel good about yourself and start fresh every day with..." became the copy platform for unscented bath soap, white cotton underwear, and laxative breakfast cereals. This idea persists today in a new laundry detergent called Fresh Start.

Even Abraham Maslow's hierarchy of needs has been pressed into service: *survival*—the Snickers candy bar; *security*—IRAs and Fixodent; *social*—Secure Circles, a club with screened and tested AIDS-free companions; and even *self-actualization*—"Be the best you can be!" (in *the Army?*)

Those less secure in the realms of psychology and motivation test copy and story boards.

This is all very curious. Since everyone concerned with developing, advertising, and selling consumer products is also a consumer, one is forced to wonder whether a little introspection and building from experience might not do better in the market than either research or psychology.

What people miss in all this are two significant facts about consumer purchasing: (1) New products are so few and far between in consumer markets that there is rarely a first-time purchase of anything, and (2) the decision is almost never whether to buy but *which* to buy. This means simply that most buying decisions are made in a context of many similar decisions in which the current buyer has been either an observer or the actual buyer.

People may buy Crest, Colgate, Aim, or Tom's of Maine; but they will buy toothpaste. Sometimes the decision will be made on purely frivolous grounds, as when people switch from whatever they use to try the Colgate pump or the Flip-Top cap. Mostly though, the decision to buy will be based on habit and some long-established notion of superiority reinforced by continual advertising & sales promotion.

Ultimately, consumer buying decisions are made based on what the market perceives to be the intrinsic quality of the product and the way it is presented.

Product Quality and Differentiation

When it comes down to it, the effectiveness of any advertising & sales promotion effort depends first upon the quality of the product and its surrounds, the ease with which it can be differentiated from competitive products, and then upon the creativeness of the advertising & sales promotion effort.

To be sure, products can be superior and yet be killed off by inept advertising & sales promotion efforts—witness the demise of the Fashion Plate switches at Westinghouse's Bryant Division. Similarly, the product can be criminally inferior and kept afloat by superior advertising—witness the Dalcon Shield or the offerings of First Jersey Securities.

For the most part, products sold into consumer markets do the job they are intended to do. Some, however, do it better than others. Some come surrounded with enough extrinsic qualities to overcome any intrinsic short falls. Woolite comes with a special reputation, but Ivory liquid does a better job.

Unfortunately, most products, especially the most heavily advertised consumer products and the ones that set the tone for all advertising & sales promotion are commodity or me-too products. With nothing else to go on, a premium is placed on the skill and ingenuity of those developing the advertising & sales promotion programs, not the product. Indeed, the recent creative director of Lord, Geller, Frederico, and Einstein is on record as preferring to do institutional campaigns for the New York Stock Exchange than mix it up in the fried versus broiled hamburger wars. One situation can get by on "production values" the other requires "breakthrough creativities." Thus, the most highly visible ads are those prepared by people who are good at manipulating visual images and words. Quality and product differentiation are ignored. Invention and gimmicks become important.

To illustrate: Gasoline is surely a commodity no matter whether it is regular leaded, regular unleaded, premium, or super premium. This commodity nature of gasoline is amply demonstrated by the practice of refiner marketers to buy or borrow from each other routinely when their local inventories are low.

Except in very special situations, retail purchases of gasoline are influenced more by station location, price, and the quality of driveway service than by the brand name. Gasoline advertising is, therefore, mostly meaningless—aimed largely at reinforcing existing preferences.

Cars burst through paper barriers on which snappy slogans have been printed. Tigers—who, by the way, also work for cereal companies—race across sand dunes and leap into gasoline pumps and gasoline tanks. Put a tiger in your tank (or a skunk in your trunk, as the competition puts it). Automobiles cross deserts or move along test tracks eking out one more foot, one more yard, or one more mile on just one more drop of fuel.

The device and the visual are more interesting than the product. When it does become possible to differentiate one gasoline from another, there is usually some distinct aspect in the product surrounds, not in the products themselves, that makes the difference. Shell's recent advertisements illustrate this point.

Shell's proposition is simple. Shell charges only one price for its gasoline whether payment is made with cash or with a Shell credit card. Mobil, Amoco, Exxon, and Chevron, on the other hand, have two-tiered pricing systems. Their gasolines cost more if purchased with one of their credit cards than if purchased with cash.

Shell's proposal is simply this: Buy a tankful from us using one of their cards, and we will give you a Shell credit card. Presumably Shell's sales will go up. In any case this advertisement is an easier and a more convincing effort to prepare.

The offer expired. After that, Shell went back to its favorite device— cars bursting through paper barriers on which snappy slogans have been printed. The competitors could move to a one-tiered pricing system or do nothing. At this writing Mobil has moved.

Parity products present all kinds of problems. Here is another example. There is a category of women's footwear that used to be known as the $14 shoe; maybe it still is. These shoes were cheap enough so that buying a new pair was certainly easier and more convenient than dyeing an old pair. Many women have several pairs of such shoes in their closets, some worn only once or twice.

How does a shoe manufacturer advertise to this market? Clearly with difficulty.

Recently, the Melville Shoe Company—Tom McAn—introduced a new line for this market, pastel slipons, with sharpened heels that pitch forward like a no. 7 or no. 8 iron. How does one differentiate this shoe from dozens of others like it? Simple. One rents a name from a celebrity licensing agency and names the line after the celebrity. If the name selected is Marilyn Monroe, this permits the well-known visual from *The Seven Year Itch,* the elevated skirt, and if things get desperate, one can turn to look-alike contests. Melville's new line is named for Miss Monroe. The TV advertisements have progressed as far as the elevated skirt.

Automobiles, too, seem to have become commodity products. Over a recent 3-month period, three out of five television commercials were virtually the same, regardless of the manufacturer. All featured cars with steel gray bodies, aluminum wheel discs, and 3.9 percent APR financing (or a substantial rebate direct from the manufacturer). Somewhere in the fine print qualifying the financing charges, the name of the sponsor was mentioned. But the overall impression was of an institutional campaign on behalf of gray paint, aluminum wheel discs, and 3.9 percent financing.

One of the things that made Lee Iacocca so effective for Chrysler, besides his ready identity, was the fact that all the good lines were saved for him: "If you want to know who builds 'em best, see who backs 'em best." Otherwise, commercials for Chrysler cars are as dumb as those of any other manufacturer. Chevrolet's Beretta swims like a shark; Chrysler's Daytona escapes from rundown chicken coops.

White goods, too, have remained commodities for nearly a generation. Major appliances have differed from one another only in price or in the number of overengineered extras. Only Maytag has set itself apart from the rest by claiming that its equipment requires less maintenance. Nothing is said about how well Maytag appliances wash or dry, only that they require less maintenance. That situation is now changing. General Electric invites its customers to "try it for ninety days; if not satisfied get a free replacement or your money back." Whirlpool goes a bit further: "Try it for a year: if you are not satisfied, we'll replace it at no charge." Both offers suggest quality in performance and are quite different from each other's claim and from Maytag's claim.

Occasionally an idea that seems to work for one marketer gets adapted by another, with curious results. Here is an interesting progression.

For years, Zenith concluded its "blind 'em with science" TV advertisements with the slogan, "The quality goes in before the name goes on." Effective. It should work elsewhere.

Next, the embarrassing Inspector 12 commercials for Hanes underwear—much angry pulling and stretching of a pair of men's briefs leading to the dramatic statement, "They don't say Hanes until I say they say Hanes!"

We move on. Next, the Clara Johnson test for Honda gasoline-powered lawnmowers. If they won't start for Clara, we won't ship them. Clara is a very nice looking young lady.

Finally, we reach Toro who cuts through all the nonsense. Toro says quite simply, "If it doesn't start for you for a whole year on the second pull, we'll fix it free."

There is a moral here. Toro offered something that could benefit the *user*—not Inspector 12 or Clara Johnson. It starts or it doesn't.

Toro isn't alone.

Recently, a full-page advertisement ran in *The New York Sunday Times* and elsewhere with a small photo and a bit of copy, which follows:

> This is a Motorola Semi-Custom Chip.
>
> Our application-specific Integrated Circuits offer an economical path to a wide variety of device. Using Computer Aided Design, our customers can develop instructions that we can transform into fully-tested prototype chips in as little as three weeks. It counts. It compares. It almost thinks. It makes new products more helpful, friendly, courteous, kind and saleable.

Sixty-three words plus the usual trademark notices. The benefits are clear to the three levels of decision makers which the advertisement addresses. Further inquiries from it enable a sales representative to get to those concerned with future generations of products—not just what's on the drawing board now.

Summary

Clearly, superior products with real benefits are easier to advertise and sell than other products. Effective advertising and sales promotion, like effective sales finesse, begins with the product, not the other way around. And products begin with the needs of the market.

7

Developing an Effective Marketing Organization

Let us now take a look at what's involved in developing an effective marketing organization. Keep in mind that it doesn't matter, really, if the goal is to refurbish an existing organization or to build a new one from scratch. The process and the concerns will be fairly similar.

Misconceptions and Preconceptions about Marketing

What will be important, however, is to understand a few of the common misconceptions, or preconceptions, about marketing. If allowed to prevail without serious consideration, these misconceptions will compromise any effort to develop an effective marketing organization.

Sales versus Marketing

Sales & marketing are not separate and distinct activities as is commonly thought. Put simply, the chief function of marketing is to maintain a firm's contacts with the marketplace in such a way that its customer franchise is maintained and enhanced. One way it does this is to optimize the sale of existing products to established markets. That is the sales function, and although important, it is not more important than other aspects of marketing. Sometimes the importance of sales is exaggerated because of the size of its payroll and the costs of its operations. As frequently, sales is underestimated because of the modest nature of the effort: a supervisor and a handful of telephone solicitors. Either way, *sales* is that part of the marketing effort concerned with moving existing products in established markets. That's enough. To expect more of it is to be unrealistic and to obscure other important responsibilities.

A second and equally important function of marketing is concerned with new products and new markets, with identifying new product and new market opportunities and developing profitable new products and new markets.

The third and equally important function of marketing is to provide all the collateral and support functions that make it possible to sell existing products in existing markets and to develop new products and new markets.

These three activities—(1) selling existing products to established markets, (2) developing new products and new markets, and (3) providing the necessary support functions—(summarized in Fig. 7.1) make up the marketing effort. Each of these three undertakings must be performed at a high level of effectiveness. This means that all three should report to a single management so that they can be coordinated and supervised.

What's missing from this mix is manufacturing, for it has the twin responsibilities of maintaining and improving the quality of the products produced and of continually bringing down costs. Both functions are required to maintain profitability and a competitive edge in the served markets.

In the ideal organization the CEO serves as the director of marketing. Only the CEO has the breadth of view necessary to coordinate all corporate functions in support of the marketing effort, and only the CEO has the authority needed to ensure that the quality of products and the welfare of customers remains paramount.

Most organizations, however, are far from ideal. Management of the marketing function is delegated. The danger lies in making the three categories of marketing activities separate and independent with no one having total responsibility for, and authority over, them all.

---

1. Optimize the sale of existing products in existing markets
2. Develop new products and new markets
3. Provide the support and services needed to accomplish the first two items

---

Figure 7.1. Three goals of marketing.

Market versus Product Management

The preconception here is a simple one and arises from the fact that most of the high-visibility experience with marketing has been gained by producers of consumer packaged goods: Philip Morris, Procter & Gamble, Johnson & Johnson, General Foods, and the like. These firms are quite successful. Their marketing efforts are organized around product managers whose responsibilities are to devise ways of keeping a product or product line alive, growing, and profitable and of expanding its distribution. In the management of products whose names tend to be generic—Kleenex, Coke, or Band-Aids—the designation *brand manager* is used. The brand manager has an additional charge: To protect the brand name and keep it from becoming generic and slipping into the public domain as aspirin, cellophane, and, recently, Monopoly have done.

Because these firms are successful and organized around product management concepts, there is a strong tendency for other firms to organize their marketing efforts around product managers too. What is overlooked in all this is that the Procter & Gambles and the Johnson & Johnsons all serve a single unique market, the consumer packaged-goods market. It is incidental to the nature of the market that most packaged goods reach the consumer through supermarkets, convenience stores, and drug chains. These products can be sold wherever there is sufficient traffic and a display of them can be built. Thus we see household detergents, dry-roasted peanuts, and adhesive bandages—occasionally, even, Band-Aid brand adhesive bandages—for sale in stationery stores, automotive supply houses, and even service stations.

Here, the package creates its own market. Producers, in effect, rent space in high-traffic areas much as a sandal maker would set up shop in a mideastern bazaar.

Not all firms, however, serve such a simple and ubiquitous market. Even William Wrigley, with its short line of chewing gums in a handful of flavors and packages, serves at least two markets: the larger, conventional consumer packaged-goods market and the smaller, but quite different, vending machine market.

Most firms in fact serve several markets. A manufacturer of offset duplication equipment, for example, serves at least four markets: instant printers, office equipment, in-house printers, and commercial job shops. A manufacturer of printed circuit boards may serve at least six markets: biomedical, information handling, industrial automation, computers, telecommunications, aerospace, and several more.

Even a manufacturer of tailored menswear serves several markets. Men's specialty stores, clothing chains, and department stores are separate markets. And because man-tailored women's wear is in demand these days, a menswear manufacturer will also serve the women's specialty shop, clothing chains, and department stores. Additionally, unused piece goods, which cannot be held over for another season, are converted into promotional items and sold to discounters. Finally, excess productive capacity is sold to large retailers on a contract basis for the production of their own house-brand clothing.

The upshot of all this is a simple conclusion. For most firms, the basic marketing effort must be organized around the markets served, plus potential or future markets, and not around the products themselves. Only if a firm actually does serve a narrow, well-defined market would it be appropriate to think about product managers to work within that market. Until then, it is the market, and not the product, around which the organization should be built.

After all, it is the way a market reacts to all the competitive offerings that is important. Only markets have needs which existing or new products can satisfy, and only markets buy or refuse to buy. More significant, perhaps, markets develop their own vocabularies and ways of talking. Mastering "customer talk" is an essential part of market management.

The distinction between product management and market management is a real one, not just a game with words. Product specialists within an applications engineering group or a customer service group are quite another matter. But, except as noted, too strong a product emphasis within marketing organization leads to overengineered products at the expense of market share and, ultimately, to the loss of competitive edge. Product managers tend to develop a vested interest in the products they manage, and the company runs the risk that products are kept alive through added bells and whistles long after they should have been replaced. Market managers can be a bit more objective about the performance of products within their markets and, hopefully, about the markets themselves. Their job is to keep the product-market combinations healthy and profitable.

Linear versus Matrix Organizations

Most of us tend to view organizations in a rather straightforward fashion, one job, one boss: general foreman, department head, supervisor, worker; national sales manager, regional sales manager, district sales manager, sales representative; general, colonel, major, captain, lieutenant; Pope, archbishop, bishop, priest.

We tend to think in terms of hierarchical organizations in which positions of increasing authority, responsibility, and salary can be arranged along a straight line. Further, we tend to believe that all the formal and functional relationships can be shown completely on a two-dimensional organization chart.

To most of us, this chain-of-command kind of organization seems normal and natural. In some situations it is. However, in many organizations, especially marketing organizations, such boss-worker relationships are only one-layer deep: manager and secretary, for example.

Marketing organizations, typically, do not lend themselves to linear relationships. Form and functional relationships cannot be shown by a two-dimensional organization chart. A few illustrations will show this.

The order-entry function provides one such illustration. In carrying out its functions, order entry is responsible equally to manufacturing and to marketing. Both marketing and manufacturing will evaluate the performance and effectiveness of the function and the individuals who carry it out. Yet someone must be responsible for seeing that people show up on time, fill out their time cards, get paid, and fulfill all the other necessaries that go along with being an employee. Order entry must report to one or the other. That is only a minor part of the picture. In military terms, there is one reporting relationship for pay, rations, and quarters, and two others for the performance of the specialty.

Similarly, the people who handle the advertising, sales promotion, and lead-generation functions will have a traditional boss-worker relationship to someone, but that someone's job will be primarily administrative. These people really *work for* one or more market managers or, in the special case of consumer packaged goods, for several product or brand managers.

It is this *working for* concept that needs to be understood. It is a client-specialist relationship, not a boss-subordinate relationship. And since most firms are not large enough to afford dedicated specialists to work with each market manager, these functional specialists must be shared by several market managers. Thus the advertising or physical distribution specialist will work for several clients as well as for a nominal boss.

With this arrangement, these specialists have all the problems of client relationship and work scheduling that a CPA or a management consultant has when working with several clients at once.

Some people are completely thrown by this situation. Others understand it instinctively and make it work. Let me illustrate.

I trained in the headquarters battery of a field artillery batallion. We were division artillery, and attached to an infantry regiment to make up a combat team. I worked for the first sergeant as did all enlisted men and, it seemed, all the 90-day wonders. He was an administrative tyrant and a disciplinary horror. We agreed that I would remain a private regardless of my job and its importance in the organization.

Once in combat, however, all that changed, Sergeant Thompson continued his morning report activities but otherwise had no special function. He happily and effectively became the battery's odd-job gofer—a coach, helping out where he could even to the point of assisting the cooks, lugging bed rolls, and carrying grub to the fire-direction center.

Our specialties assumed paramount importance, and we worked for our clients, the regiment, several forward observers, and, on occasion, for division and corps. Except for the goal setting, coordinating, and supply functions, the hierarchical structure by which the army is presumed to function evaporated. We worked for clients.

There is also one more consideration here that plays hob with the traditional linear notions of organization: In business, the specialists may be paid more than those they work for, the clients or the administrative boss. Pay for specialists is, more often than not, determined by an outside market. To keep or recruit good people requires meeting or beating that market price. Pay for these specialists is, therefore, frequently outside normal hierarchical salary grades.

Eventually, in the growth of a firm, the served markets may reach such a size that they require a complete, dedicated marketing organization as well as completely dedicated manufacturing capabilities. Thus, recently, IBM has restructured its operation into seven independent business units, each more or less autonomous and each with its own product development, manufacturing, marketing, service, and finance functions and each serving its own well-defined market.

What this all boils down to is simply this: A marketing organization is not a linear or hierarchical organization in which everyone plays unchanging and well-defined roles with fixed relationships to everyone else. Rather, it is a matrix in which everyone has several reporting and working relationships. Furthermore, it is a variable matrix in which those relationships continually change as products and markets and competition change.

In view of all this, it is easy to see why a two-dimensional organizational chart can be misleading and why it can even obscure the real challenges and problems that marketing is supposed to solve.

For example, the problem is not to find an advertising manager at salary grade 15 or whatever. That's the organization chart problem. Rather, the goal is to provide advertising, sales promotion, and lead-generation support for 12 product lines in 4 separate markets which, by the way, might soon be 10 product lines in 5 separate markets.

Functional Model of a Marketing Organization

Figure 7.2, a functional model of a marketing organization, suggests a way of looking at a marketing organization without the restrictions imposed by a conventional organization chart.

Two things are significant about Fig. 7.2. The first is simply that the functional responsibilities have been sorted out in relation to sales. Some come into play before a sale is made, and some are not important until after a sale has been made. Viewing these functions in this way makes it easy to establish priorities in startup situations or in building an organization to support a new product or a new product line.

With this way of looking at things, there is a checklist of what must be accomplished to ready a product for market and of what must be in place before that product can be sold. The danger of overlooking something is considerably reduced if not eliminated entirely.

The second significant point about Fig. 7.2 is the clear separation of support functions from line or operating functions. It is the nature of these support functions that they may be shared and may support several products or product lines in several markets. Further, several may be combined and made the responsibility of one person or of a small group. Thus in smaller growing firms, it is not unusual for order entry and customer service to be combined. This creates a situation which marketing shares with manufacturing. Similarly, advertising, sales promotion, and lead generation may become the responsibility of a single person or a small group.

A problem commonly encountered with the automated process equipment that is becoming more common with manufacturing is monitoring the process at each step along the way. Manufacturing management has to be sure that at the end of each step, the process has done what it was supposed to have done within the allowable tolerances. Manufacturing management cannot assume that everything is proceeding as it should. Management must look inside the black box and be sure.

A similar situation exists with the less visible functions of marketing. With the conventional organization chart which displays job title and not job function, this becomes very difficult to do.

Viewing a marketing organization as in Fig. 7.2, rather than through a *conventional organization chart,* makes it easier to locate problem areas and to expand or contract staff without losing something essential in the shuffle. It is the function itself that is being displayed, not a job title. This idea may not be as soothing to management egos as a conventional organization chart, but it gets the job done.

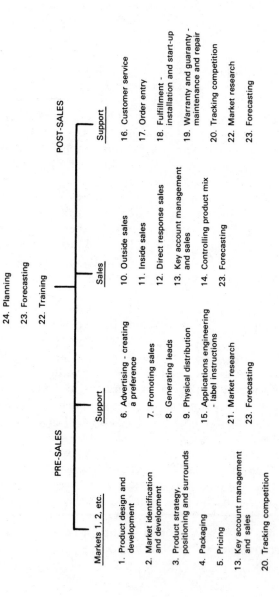

Marketing Management

25. Managing it all
24. Planning
23. Forecasting
22. Training

PRE-SALES

Markets 1, 2, etc.

1. Product design and development
2. Market identification and development
3. Product strategy, positioning and surrounds
4. Packaging
5. Pricing
13. Key account management and sales
20. Tracking competition

Support

6. Advertising - creating a preference
7. Promoting sales
8. Generating leads
9. Physical distribution
15. Applications engineering - label instructions
21. Market research
23. Forecasting

Sales

10. Outside sales
11. Inside sales
12. Direct response sales
13. Key account management and sales
14. Controlling product mix
23. Forecasting

POST-SALES

Support

16. Customer service
17. Order entry
18. Fulfillment - installation and start-up
19. Warranty and guaranty - maintenance and repair
20. Tracking competition
22. Market research
23. Forecasting

Figure 7.2. Marketing organization: functional model.

Building a New Marketing Organization or Auditing an Existing Organization

With the foregoing as rather extensive background, we can now take a detailed look at what's involved in building a new marketing organization or in auditing an existing organization. Neither undertaking is without its difficulties, but as we shall see, both undertakings are made easier because of the approach we have taken and both efforts are remarkably similar.

In each instance the starting point is the same, a close look at each market being served or each market to be served. The objective is to establish the relative importance of each functional marketing responsibility for each of the markets served. As we have seen, the importance of these functions varies considerably over time and from market to market. Moreover, since most firms have limited resources, it is important to know which functions are important and which are less so. Otherwise those resources may be applied indiscriminately and ineffectively.

More than one firm, for example, has tried to solve a problem of declining sales with a massive advertising effort. A correct appraisal of the market being served might have shown that the trick could be turned quite simply by more careful attention to key account management and sales or more simply by following up the bingo cards already in-house.

A worksheet for evaluating these functions on a market-by-market basis is provided in Fig. 7.3. A rating scale has also been proposed: 1—for moderate importance, 3—for normal importance, and 5—for critical importance. However, it doesn't really matter what kind of a rating scale is used as long as the three categories—nice to have, important, and absolutely essential—are made clear in the analysis and a spread in ratings is forced.

This step is the most critical in making an audit of an existing organization and the most difficult when the job is to plan a new one. Misjudging the characteristics and requirements of a market can lead a firm to be underequipped to serve it or, what is just as bad from the viewpoint of resources allocation, overprepared. If a firm and its people have been working in a market for a period, there should be no difficulty in figuring out how that market works and in providing the organization to serve it. This is the situation encountered when an existing operation is audited or when experienced people start a firm of their own.

Similarly, there should be little difficulty when a large served market begins to segment. The special characteristics and requirements of the

	Market Importance	Perfor-mance	Market Importance	Perfor-mance	Market Importance	Perfor-mance
1. Product design and development						
2. Market identification and development						
3. Product strategy, positioning, and surrounds						
4. Packaging						
5. Pricing						
6. Advertising: Creating a preference						
7. Promoting sales						
8. Generating and following up leads						
9. Physical distribution						
10. Outside sales						
11. Inside sales						
12. Direct response sales: Telephone, television, direct mail						
13. Key account management and sales						
14. Controlling product mix						
15. Applications engineering: Label instructions						
16. Customer service						
17. Order entry						

1 = Moderately important/needs improvement, 3 = Necessary/Acceptable, 5 = Critical/Done well

Figure 7.3. Functional responsibilities of marketing: evaluation by served market.

	Market		Market		Market	
	Importance	Performance	Importance	Performance	Importance	Performance
18. Fulfillment: Installation and startup						
19. Warranty and guaranty: Maintenance and repair						
20. Tracking competition						
21. Market research						
22. Training						
23. Forecasting						
24. Planning						
25. Managing all of the above						

1 = Moderately important/needs improvement, 3 = Necessary/Acceptable, 5 = Critical/Done well

Figure 7.3. (*Continued*) Functional responsibilities of marketing: evaluation by served market.

segment should be easily discovered and organizational adjustments made to serve them.

IBM's recent reorganization into seven independent business units recognizes the fact that the computer market is not a monolith. Rather, the computer market is at least seven markets, each with its own requirements and, as important, its own ways of thinking and talking about these requirements.

Often, however, a particular management does not recognize that a market has begun to segment, and it suffers accordingly. The classic example of this was Detroit's failure to recognize the growing market for small fuel-efficient cars. Even when that market segment had grown to 20 percent of the total, Detroit continued to ignore what was happening.

Evaluating New Markets

Management myopia aside, problems do arise when a firm faces an entirely new market. In such situations, the tendency seems to be to project upon the new market the characteristics of the known served markets and to proceed accordingly. That way lies folly or, even, economic disaster.

The opening plays in the effort to establish a home computer market illustrate this quite well. Here, we have seen excellent firms, with broad experience in the industrial commodities, make-or-buy consumables, and capital equipment markets, stumble and fall soon after entering the consumer durables market. Many, eventually, went outside to hire senior managers experienced in the marketing of consumer products. Some may even recover their lost ground.

Here is another example in a bit more detail: The firm was a highly regarded manufacturer of components for the electronics industry. In order to better control its own production, it equipped its major machines with programmable controllers. These were homemade and extremely user-friendly. They even spoke English.

The firm greatly benefited from these devices and thought that others would too. So, it priced them and put them into production.

Since the controllers were homemade, the firm knew nothing about the market it was entering. It was quite a surprise when the firm's own manufacturing vice president said that he would not buy the devices at the proposed prices because there were better controllers available at less money.

At this juncture, the firm decided upon a market test for the device. A sales force was selected, trained, and equipped to sell it. Their efforts proved the manufacturing vice president to have been right. The program was abandoned.

The test to determine when a really new market is being faced is a simple one. If, when, management runs through the list of 25 functional responsibilities, it can only certify the importance of forecasting, planning, and managing numbers 23, 24, and 25, and is uncertain about the rest, it can be sure that it faces a new market. When it finds itself in this situation, several courses are open to it.

It may, for example, go outside and hire management talent familiar with that market and let the new management make the organizational and operating decisions. The hazard here, of course, is that lacking understanding of the new market, management may have difficulty in judging the qualifications of the candidates being considered. However, from the information provided here, together with a thorough familiarity with the established markets being served, management should be able to carry out reasonable screening interviews and make educated guesses as to the qualifications of candidates.

A second course open would be to detail someone already on staff to become familiar with the new market. If need be, even a small task force can be assigned to do this. Eventually, someone from that group could become manager of that new market.

Of these two approaches, the second is to be preferred. A new hire, coming in, would have to learn how to use the resources of the new employer before becoming effective. The chances of this happening quickly and effectively are less than even. In contrast, an insider, reasonably free of preconceptions, can learn the ways of a new market much more readily than an outsider can learn the ways of a new employer. Of course, colleagues may have difficulty accepting the insider in the new position.

There is a third approach to cracking a new market which has most of the advantages of the other two and few of the disadvantages. This approach is to turn to an experienced management consultant familiar with similar firms and the markets they share and let the consultant as an impartial observer evaluate the new market as well as the firm's capabilities. Based on this study, the outsider should be able to recommend whatever changes are needed so that the firm can serve the new market and the person to be hired can manage it.

This is not simply a job of market research; it goes quite a bit deeper than that. The evaluation of a firm's capability to serve the new market is often more important than the assessment of the market and the way it works.

However, opening up a new market or building a marketing organization from scratch is not a common challenge. The challenge most marketers face is simply doing a better job of exploiting the markets already served. In simple terms, finding out how to do this means taking a close look at how well each of the 25 functional marketing responsibilities is being carried out and improving those that need help. (For a discussion of measurement, see Chap. 24.) Fig. 7.3 shows how to evaluate the importance and the performance of these responsibilities for each of the markets served. Clearly those functions get attended to first that are most important in terms of the markets being served.

Summary

Certainly, there are more than 25 responsibilities involved in marketing. We have already pointed out that each function on the list, is made up of a number of subfunctions. Therefore, an effective audit must go much further than a superficial appraisal of broad categories. The performance of each of these functions must be considered in all its ramifications for each market served.

As we have pointed out, none of these functions exists independently of the others or independently of the health of the marketplace or of the competitive forces at work within it. What this means is that an audit is a serious undertaking and often must be carried out when there is the least time available to do it.

However, because of the approach we have taken, it is a much less difficult task than it might otherwise be. Further, because of the view taken of the entire marketing operation (Fig. 7.2), evaluating the performance of these 25 marketing responsibilities ought to become a continuing effort. In fact, conducting such audits on a continuing basis can be thought of as the prime responsibility of marketing management.

PART 2

New Products—The Dimensions of the Challenge

Among marketing people, it is an article of faith that continued success in the marketplace requires a continuous flow of profitable new products. The number of new products each year will vary from situation to situation, but the need for them is continuous. Established products eventually become obsolete, and markets shrivel and die. Even Big Macs have peaked, and a McDonald's franchise is no longer the money maker it once was.

In these days of slow growth, especially, new products take on an added significance. The income new products generate is *found money*. If the product is new and aimed at an established market, its superior benefits will ensure sales at the expense of existing competitive products, sometimes our own. And if the market itself is new, so, too, will be the income for everybody.

So important is the subject of new products that the literature is studded with articles concerning the life cycle of products and of markets. Such articles tell us how much time we have left before a new product will be required or before a new market must be found. Further, it is not difficult to find good meaty articles about the techniques for launching a new product or about the management of products in the marketplace. One can even find learned articles about the life cycles of industries and technologies. MIT's Systems Dynamics Group, for example, writes and talks about the 40- to 60-year Kondratief waves that control the lives of basic industries. (Nikolai Kondratief, himself, wrote about 54-year life cycles for capitalist economies.)

Surely it is important to know how to bring a new product to market and how to manage it once it is there. It is also important to know where it is in its life cycle, although some products like Ivory Soap, Wrigley's Doublemint, and Campbell's Tomato Soup seem to go on forever (would that we could be as lucky with our own). But first, we ought to know what an acceptable new product is and just as important, we ought to know where to look for and how to recognize viable new-product ideas.

A story will illustrate this.

A friend of mine is a mechanical engineer—and a good one. At the time I am referring to, he had been out of school for about 8 years and had just started his third job. His first was with a manufacturer of electronic controls where he worked with a new-product group. In the 6 years that he was there, he had a hand in developing and bringing to market five or six new products.

Then another electronics firm made him an offer he couldn't refuse. He accepted and was put in charge of new-product development. He was given a secretary, a nice office, two telephones, all the credit cards he could use, and a fine budget. And he was told to go develop some new products.

He was very conscientious, and after a year of traveling and talking with customers, he proposed five new-product ideas. Three were turned down by management as being unsuitable. Two went to engineering for further study. Six months later, he proposed three more new-product ideas. These, too, were turned down. At that point he said to management, "Look, you have turned down six new-product ideas because they were unsuitable. What is an acceptable new-product idea?" The answer he got was this, "You are the new-product expert, you should know."

He quit, called his former employer, and returned to the old company in charge of new-product development.

Clearly, any continued and successful effort to identify, evaluate, develop, and launch profitable new products ought to begin with an understanding of what constitutes acceptability.

The second story concerns the operating vice president of a machine tool firm, a firm with a reputation for innovation. In discussing new products one day, he said this to me, "We really don't know what we are doing. Half, maybe two-thirds, of our new products die. We try to bury them quickly before anyone notices. What it boils down to is this: We take a hard look at who is proposing any new product. If we trust him and think he is mature and aggressive enough, we let him go ahead. It is as simple as that."

This might be called the advocacy approach to new product selection and development. However, there may be no necessary relationship between the quality of a product and the quality of its *champion*. The danger here is in institutionalizing the selection of a product *champion* and not institutionalizing the identification, evaluation, development, and launching of profitable new products.

These two situations may not be typical, but they are common enough. For most firms, developing new products is a chancy business. There are few guidelines for an acceptable new product. We do not know where to look for new-product ideas, although we are assured that they are all around us—somewhere.

When we do eventually have an idea, our procedures for evaluating it and putting it into development are neither clear nor firmly established. Finally, once we have the new product, we may not be able to get it off the ground as quickly as we would like.

In view of all this, we need to explore the requisites for a successful system for identifying, evaluating, developing, and launching new products. There are five of these:

- *First,* we need some broad guidelines to show us the kinds of new products that are best for us and for our firms. We'll explore this subject in some depth.

- *Second,* we need to know where and how to look for new-product ideas. Since the possibilities here may be new to most, we'll explore this subject thoroughly.

- The *third* requisite for an effective system for identifying, evaluating, developing, and launching new products is a simple way of auditing what's going on in the marketplace and conducting necessary market research so that we do not get led astray or zonked by competition.

- *Fourth,* we need a final evaluation screen which will tell us which of several new-product ideas should go into development. This important subject will also be covered.

- *Finally,* we need an effective process for actually launching the new product, and as we shall see, it is a much simpler process than many of us think.

There is a caution. I'll be talking about ordinary, run-of-the-mill new products—anything from a nut or a bolt to a robotized assembly line, from freeze-dried snow peas to a food processor. Most new products are not breakthroughs. They are rather unglamorous and ordinary. All they do is make or lose money. Those are the ones we will be concerned with.

8

Developing Guidelines for New Product

As a starting point, let's take a close look at what we know about successful marketers. We'll examine a few characteristics which successful firms seem to share and which are absent from the not-quite-so-successful firms. And, by *successful* I don't mean anything extraordinary or hard-to-understand, I mean quite simply that they make more money than other firms in the same business, while serving a broader and happier customer base.

These firms are successful today because of the things they have done in the past. Firms that have met our definition of success do not achieve that position overnight. They have earned it by what they have been doing for a long time. And, one of the things that has made them what they are is that over the years they have introduced a number of successful new products. Today's standard products were, after all, yesterday's successful new products.

My thesis here is a simple one. We can identify a number of characteristics shared by successful marketers. We can relate those characteristics to the identification and development of new products. Thus, we have useful guidelines to aid us in the selection of successful new products. If we follow these guidelines, over time we too will become increasingly successful.

Put another way, what I propose to do first is to establish a few long-term goals to guide us in the initial selection of new-product ideas. How to achieve these goals will, of course, vary from firm to firm. The goals themselves, however, which we will express here qualitatively, will be the same for all of us.

Over the years, and in connection with the problems of strategic planning, a number of organizations—among them the Strategic Planning

Institute of Cambridge, Massachusetts—have been looking at or looking into what makes one firm more successful than another.

Return on Investment (ROI) is the criterion used to measure success. The ROIs of firms in the same businesses (that is, serving the same markets) were compared with one another. The leaders in each group, regardless of the kind of businesses, shared 30 or so characteristics, each of which influenced ROI independently of the others. Among them are the 11 characteristics shown in Fig. 8.1.

These 11 characteristics seem to have the most use to us in establishing guidelines for the selection of new products.

These 11 characteristics separate nicely into two main groups. The first five relate to the product-market combinations that generate income. The last five relate to the changes that a new product produces internally, and so it influences our ability to hang onto the money it generates. The middle, or sixth characteristic—advertising & sales promotion—is the interface between the two groups.

Throughout what follows, real products will illustrate the points being made. However, for the most part they will not be industrial products. There is a great diversity among industrial products, markets, and methods of distribution. There is little in common between say, marketers of office supplies and microprocessors, alkyd resins and bus ducts or chip carriers and horizontal boring mills. Industrial products, therefore, do not always make useful illustrations. However, we are *all* consumers. We shop for the same kinds of things at supermarkets, auto

1. High-quality products
2. Broad product offerings
3. Narrow market segments
4. High market shares
5. Healthy margins
6. Marketing efforts which stress direct sales and minimize advertising
7. Moderate new-product activity
8. Low-to-moderate investment intensity
9. High value added per employee
10. Vertically integrated
11. Low-to-moderate research and development aimed at product and process improvement

Figure 8.1. Common characteristics of successful marketers.

dealerships, and drugstores. Therefore, consumer products, for the most part, will be used to illustrate the points to be made. These points apply equally to all seven markets discussed in Chap. 2.

1. High Product Quality

This may be the most important characteristic of successful firms.

Product quality is the basis of reputation, and reputation is what makes it easy to sell existing products and to get new products accepted quickly. As simple as this notion is, some firms don't seem to grasp its significance, let alone implement it.

The domestic passenger car market provides a good example of the importance of quality. Here's the way things stand with the five principal suppliers to that market.

General Motors, plagued with an unsafe-at-any-speed history, low gasoline mileage, and innumerable model recalls, has seen its market share drop from over 62 percent in 1980 to 56 percent in 1985 and 49 percent in 1987.

The Ford Motor Company's TV commercials stress that "At Ford, quality is No. 1 (*and has been since 1982*)." Full-page newspaper advertisements deliver the same message. One wonders, if quality at Ford has been important for such a short time, with which model year can one begin to take the quality of its products seriously.

Chrysler appears to have taken a deep breath and offers to warrant its cars for 5 years or 50,000 miles. GM and Ford went for 2 and 20,000.

American Motors, with a long history of extended warranty, makes the same offer as Chrysler (and is now owned by Chrysler).

"Foreign"—which is the easiest way to identify the fifth supplier—has seen its market share grow from 5 percent 20 years ago to over 25 percent today. Its share continues to grow.

Since length of warranty is assumed to be an indicator of quality, in the spring of 1987, General Motors increased the warranty period on one model to 6 years or 60,000 miles. Then, overnight, everybody had to play catchup. Suddenly Chrysler had 7 years and 70,000 miles, and the rest 6 years and 60,000. This seems suspiciously like quality by *fiat*. But in any case, getting satisfaction at the end of an extended warranty remains a lawyer's game.

As one more commentary on the quality of passenger cars, consider this. Nearly one-third of the new vehicles sold as passenger cars in the period 1980–1987 are, in fact, pickup trucks. Pickups—and it doesn't matter whether they are domestic or foreign—are perceived by one-third of the market to be of higher quality than the vehicles actually designated to carry passengers. A new fashion and a new market may be developing. Some manufacturers are actually developing new models with enhanced passenger-carrying capabilities.

Further, quality is such a chancy business that many states have seen fit to enact "lemon laws" to protect customers.

The implication here for new-product development is quite clear: High quality is essential. Even though some aspects of quality are subjective, no one should have trouble establishing what high quality is for the market being served.

One more point—just to make sure there is no misunderstanding: *High quality* does not necessarily mean *high-priced*. There is, for example, no more effective general-purpose writing instrument than the 10-cent BIC Stick. Both the Cross or the Mont Blanc pen have other attributes which justify high price.

2. Broad Product Offerings and Many Markets Served

Another characteristic of successful marketers is the breadth of their product offerings and the many markets they serve. Eastman Kodak provides a fine example of this. If you need film for whatever purpose—medical x ray, industrial x ray, measuring radiation exposure, making offset printing plates—the list can go on and on—or just for the ordinary, garden variety of picture taking, Kodak has a high-quality film available.

To clarify another important point. New products must really be new for the producer and not merely extensions of existing product lines. For example, if Campbell comes out with another kind of soup, Crispy Vegetable condensed soup or Chunky Style single-strength soup, these are only line extensions. That new soup will still wind up on the soup shelves at the supermarket. A new product would wind up in a new section.

The new product should actually increase the number of markets served or broaden the offering to them. Merely offering a new size or color is not enough.

3. Serve Narrow Market Segments

Successful firms serve very narrow, well-defined market segments.

It must be remembered, however, that neither markets nor market segments last forever. Let me illustrate: Once there was a sneaker or athletic shoe market. Keds was the big name. Then came Etonic, which carved out the golf shoe market. Then Topsiders carved out a sailor's, or yachting, market. Adidas took care of the tennis people, Nike the joggers, and Converse the basketballers. Five new markets, where once there was only one.

This situation lasted for a while. Then Reebok carved out the aerobics market. Rockport developed a shoe for people who walked not jogged. Then Reebok acquired Rockport and started to "play Pac-Man" with the rest of the industry.

Trying to find a simple pair of sneakers under these conditions is nearly as difficult as finding a bottle of Moxie. It is much easier to find a pair of sneakers that records distance and the time worn and calculates the number of calories burned (Puma's R S computer shoe).

The implication here for new products should also be clear. The new product should serve a narrow and well-defined market. If possible, the new product should help define or create the market which it will serve.

To illustrate this point further and to provide an introduction to the next guideline, consider this. Stratus Computer makes only fault-tolerant computers for the on-line transaction processing market. Stratus is number two, behind Tandem, but ahead of IBM whom it supplies. Its sales and income continue to grow while those of most other computer firms stagnate or decline.

4. Secure a Healthy Share of Served Markets against Few Competitors

Successful firms enjoy a healthy share of the markets they serve and generally compete against only three or four others. The market shares of the successful firm tend to peak at between 30 and 40 percent. The ROIs tend to peak at about this share level, too.

If the importance of market share needs to be illustrated, the cigarette market provides a ready example. It is roughly an $18 billion market. One share point (1 percent) is worth $180 million. Philip Morris holds 36 percent of the market; R. J. Reynolds, 32 percent; Brown Williamson, 11 percent; and everyone else, Lorillard, American Tobacco, and Liggett & Myers, under 9 percent. If any of these low performers gets just one more share point, it will add $180 million to its sales.

Campbell's, which serves many segments of the grocery market, provides a good illustration of high market shares against few competitors, one that is easy to see the next time you are in a supermarket.

As far as soups are concerned, Campbell's dominates this segment of the grocery market. Its share is way above the 30 to 40 percent just mentioned. Heinz is there, plus a couple of gourmet brands and some generics, but no serious competition. Campbell's *owns* the canned soup market; its other products are more illustrative of the point we want to make.

Walk to the bread shelves, and after setting aside the common white breads like Wards, Sunbeam, and Wonder, you will find Campbell's Pepperidge Farm, Arnold's, and a few regional ethnics.

For canned citrus juices, there are Campbell's Juice Bowl, Ocean Spray, and various house brands.

With baked beans, you have Campbell's, B & M, Friends, Van Camp, and perhaps a house brand or a generic.

You'll find the same situation in the potted meats section. If you want chicken, there are Campbell's Swanson, Richardson & Robbins, Wm. Underwood, or Hormel.

If you want tomato or mixed vegetable juice, it is Campbell's tomato or V-8 against Stokeley, S & W, Del Monte, Ocean Spray, Welch's, and the house brands.

If it's pickles you want, you'll find Campbell's Vlasic against Heinz, Clausen, and some locals.

Then, there are "oh, oh, Spaghetti-Os", Prego Spaghetti sauces, LeMenu frozen dinners and Mrs. Paul's frozen fish. There's more too.

Again, the implications are clear. Where possible, the new product should serve a market segment where there are few competitors and where a sizable market share is possible.

5. Healthy Margins

This characteristic should come as no surprise. It is what would be expected from high-quality products enjoying strong positions against few competitors in the markets which they serve. Beyond this obvious benefit, there are others.

Because of the broad-based product offerings, if a single product were to come under price pressure and require that its margin be shaved to maintain share (a bad move, by the way, in most situations), the impact on totals would be small. Additionally, high margins mean that finished goods inventories do not have to turn rapidly to sustain a high ROI. Because of this, the business can proceed in a much more controlled, deliberate, and orderly fashion.

The implication here for new products should also be clear. The successful new product should support a high margin, certainly no lower than the company average and much higher if possible. (For a full discussion of pricing, see Part 3).

These five characteristics of successful marketers and the new-product guides we have extracted from them all relate to the generation of income. However, we must also be concerned with how the new product affects our ability to hang onto and convert that income into profits. The next characteristic of success which we will review serves as an interface between these two kinds of concerns.

6. Marketing Efforts Stress Direct Sales and Minimize Advertising

With successful marketers, the main thrust of the marketing activities is in sales and promotional activities. That this should be so, I think, follows from the first five considerations. If the market segments served are narrow, customers and prospects should be easy to identify. For this reason, lead generation can be minimal. Further, because of the firm's established reputation and market position, claims for new products should gain ready acceptance. Therefore, the need for advertising to educate and condition the market, to create a preference, should also be minimal.

"Japan, Inc.," is in the enviable position of being able to introduce a new product in almost any market and having it accepted immediately. The consistently superior quality of its cameras, cars, office equipment, electronic devices, and earth-moving equipment has conditioned us to accept its new products almost on faith. Indeed, so strong now is its reputation that some claim that the governor of New Hampshire owed his election in the mid-eighties to the similarity of his name, Sununu, to that of a Japanese car, Subaru.

However, there will be occasional missionary activities in which advertising plays a heavy role. The firm, for example, may be unknown in the market it wishes to serve. The product itself may satisfy a need that is not well-recognized. Or, a technology may be involved that is neither understood nor accepted.

The optical scanners which are found at the checkout counters of some supermarkets provide a case in point. They were introduced in

1970. By 1976, they were in operation in only 64 supermarkets. By mid-1985, they were operating in only 6000 of the nation's more than 40,000 supermarkets. By the end of 1986 the number of supermarkets had declined to 35,000, and half of them had optical scanners.

The Polaroid film pack and camera, for example, required massive missionary work to gain the rapid market acceptance it received. When IBM, Phillips, and Burroughs first introduced the small, (for its time) self-contained business computer, there was enormous resistance from people who were accustomed to the NCR bookkeeping machine. And, of course, some of us even remember Mr. Reynolds demonstrating his new ballpoint pen at the bottom of a swimming pool.

Therefore, our goal in this area is to have a new product that requires minimum advertising support and which responds well to direct selling and promotional efforts. Properly selected launching tactics can help achieve this goal.

Now, let's take a look at five characteristics of successful marketers that relate to their ability to hang on to margins and convert them into net profits.

7. Moderate New-Product Activity

Successful marketers have very little new-product activity. In this context, by a *new product* we mean one that has been on the market for under 3 years. ROI is usually greatest when new-product sales are between 3 and 10 percent of total sales.

Sometimes, I think, we forget that untested new products have a way of tying up capital in raw materials, finished goods inventory, equipment, space, spare parts, sales literature, etc. But more importantly, perhaps, each new product also ties up a considerably greater portion of management and sales time than do established products of proven profitability. It takes a while for the twin investments of time and money to begin to generate a return. Successful firms do not have too much at risk in this area.

The goal here would be to limit new-product introductions to some small number, four or five per year, or to limit them in such a way that demands on time and money are limited.

We need not be so careful in this area as the Zippo Manufacturing Company of Bradford, Pa., which waited 53 years between new products. In the summer of 1985 it added a butane-fired CONTEMPO to its line, aimed at the Yuppy market.

Please don't misunderstand what's being said here. We are talking about run-of-the-mine new products, not significant breakthroughs. If, however, we should turn up our own version of the microchip or self-developing film or the Xerox process, it would be another proposition entirely.

8. Low-to-Moderate Investment Intensity

It may come as somewhat of a surprise, but another characteristic of a successful industrial marketer is a lower ratio of invested capital to sales than with less successful firms. This ratio seems to vary inversely with ROI: low investment intensity, high ROI; high investment intensity, low ROI.

For a simple example of this, consider John Deere & Company. Until 1986, the firm had not shown a loss since the days of the great depression. It took advantage of its position in the marketplace to concentrate all its manufacturing of agricultural equipment into a single, highly automated, heavily robotized, and completely integrated facility in Waterloo, Iowa. The plant went on stream in 1982 about the time the worldwide market for agricultural equipment began to shrink. Deere's monster machine is now running at 10 percent capacity with no way of shutting down what's not needed.

We have all been led to believe that machine-made products will not only be somehow better, but cheaper as well. In some ways this is true. But, what is certain is that as labor-intensive manufacturing converts to machine-intensive manufacturing, the ratio of investment to sales increases. Firms change from being aggressive marketers to being defensive marketers. The emphasis shifts from finding profitable new marketing opportunities to keeping expensive plants and equipment busy. If the whole industry is investment-intensive, then everyone's prices and margins keep eroding.

Steel provides a good example of a high-investment, low-margin industry.

Here is another example. Not far from my office is a firm I'd prefer not to identify. This firm worked two shifts to satisfy sales. Then it bought an enormous piece of equipment which could stamp out everything it needed on just one shift. The firm saved money and the machine paid for itself on this one-shift operation. However, the machine was idle for 16 hours every workday and for 48 hours on weekends.

This thought horrified someone who could only calculate carrying charges. A decision was made, therefore, to put the machine to work for two shifts. This resulted in twice the production needed to satisfy the market. The only way to move all of this product was to cut prices with a consequent reduction of margin, profitability and, ROI.

The whole thrust and mind set of industry is biased toward mass production—efficiency, long runs, and increasingly lower costs, all measured by labor productivity. These were powerful and novel ideas when introduced by Frederick Taylor in the last half of the nineteenth century.

Times have changed. Now the demands are for product superiority, achieved through short runs and flexible production which may mean lowered worker productivity and the risk of higher costs. The trade-off is between incremental cost increases on the production floor and happy customers. The customers are beginning to win.

The implications here are readily understood. A new product should not require that a firm increase its investment intensity but should tend to decrease the ratio of invested capital to sales.

9. High Value Added by Each Employee

Among successful firms, the value added per employee is higher than that with less successful firms. This is, of course, another way of describing productivity and of recognizing that labor-intensive production is, on occasion, more profitable than investment-intensive production.

Increased labor costs are invariably handed on to customers with no necessary negative impact on profitability. However, when automated production is substituted for handwork, any savings tend to be handed on to customers through lower prices with a necessarily negative impact on profits.

What with payroll costs, equal pay for equal work, union threats, equivalent worth, and all the other problems that come with hiring people, it is no wonder that the attractiveness of machines persists. They never join unions or ask for maternity leave. Machines just do the job they were built to do—no more, no less. And that's the problem.

People, in contrast, are infinitely programmable and, for the most part, self-programmable. But while machines require maintenance only, people require motivation. That ain't easy, but the results are worth it.

In 1982, General Motors (GM) closed its Fremont, California, assembly plant because it couldn't manage its 5000 employees and turn out automobiles profitably. Shortly thereafter, GM formed a joint venture with Toyota Motors and turned the plant over to them. With only minor changes in layout and equipment, the plant now turns out a quarter of a million cars a year with only 2500 of the former employees. It now requires only 21 hours to assemble a car; under GM management, comparable models required 38 hours to assemble.

These are not isolated situations. Similar results can be found in other industries—rubber and steel, for example. No wonder the robotics industry expects its sales to decline by 30 or 40 percent over the near term.

The implication here is also obvious. New products should increase the value added per employee without necessarily increasing the investment intensity.

10. Vertical Integration

Vertical integration seems to be characteristic of successful marketers. Conventional wisdom, however, says that when markets are unstable and product technology changes rapidly, it behooves a marketer to remain flexible—horizontal. This means buying and assembling, not making, items supplied by others and letting the others take care of frequent design changes and retoolings.

Something like this has happened in the silicon-chip market. As the chip capacity increases—64, 128, 256...—firms that used to grow their own, no longer do so. They buy excess production from fewer and fewer sources who enjoy fewer and fewer competitors in a narrowing and increasingly defined market.

Conventional wisdom also says that in stable markets with stable technologies and products, vertical integration is to be encouraged. However, who is to judge stability? It is ironic to note that the chip market, which appears so turbulent to some, is apparently quite stable, at least to the remaining manufacturers of chips, who we assume are making a killing.

The implication, once more, is clear. The new product ought to encourage vertical integration.

11. Moderate Research and Development Aimed at Product and Process Improvement

Finally—and this may come as a shocker to many—the successful marketer has a low-to-moderate research and development (R&D) effort compared with others in its field. Further, those R&D efforts are aimed mostly at improving the quality of existing products, improving the processes by which they are made, or investigating new applications for existing products.

There are a couple of important points here. Large R&D expenditures are not necessarily a sign of patriotism, even though our government has urged industry to spend more. What's significant is not how much is invested in R&D, but *how* it is invested. The aim must be to make good products better and happy customers happier.

Occasionally the goal is cost reduction to help hold and expand a market. Sony, for example, introduced the Walkman in July of 1979. Eighteen months later, the number of parts had been halved, sound quality was improved, and the unit was smaller. Now, 9 years after it was introduced, another third has been cut from costs, and the basic model lists for only $32.

Frequently, a goal is product improvement which will help expand a market. Often cost reduction is a side benefit. For example, in 1982, a 32-bit super-minicomputer with 2 million characters of main storage, 100 million in disk memory and two video display terminals plus a dot matrix printer cost about $44,000 to build. Three years later, costs had been reduced by about one-third to about $28,000. Most R&D is not quite as focused.

Basic research aimed at increasing our understanding of the universe is a luxury few firms can afford. Often such research is funded with full recognition that the results will have little or no immediate impact on earnings. Bell Labs appears to have been such a situation. Fiber optics and satellite communications technology, which are so important to phone communications today, were developed outside the Bell System, and most of the improvements in existing telephone equipment originated with Western Electric, the manufacturing arm.

Another much smaller firm, which I will not name, quite consciously and courageously invested a large portion of its income in the development of a new technology. It did so knowing full well that it might be 10 or a dozen years before a market would develop for the new technology. That market is now slowly developing. Such firms are, however, unique.

Each industry has its own built-in level of research and development activities. Generally, 10 or 11 percent of sales would be a large investment. Firms with the more moderate activities seem to make more money than the rest. The all-industry average is something less than 3.5 percent. The range seems to be from 0.5 percent for steel to over 12 percent for semiconductors.

The pharmaceutical industry is commonly thought of as being a high-level R&D industry (8 percent of sales). However, when looked at closely, that R&D is concerned with compliance and product liability, with the production and the prefabrication of more useful molecular building blocks, and with the further exploration of technical literature to see what of value remains in the public domain. Most new ideas for this industry come from external sources and are often the result of university research grants.

The computer (8 percent), telecommunications (5 percent), and medical instrumentation (7 percent) industries are other industries where high levels of R&D are expected. *Inc. Magazine* has published figures from these industries showing that the fastest-growing among them are also the ones who spend the most for R&D. (Growing firms commonly have very low ROIs.) Even here, the R&D expenditures among the faster-growing, are in the 10 or 12 percent of sales range and are budgeted for product improvement, expanded applications, or improvement in the manufacturing processes.

One final example here.

Research and development at General Motors concerns product and process in a very hard-nosed way. For them, it is cheaper to achieve improved fuel economy by reducing drag and wind resistance—that is, by just changing body contours—than it would be by designing a more fuel-efficient engine or by fiddling with weight reduction. Even a firm like General Motors will let someone else do the basic developmental work and make the basic breakthroughs, occasionally to its own disadvantage.

Honda, for example, through its own R&D efforts, has made substantial improvements in the design of the cylinder head and combustion chamber of the internal combustion engine. Honda continues to gain market share while GM's declines.

As far as new-product development is concerned, two implications follow from this modest R&D characteristic of successful industrial marketers: (1) Ideas for new products come from the marketplace, not from the lab. (2) Each new product should contribute to holding down the R&D burden.

What the 11 Characteristics Mean

Thus, these 11 characteristics of successful firms are readily converted into goals for new products to achieve, or to put it another way, they are easily converted into new-product selection guidelines (Fig. 8.2). None of them, by the way, aim merely at cost reduction. The goal is improved quality.

1. Provide higher quality than is usually seen in the market served
2. Broaden the offering to the market served
3. Help narrow and bring into high focus each market served
4. Afford an increased share of the market served
5. Provide above-average margin

6. Respond to direct selling and promotional activities, require minimal advertising

7. Limit annual new-product introductions
8. Require below-average investments
9. Enhance productivity
10. Encourage vertical integration
11. Give priority to ideas generated by the marketplace

Figure 8.2. New-product selection guidelines.

Folding Them into the Corporate Culture

These considerations ought to become part and parcel of the way we think about new products and evaluate them before we invest heavily in their development. It is apparent, for example, that the management—the boss, if you will—of young, successful, growing firms evaluates new products in this way almost by instinct.

However, as firms grow, the number of markets served increase, and more people become involved in the selection and development of new products, that instinct becomes dull and blunted. New-product people are selected because of their strengths or expertise in only a few of these areas. They know a product class, for example, and understand its technologies and quality requirements. Rarely, however, will they understand either intellectually or by instinct, all eleven of these goals and guidelines.

The organization itself must make up for these personal lacks. It can do this through training and indoctrination. It can, by the use of procedures and checklists, establish formal screening processes. Further, it can, through example and attitude, build these considerations into the organization's value system and culture.

The larger the organization, the more likely it will be that all three—training, procedures, and examples—must be employed to ensure that these considerations are not overlooked.

It is hard to tell exactly what accounts for the ability of firms like Hewlett-Packard, 3M, P&G, or John Deere to introduce a stream of high-quality new products year after year. It can be assumed that these 11 new-product considerations or their equivalent are part and parcel of the corporate culture.

What I propose here is that the entire organization, not just its new-product people understand all eleven of these considerations. And I also propose that each new-product idea selected for consideration also satisfy each of them. Difficult at first, perhaps, and progressively easier, but, in any case, essential to long-term success.

Obviously, if there is a business plan, these new product guidelines must conform to it. They will, in fact, help to flesh it out. And if there is no business plan, these guidelines for developing new products will be a start in formulating one.

With these goals, therefore, with these new-product selection guidelines established, we have a foundation on which to stand as we begin to think about and examine new-product ideas. We ought next to think about how we find them. Where do we look for, where do we find new-product ideas?

9
Finding New-Product Ideas in the Marketplace

There are just five ways in which new products come into being for a firm. That's all, just five. These are summarized in Fig. 9.1.

New products are invented, they are acquired, they evolve from existing products or existing technologies, they are picked out of the wastebasket, or they are developed from the requests and suggestions of customers.

1. Invention

Most people, including the tyros in our business, are inclined to think that new products are invented. There is a flash of inspiration, a stroke of genius, and—presto—a new product is born. This happens, but not very often. It is possible that the Phillips head screw and screwdriver came about in this way. Mr. Morita says that the Sony Walkman came about this way, too. Perhaps it was also the origin of Le Funelle, a device that lets women relieve themselves standing up.

More usually, however, the invention starts with an idea of the finished product—an incandescent lamp or self-developing film—and the process of invention is a lengthy series of trials and errors until the product comes into being, together with an economic process for making it.

The development of xerography provides a good example of how a breakthrough comes to market. The concept was of a dry, nonphotographic process for making multiple copies. Chester Carlson filed his first patent application in 1937. Ten years later, he formed a partnership with the Haloid Company for the manufacturing development of the process. Ten years later, English flour miller and motion picture

1. Invention
     Strokes of genius
     Concept and hard work

2. Acquisition
     Purchase
     License
     Theft
     Copying

3. Evolution
     Fill-in
     Extension
     Repackaging
     Combination and integration
     Specialization
     Adaptation
     Pruning

4. Rejects and failures

5. Customers' requests

Figure 9.1. Common sources of new-product ideas.

producer, J. Arthur Rank supplied capital for its commercial introduction. In 1959 the first Xerox machine was introduced.

The development of the Land Camera provides another illustration. The idea of self-developing film came to Edwin Land when his daughter asked why she had to wait to see the photograph he had just taken of her. Within an hour, Land had the whole process outlined—camera, film, and chemicals. That was 1944. Four years later, after the design, manufacturing, and marketing problems had been solved, the Land camera was introduced successfully. It was profitable from the start.

Breakthroughs are rare, very rare indeed. Developing new products in this way is not a field for the typical industrial marketer to plow. We must look elsewhere for reliable sources of new-product ideas and new products.

2. Acquisition

Acquisition of an idea or a product from a third party is a common source of new products. Sometimes the acquisition results from an outright purchase. Sometimes not. Either mode has its kosher and not-so-kosher exemplars. Parker Brother's Monopoly, Selchow & Righter's Scrabble, and Ideal Toy's Rubik's Cube are all simple examples of new products acquired through purchase. In each of these situations, the company and the inventor have benefited enormously. Many firms routinely add to their product lines through purchases.

Johnson & Johnson, for example, has a long history of acquisition. It acquired its Reach toothbrush from E. I. Du Pont for a considerable sum, added it to its health and beauty aids products line, and seems to be doing reasonably well with it. Not all its acquisitions, however, have been as successful. Johnson & Johnson recently acquired the firm of Stimtech which owned a new painkilling technology. Here the goal was not to broaden product offerings but to suppress what was viewed as a threat to Tylenol, another acquisition. The courts have declared it to be an illegitimate acquisition.

Licensing is another common means of acquiring new products. In the fashion industries, many manufacturers are able to introduce new products through the simple expedient of licensing designer names. Designer names are attached to everything from bed sheets to jock straps and, even, pasties for women. Recently, designer cigarettes appeared on the market.

Coming closer to home, many of the newly formed manufacturers of telephone equipment owe their product lines to licensing arrangements with AT&T. Most video games are manufactured under license from Magnavox, a subsidiary of North American Phillips; the original patents are held by Sanders Associates which has licensed them to Magnavox.

Acquisition through purchase or license is just one kind of acquisition. There are others which do not involve any form of compensation.

Outright theft is one means of new-product acquisition that involves no compensation. Stealing new products and new-product ideas occurs more often than we would like to think. Complex patents and ponderous court procedures occasionally make it hard to tell outright theft from situations in which great minds have come to think alike. It is likely that Kodak's infringement of Polaroid patents on instant photography arose as much from the difficulty of reading patents on complex procedures as from a desire to stay even with a competitor. However, the courts cough up guilty bluechip firms often enough to suggest that acquisition through theft is not unusual. Johns-Manville, for example, was recently found guilty of stealing the design of a patented lighting fixture from the much smaller Massachusetts firm that developed it. And even mighty Sears Roebuck has been found guilty of shortchanging the inventor of a patented socket wrench.

While thievery is a reprehensible means of acquiring new products and new-product ideas, there is another quite legitimate means of acquiring them without paying for them.

Some call it copying, and occasionally that is just what it is. Knockoffs are a way of life in the garment industry.

As soon as the first Hula-Hoop hit the market, anyone with spare garden hose and a knife was in the business. Copying is an honorable tradition with large payoffs so long as discernment and discrimination are used to select what to copy. The first Datsun, for example, which Nissan Motors introduced into this country was nearly an exact copy of the Crossley, even to the location of the impossible-to-reach block drains.

Copying is not, however, a technologically elegant term. Some prefer to call the process *reverse engineering,* which comes closer to describing what actually happens. Perhaps the classic example of the reverse engineering technique was the conversion of the woven Chinese finger-trap toy into highly effective, low-bulk industrial cable pullers.

A more current example is the Merrill-Lynch Cash Management Account. It was introduced in 1977 to a chorus of "Who needs it?" from competitive firms. Four years later, Merrill-Lynch's CMA had nearly 600,000 customers and over $35 billion in assets. In the money management industry, copying Merrill-Lynch then became the thing to do.

A marketer's goal, after all, is not to have a completely original product line. Rather, it is to have profitable products with long lives, products that conform to the 11 goals and guidelines just discussed. If someone else's product provides us with an idea which we can adapt and improve upon (*improvement* is the key word) and which will contribute to the health of our business, we would be foolish not to take advantage of it.

The genius of Japan doesn't lie in its innovativeness or in its ability to buy IBM secrets from the FBI, but rather in meticulous attention to high quality and the consistent production which ensures it. However, some may say that that in itself is an innovation.

3. Evolution

Invention and acquisition are not, however, ever likely to become the major source of new products. Like it or not, we are going to have to develop most of the new products we require by ourselves. That is a big challenge. An immediate response to it might be, "Yes, but I am not a scientist or an inventor. I'm a marketer or a financier or a manufacturer or an engineer." Fortunately, that challenge is not as difficult as it might seem.

Most products develop through an evolutionary process of change and adaptation in response to the needs and opportunities of the marketplace. It is our obligation, therefore, to know our markets, our customers, our products, and our manufacturing and technological capabilities and limitations. We must know them well enough to recognize both the market's needs and our opportunities when they manifest themselves.

Where many of us have problems is in failing to recognize those situations which may be signaling a need or an opportunity. New-product development activities seem to be random and seem to be carried out on a hit-or-miss basis. However, if we can identify those sources from which the signals are most likely to come, we can focus our attention on them. We won't have to scan the horizon or grab for a brass ring that may not be there. Knowing where these signal sources are, we can keep them under continuous surveillance. Then, we hope, we will be the one to receive the new-product signal and not our competitors.

There are seven such areas (See Fig. 9.1) which we should explore periodically. Each could provide us with a viable new-product idea. Let's take a look at each of these potential sources.

Fill-ins

It is generally assumed that the products offered to a market form a price and quality continuum; that is, if they were laid out side by side in order of increasing quality and increasing price, there would be no gaps or discontinuities. Occasionally, this is so; more often, it is not. Wherever the continuity is interrupted, there may be a new-product opportunity. Periodically, it is important to lay out all the competitive offerings to a specific market segment to see if there are large holes or discontinuities in quality, price, or, best of all, both. Where such a hole does appear, we need to find out if we can profitably plug it with a new product.

Let me illustrate (See Fig. 9.2).

Six firms filled the same market need with essentially the same three products at the same price and quality levels: the quick-and-dirty models cost 1 cent each and had a 30 percent share of the total market; the model which was adequate cost 2 cents each and had a 50 percent share;

	BEFORE		AFTER	
Quality	Unit price	Share	Unit price	Share
Overkill	6¢	20%	6¢	10%
Superior			4¢	25%
Adequate	2¢	50%	2¢	45%
Quick and dirty	1¢	30%	1¢	20%
		100%		100%

Figure 9.2. Filling-in competitive offerings.

finally, the quality overkill model cost 6 cents each and had a 20 percent share.

One of the six firms looked at this situation and saw a new-product opportunity. It modified the performance characteristic of its 2-cent model and nearly matched those of the "Tiffany" model. The result, a superior model at 4 cents each with an extra margin of nearly 2 cents. Through a very adroit launching effort, it captured 25 percent of the total market before competition knew what had happened. This was calculation. Luck made the results even sweeter. Capacity was limited, and as the 4-cent volume built, something had to give. The 1-cent quick-and-dirty model, which had become a price football, was abandoned.

Extensions

The same technique of laying out the entire competitive offering to a market by price and quality may show that the opportunity is to extend the series, not to fill a hole in it. The new product may extend the series upward from the high end, or it can be downward toward a lower price. However, being forever mindful of the strategic guidelines discussed above, there should be no diminution of either quality or margin should the new product fall below the low-priced end of the range.

Recently, we have seen this kind of thing happen in the United States' writing instrument market. BIC, for example, looked at the range of offerings and decided that it could be extended downward. It introduced its low-cost models. Koh-i-noor, on the other hand, looked at the same market and saw its opportunity at the high end. It began importing Mont Blanc fountain pens which topout at over $7000 each.

Repackaging

Often it is possible to create a new product simply by repackaging an existing product or changing the way it is brought to market. Repackaging takes many forms, but is always aimed at easing the movement of the product into the market. Blister-packed nuts, bolts, and other small hardware items are simple examples of this kind of opportunity. Rental or lease-purchase plans which make capital equipment available from operating funds may be another example.

The reconstituted orange juice which Minute Maid offers in cartons was not merely just another way of making its frozen concentrate available; it opened a new market. For, in addition to being a new product, it has a new buyer. Minute Maid now sells to the supermarket dairy buyer as well as to the frozen-food buyer. The basic Polaroid camera, for another example, has been repackaged to produce drivers' licenses and employee identification cards with photos attached.

One final example. *The National Business Employment Weekly,* a publication of the *Wall Street Journal,* is a gathering together of all the employment advertisements from the regional editions, and TRW has repackaged the personal credit ratings it supplies to commercial subscribers. Now for $35 you can easily get a copy of your own credit history plus information on who is asking questions about it. A simple idea and a new product.

Integration and Combination

Frequently the market signals a situation in which new products can be developed through the combination or integration of existing products or processes. Prefabrication and preassembly are simple examples of this.

For a homey example of the combination of products, there are packaged cake and piecrust mixes. An example on the process side would be the Cuisinart which combines a blender, a slicer, and an old-fashioned electric mixer.

An industrial example of process integration is provided by the Sanborn coolant and cutting-oil recovery system for the metals-working industry. Metal-working fluids become contaminated by solids, by bacteria and fungus, and by other fluids, all of which limit their lives. Conventionally, coolant life is extended somewhat by separate processes which screen out solids, add disinfectants, and skim off tramp fluids. The Sanborn Process accomplishes all of this in a single system which extends the life of these fluids indefinitely.

Market Segmentation

Often a market which appears to be monolithic turns out to be neither uniform nor continuous. Sometimes this occurs because the market itself grows and changes. Where once there was one market, there now are several. Earlier we discussed the men's footwear market and saw how the market for sneakers had become several separate markets. Here, growing affluence and sportsmindedness has led people to think about and afford more specialized footwear.

Market segmentation occurs in other ways as well. (See also Chap. 3.) Frequently, the change comes about because we have acquired a greater mastery of our own technology and can satisfy narrower needs. Changes in the offset duplicator market illustrate this.

The original offset duplicator was sold to a market made up of those who needed a sheet-fed press capable of turning out a moderate volume of fair-quality work at a modest cost. The equipment used photoetched zinc plates, required a skilled operator, and needed constant monitoring. It found a ready market among small commercial printers and in-plant duplicating operations. As the technology improved, operations became more reliable and high-volume high-quality paper plates were developed. Coincidentally, the quick-printing market, exemplified by such firms as PIP or KWIK-KOPY, was being established.

One manufacturer of offset equipment, A.B. Dick, Inc., took advantage of the improved technology to develop a lightweight, simple-to-operate high-speed press which delivered moderate quality and occupied very little floor space. This manufacturer now dominates the quick-printing business, the fastest-growing segment of the printing industry, and has a 50 percent share of the total.

Adaptation

Another evolutionary source of new products is the adaptation of an existing product to another use or the adaptation of an existing product idea to another market. Here the examples are endless. One is staring at me as I write. Roger Tory Peterson's *Field Guide to the Birds* was first published by the Houghton Mifflin Company in 1934. The idea of this kind of guide was then adapted to other areas of interest. There are now 25 titles in a series that covers animals, flowers, trees, etc., each with its own distinctive market.

And there are other examples. The miniaturization of commercial ammonia refrigeration systems with freon has produced the home freezer and refrigerator. Miniaturization of industrial forced-air space heaters has produced the common blow dryer. And, going in the other direction, beefing up the common desk stapler has provided packers and shippers as well as the construction industry with a most versatile tool. The Remington Surgical Clipper is our old friend the Lady Remington dressed in specially designed surgical garb from 3M. Further, the Ramset device, for fastening wood, metal, and plastic to concrete, is merely a special 22-caliber single-shot pistol with a spike or bolt in the place of the bullet. And for one final example, a child's toy and laboratory curiosity has become the gyroscopic stabilizer.

Pruning

Additionally, there is another drastic, but natural, means of encouraging the development of new products—pruning. When a tree or shrub stops producing or becomes rank, the gardener prunes it back drastically. Horticulturalists are used to this kind of surgery; marketers are not.

Once in a while, the only way to stimulate the development of profitable new products is through the ruthless cutting away of the dead, the dying, and the unproductive from existing offerings. With the deadwood removed, existing opportunities are more visible. Often the market responds with a new product suggestion or two of its own.

Let me illustrate. Davis-Standard, a division of Crompton and Knowles makes extrusion equipment for the plastics industry. Over the years its product lines had expanded downstream so that each extruder sold was part of a specially engineered system. Davis-Standard shared a highly fragmented market with 160 known equipment manufacturers. No one was the clear leader in the manufacture of the basic extruder, Davis-Standard's original business. The firm saw its earnings evaporate as it sank further and further into this mess. It decided that it hadn't the resources for this game and withdrew. It slashed away all auxiliary equipment and focused again on making single screw extrusion machines. Within 4 years it had become the market leader, manufacturers of auxiliary equipment adapted to the Davis-Standard extruder, and ROI increased by a factor of 10.

Pruning is becoming commonplace on a large scale as firms divest themselves of acquisitions which "no longer promote strategic goals." Some people call this "movement back to the core business." It is pruning nonetheless. When properly done, both the parent and the cutting flourish.

Catalogs, too, require frequent pruning. A common practice involves setting an income or profit goal for product categories, part numbers, or, even, pages and dropping anything that does not rise above that threshold. Often, as a result of this process, it is possible to combine several of the eliminated items and from them make a new and viable product.

This leads us to the next large source of new-product ideas.

4. Rejects and Failures

Often, quite viable new-product ideas can be found among our rejects and failures. This does not mean that we become bag ladies or archeologists rooting around in the trash. What it does mean is that we should

154 New Products—The Dimensions of the Challenge

be aware that available materials change, markets change, and so do technologies.

The advent of a new material, Teflon, for example, made it possible to manufacture many high-performance parts of molded plastic. Thus were eliminated less reliable and more costly parts of cast or machined metal, as well as the cheap, molded plastic parts that guaranteed unreliable performance.

Many product ideas are rejected because existing technologies cannot produce the product at a reasonable cost or permit it to be sold at a reasonable price. Many products fail because there isn't a market large enough to support them at the time.

Light, or low-calorie, beers provide excellent examples.

Twenty years ago, Gablinger's, a low-calorie beer produced by a complex Swiss process, was introduced. It failed miserably. Shortly thereafter, Piel Brothers introduced another low-calorie beer made by a more conventional brewing process. It, too, was a marketing disaster. More recently, however, consumers seem to be acutely conscious of physical fitness, nutrition, and calorie intake. As a result, even respected vintners tout their low-calorie wine. In this market climate, low-calorie beers are a marketing success.

5. Customer Requests

Finally, of course, there are customer requests. These can be a powerful source of profitable new-product ideas. However, because the ideas come from customers, they tend to be less carefully screened than homegrown ideas. They can, therefore, become serious distractions and even profit drains.

Occasionally, the simple suggestion or request of a customer or prospect can result in an extremely profitable new product. Thus, a simple request to Henry Ford to replace the rumble seat on a Model-T coupe with a small truck body resulted in the pickup truck.

More frequently, however, we find that what should have been a special order or a specially engineered device has, in fact, become a standard product, often merely a line extension. The catalogs of stationers, fastener houses, and the manufacturers of washers, gaskets, and electronic interconnection devices are replete with items which have no potential beyond the original order or which differ from one another only in color or in an unimportant dimensional characteristic.

Padding catalogs in this way is a common device used by new firms to give themselves a greater presence than is actually warranted. The large numbers of essentially similar products may even suggest a special order to a customer. Mostly, however, this effort is self-deluding.

It is a general rule that when customers talk problems or performance, the marketer should listen; there is the possibility of a new product idea. But when customers talk color and dimensions, dig out your pencil; there may be a special order in the offing.

10

Conducting Market Audits and Market Research

From the discussion of the sources of new-product ideas, and as a clear implication of the 11 new-product guidelines discussed in Chap. 8, it is obvious that nearly all new-product ideas will and should come from the marketplace. This, in turn, suggests that we do a little formal market research and make a periodic audit of our product lines, of the markets those products serve, and of the competitive offerings in those markets.

Market Audits

Two points are critical here. The first is simply that in looking at a market or market segment, we should consider all the products that are offered to it, our own as well as those of our competitors. And, to the extent we can do so, this means looking at these offerings from the customers' points of view. It means, if an illustration is needed, that we should look at the Bics, the Papermates, the Parkers, the Schaeffers, and the Crosses, as well as the Mont Blancs and all the no-names. Looking only at our own offerings and those of the competitors at our price points is to wear blinders. Further, we should not limit ourselves to our own technology. If our product is ballpoint pens, we should also look at fountain pens, felt tips, and any other hand-held writing device. The audit should include anything that accomplished the same purpose for the customer as our own product.

The second critical point is how often we conduct the audit. Periodically to be sure; but how often is periodic?

For most product lines in most markets, a once-a-year audit might be enough. For more volatile markets, more frequent audits would be required. And for some markets, consumer packaged goods for example, perhaps the audit should be continuous.

Audit Questions

The goal, of course, is to find clear opportunities for new products or at least clues and suggestions that a need may exist. The audit should answer questions like these:

- Where can we plug a hole in or extend the offerings made to a market?
- How can we repackage an existing product or service to expand a market or create a new one?
- Where can we integrate or combine several products or processes (our own or competitors') to create a new product or a new market?
- What segments of an existing market are beginning to develop different needs and requirements? Do these changes create a new-product opportunity?
- How can we adapt what's offered in one market to the needs of another?
- Which of our products need simple improvements to maintain or improve their market position?
- What products have outlived their usefulness to the market, and how do we replace them?
- What do customers and prospects say about their current problems and future needs that suggest new products?
- Which of our failures or rejections deserve another look?

The answers to these questions come from many sources including analyses of competitive advertising, product literature, pricing, distribution, available share information and the occasional testing of competitive offerings.

Informal Interviews

As important, the audit should also include discussions with the decision makers and the buying influences of representative customers and prospects: Buyers and buying committees of retailers, for example, and purchasing agents, engineers, and manufacturing people at industrial accounts.

In this process, we can rely on our sales force to provide some of the input required. They can provide lost business reports as well as some of the other information needed: competitive advertisements, literature, and prices. They can provide information on distribution and even product samples. They should also be able to identify both the buying influences and the decision makers at important accounts in their territories.

There is one thing, however, they cannot do for us. They cannot pick the brains we need to have picked. They cannot have the freewheeling discussions of current problems and future needs that lead to the identification of new-product opportunities.

Salespeople have one job: to sell current products. This imperative colors the way they react to customers and prospects. More important, it colors the way customers and prospects react to them. The potential for a sale blinds the sales representative to all else, and it causes the customer to become guarded. There are exceptions, but they are rare. When they occur, consider yourself lucky. For the most part, the kind of field research I describe here will have to be done by management. It cannot be delegated to the sales force.

No matter how unfamiliar we are with a market, after one or two conversations with a few key customers and prospects, a sense of that market will begin to grow. That sense, coupled with what we have learned from other parts of the audit may eventually lead to a new-product idea or two. These ideas will be further refined and eventually will be either abandoned or tagged for serious investigation.

So far so good. But here is where a potentially serious problem begins to arise.

Unless we have been extremely lucky and can devote all our time to new products or unless we are concerned with only one market or market segment, we will have been able to talk with people at only six or eight firms. If these six or eight have sufficient buying power, their inputs may be enough to justify moving ahead on a new-product idea.

Formal Market Research

Usually, though, the people we are able to talk with are not representative enough of the marketplace. Their needs may suggest an idea and a good one, but before it gets more serious attention, we will need the reaction of a broader sample of the potential market. This means market research of a more formal kind.

Market research of the complex and sophisticated kind practiced by the manufacturers of consumer goods has received quite a bit of publicity. The importance of research in this market becomes clear when it is realized that only 35 percent of new consumer products ever survive market tests and go on to win consumer acceptance. Perhaps information like this has colored our understanding of what and how much market research is necessary and of what we can expect from it.

The curious thing about most consumer goods market research is that it rarely has anything to do with new products. For the most part it is concerned with testing advertising copy, finding appropriate buzz words for discrete market segments, evaluating brand-name recall and recognition, and other related concerns. Even taste and package tests are more promotional devices than sources of useful information.

Many within the advertising profession question the value of such research, suggesting that it gets in the way of good advertising and wastes a client's money. The point that is always overlooked is that everyone concerned with the development, manufacture, and sale of consumer products is a consumer. Formal outside research is rarely needed.

One of the results of applying the 11 guidelines discussed in Chapter 8 should be a product which serves and helps define a very narrow market. This, in turn, should make our market research burden that much lighter.

Sample Size

A sample of 50 well-selected firms in a market is more than sufficient to qualify a new product. Within each firm that makes up the sample, we need to be concerned with only three functions—the specifier, the user, and the buyer. With most firms and for most products, we need to be concerned with only engineering, manufacturing, and purchasing. Our 50-firm sample becomes at most 150 people. This brings the size of the market research project within the means of any firm.

Each of these three functions will have a different and predictable interest in a new product or process. The specifier, the design engineer, is interested in the performance and reliability of the final product. The user, the manufacturing or production supervisor, is interested in what, for want of better words, we can call the "handleability," or workability, of our product in the manufacturing processes. And finally, the buyer or purchasing agent, is interested chiefly in the availability of our product when it is needed. All are interested to one degree or another in costs or cost effectiveness.

A similar, simple process works as well with consumer products. We and our colleagues represent customers and prospects. The other functions are filled, of course, by the retail buyer and those involved with distribution.

Simplifying Factors

The small size and the predictable interests of those in the sample should begin reducing the market research task to a more manageable proportion. Its difficulties become easier when we take into account considerations like these (and here I may be giving away a few trade secrets):

- With samples of this size, the people to be included can be identified by name. If one person isn't available, an acceptable stand-in can be found readily.
- Unless the level of the people to provide the inputs is so high as to require a personal visit for courtesy's sake, data is most conveniently gathered by phone. Mail surveys are not recommended; too much time is lost before the number and the quality of inputs is known. With in-person or by-telephone interviews, the desired kind of feedback is immediate.
- Elaborate or multipart questionnaires are to be avoided. They complicate the task of analysis, exhaust the patience of those being questioned, and seem to provide more useful information than they actually do.
- Only those questions should be asked which the respondent is competent to answer. Too many questions that must be answered "I don't know" discourage conversation and end the interview prematurely. In surveys of this type, it is often the volunteered information, not the answers to the questions asked, that provides the substantive inputs.
- The questions used should be tested by the first few interviews. If they do not produce useful information, they should be reworded. Then they should be used without change for the balance of the interviews.

Questionnaire

For most research of this kind, only five or six questions are required to develop all the information needed. Interestingly enough, the same series of questions works equally well with specifiers, users, and buyers. (Fig. 10.1 shows a typical questionnaire).

The simplicity of the questionnaire and the directness of the questions may come as a surprise to many, but it should be remembered that

1. Do you specify, use, buy _____?
2. When you consider a new _____, what's most important to you?
3. How many _____ do you think you use?
4. In considering a new _____, what information is important to you?
5. Are you familiar with the following (products) (manufacturers of _____)? If so, how would you characterize each?

Figure 10.1. New product, new market evaluation questionnaire.

this kind of research is conducted not so much to develop new information as to confirm hunches and near-certainties arrived at through other means.

By the time this kind of research is required, competitive literature will have been analyzed; competitive products examined and tested; and specifiers, buyers, and users from key prospects will have been interviewed face to face. Under these circumstances, the handful of questions shown in Fig. 10.1 are more than sufficient.

The *first question* must always be the qualifier. There is no point in running up the telephone bill by interviewing the wrong person.

The *second question* begins to develop substantive information about the subject of the inquiry. Here, and in question 4, it may be necessary to furnish the interviewer with a list of "for instances" to be used as thought starters.

Preliminary information may suggest that it would be desirable for the product to meet third-party specifications—a military specification, an Underwriters' Laboratory test, or the Pennsylvania Department of Agriculture regulations. If so, it may be necessary to suggest this possibility to the person being interviewed.

Perhaps packaging is important. If so, maybe a few packaging options should be suggested. The results of the first few telephone interviews will tell if such thought starters should be furnished to the interviewer.

The *third question* asks for quantitative information which the respondent may or may not be competent to provide. Discrepancies among the numbers furnished by user, specifier, and buyer may be significant.

The *fourth question* gathers more of the kind of information asked for in question 2. It is not uncommon to find contradictions between the answers to questions 2 and 4. During a telephone interview these differences can be easily explored and resolved. Such problems are impossible to resolve in mail surveys.

The *fifth question* establishes the images, the perceived qualifications, of everyone serving the market or market segment.

There is a small caution to be observed in interpreting the results of such a survey and, particularly, question 5. The information supplied in answer to any question requiring qualitative answers will follow normal distribution patterns. Even though the sample is small, the answers will tend to fall under a bell curve.

People being what they are, the significant answers will be found under the end of the curve and not under the center. Answers generally sort out like this: a few reflect history, the way things were; most reflect the immediate past or the present; and a few predict the future, the way things will be, have to be. In understanding the results, the IFUM principle applies: One has to be able to separate the Important Few from the Unimportant Many.

On occasion, it is necessary to offer a brief summary of survey results to get willing participation. If there were a sixth question, it would probably be: "May I have your title and mailing address?"

As a means of gathering important and useful information about the new product and its market, this process is straightforward and simple. All that's missing is the person to do the phone interviewing. In selecting someone for this purpose, there are a few simple, but important, requirements:

- Your anonymity must be preserved. As long as the interviewer remains a bland, nonthreatening third party, accurate and useful information will be forthcoming.

- The interviewer must have a plausible, nonthreatening reason for gathering the information. Consultants, reporters gathering background for a story, and researchers for banks and brokerage houses are acceptable covers for interviewers.

- The person doing the work must be an experienced phone interviewer. Interviewing skills are more important than technical knowledge, although the more of each, the better.

- Finally, the results of the first few calls must be reviewed. Generally, after eight or ten calls, enough information will have been gathered to indicate the quality of on-going responses. Usually, there are no problems, but occasionally you'll find that questions 2 and 4 need to be made a bit more directive to provoke useful information.

Most such information is gathered by a market research or by a sales or marketing consultant. They have the skill and experience; they can easily preserve the anonymity of the sponsor, assure the anonymity of the respondents, complete such assignments swiftly, and interpret the results accurately. However, with all due respect to the profession, the job can be done almost as well by an experienced secretary working at home on maternity leave.

Eventually, through research like this and through the market audit which you have made, enough preliminary information will have been assembled on the new product idea to indicate that a formal evaluation is in order.

11

Selecting New Products for Development and Launching Them Successfully

Developing and launching a new product requires the investment of considerable time and money. The decision to proceed with a new product cannot be made lightly. It should only be made after a number of tough questions have been considered and answered.

Decision Screen

My own list of such questions is shown in Fig. 11.1. The list is 32 questions long. It is not a static list, but changes a bit to fit each client organization with which I work. What's important is not the actual questions on the list, but the attitude toward new products which the list reflects. Frequently, questions are combined. Questions 13 and 14 of the current list, for example, are often combined.

When push comes to shove, what's important is the thoroughness with which a possible new product is explored, not the list of questions which provokes and guides the exploration. It is the assessment of the product and the market it will serve that is critical and not the checklist of things to be considered.

Providing Answers

Providing answers to such questions requires serious efforts and careful inputs from marketing, sales, engineering, manufacturing, purchasing,

Figure 11.1. Final decision screen. New product: develop and launch, or reject?

1. What is it? What does it do? What are its performance specifications? Its physical specifications?

2. What are our qualifications to make it? Mastery of the technology? Ownership of the manufacturing processes? Knowledge of its market? Knowledge of the channels of distribution to the market?

3. Who can use it? Why should these people be interested in it? (Specific customers and (SICs).)

4. Are we currently serving these markets?

5. How does the market view our qualifications to make it? To service it? To sell it?

6. How many can be used (by specific customer and by SICs) at various price levels? On introduction? In 6 months? In 1 year? Etc.?

7. What does the competition have that comes close?

8. What would our competitive advantages be?

9. Is the technology available to build it? Do we have it? Do others?

10. What's required to build it? Tools? Machinery? Space? Personnel? Storage? Test equipment? Other requirements? What do we have? What do we need to acquire?

11. Are the materials needed to build it available? From current suppliers? Elsewhere?

12. What are the approval lead times and ordering cycles likely to be?

13. How will samples or test and approval models differ from production models?

14. How long will it take to have samples and test models available? Production models?

15. What will it cost to make at various levels of production? In various modes of production?

16. Are subcontractors available? For parts? For major components?

17. How will it be distributed and sold? Our own distribution and sales organization? A new distribution and sales organization?

18. What will its impact be on competitive products? On our own products?

19. What is the competitive response likely to be? Overall? By specific competitor?

20. What are the sales support requirements? Training? Literature? Service? Spare parts? Other?

21. What should our pricing, sales, and marketing strategies be?

22. What are the advertising, lead generation, market conditioning, and sales promotion requirements?

(Continued)

23. What product performance tests have been made? In-house? By customers? What were the results?

24. How will it be introduced? Customer by customer? Regional rollout? Nationally? What are specific plans? Timetable?

25. What serious sales and manufacturing problems can we anticipate? How will we handle them?

26. What will it cost to bring the product to market? How long will it take to get our money back? Thereafter, what will be our rate of return?

27. If we do not make it, how will it affect our manufacturing capability, growth, market position, customer base, and profitability?

28. If we do make it, how will it affect our manufacturing capability, growth, market position, customer base, and profitability?

29. How does it satisfy each of the 11 strategic guidelines?

30. How does it compare with our other new-product options?

31. What assumptions have we made (Questions 1 through 30 above)? Are they valid?

32. *What is our decision? Do we make it? Or, do we set it aside and move on?*

Figure 11.1. *(Continued)*

finance, and perhaps, even a few others, customer service, for example, or even field service.

This kind of joint activity has demonstrated its value in manufacturing. Production time on new products—from engineering design to the test of new products—has been chopped by 60 to 75 percent, simply by integrating manufacturing, quality, and test engineering into the design process. CAD/CAM makes this easy to accomplish. What we propose here may not be as easily accomplished. Nevertheless, we propose that everyone who will be involved eventually be involved at the outset. Their contributions should be made simultaneously and not one at a time. When this comes off successfully, quality goes up and lead times go down.

In some organizations, where the 11 new-product guidelines are part of the corporate culture and there is a long history of successful new-product development, the list of questions can be a short one. In other organizations, where this kind of new-product effort is new, the list must necessarily be long and exhaustive. Many of these questions would be divided and subdivided.

In smaller growing firms, the necessary answers are provided by the managers of the input groups involved: sales, manufacturing, finance, etc. However, as the size of the firm increases, other duties and responsibilities may prevent these department heads from sitting in on the new-product evaluation process. A practice has evolved, therefore, of establishing a basic cadre of regulars to provide continuity for the effort and supplementing it with others to form an ad hoc evaluation group for each new product.

The group is variously known as a *new-product evaluation team,* a *core sales group,* or a *new-product task force.* Its job, of course, is to consider the answers to the questions asked on the new-product evaluation screen, arrive at a recommendation for the new product, and eventually, even, supervise the successful launch of the new product.

The composition of such groups varies from firm to firm and from product to product. The most effective way of determining who should belong to the group is by use of the list of questions. Whoever is in a position to supply the most authoritative answers to blocks of questions belongs on the task force. When carefully managed and supervised, such task forces can become important elements in a firm's motivation and reward program and can be a useful means of identifying promotable talent (see Chap. 20).

Such groups are, however, only as good as their management. The team leader must make certain that the tough, but significant, questions are seriously considered and not glossed over and that realistic answers are found to them. Top management must support the group's efforts, provide the policy guidelines discussed earlier, demand excellence, and abide by the group's recommendations. This may even mean an occasional failure. Second guessing the group's efforts will only subvert a very essential process.

Important Questions in the Final Screen

Several of the questions listed in Fig. 11.1 have proved troublesome and should be discussed. Others are a bit more straightforward and obvious.

2. *What are our qualifications to make the new product?*   There is room for extensive self-deception here. A simple example will illustrate the kind of pitfalls that await those who make emotional decisions, not decisions based upon a hard-nosed evaluation of qualifications. The management of a respected manufacturer of miniature electronic components coveted the hobby and prototype shop markets. Customers bought in small quantities (blister packs) and paid high unit prices. The firm reasoned that it could supply these market requirements from its regular production. It surveyed the

hobby shop markets and distributor markets to see what was available in small-quantity prepacks. It then selected from its own catalog the items that would complement what was available. It designed packages, installed packaging equipment, and commenced to develop its line. It then discovered that it knew nothing about the hobby shop market, nothing about its economics or how it was supplied. Further, it discovered that the distributors it had surveyed were phasing out the blister-pack lines because they did not move except through pilferage. The effort was costly.

5. *How does the market view our qualifications to make it?*   Action on a new product, even a good one, may have to be postponed until the firm has earned the right, in the eyes of the market, to make, sell, and service the product. In a classic example of this, in the late fifties Lionel Trains hired the Army's Chief of Ordnance and tried to solicit defense business. Even with its very capable figurehead, the firm was never perceived as being capable of doing defense work and the effort failed. RCA and GE failed to crack the computer market primarily because the market did not see them as being qualified to do so.

7 and 8. *Competitive offerings and competitive advantages.*   Evaluating competitive activities requires very clear eyes. For example, the new management of an old established firm which manufactured the most reliable liquid flow meters available viewed with contempt the failure of a competitor to launch another type of meter. It reasoned that because of its experience with the most basic technology, it could succeed with the new, but imperfect, technology when the competitor could not. Its ego trip became an extremely costly failure.

13. *How will samples differ from production models?*   Samples which differ significantly from production line models are a common source of new-product failure. Samples from a prototype shop typically are more carefully made than the items which will come from regular production. This situation is commonly encountered in the clothing business where samples are made in a sample workroom. Detailing of the garments and the amount of handwork give the sample garment a look of higher quality than will be available in production models. The result is that the retailer's expectations are seriously disappointed.

18. *Impact on competition or on our own products.*   Failure to consider this question often leads to the introduction of a new product which competes head-on with another of the firm's products. Diet Pepsi and Tab provide a good illustration of this. Tab, for example, cre-

ated its own place in the diet-drink market and achieved its sales goals without cutting into the sale of its sister product, Coca-Cola. Because of similar names, however, Diet Pepsi and Pepsi competed head-on, forcing the customer to select one or the other. As a result, Pepsi sales declined a bit, and Diet Pepsi never achieved the goals expected of it.

More than one manufacturer of sterling silver has seen its market deteriorate because it duplicated its sterling patterns in plate.

Western Union provides another example of this kind of competition. At present, its basic income is derived from the 100,000 subscribers to its TELEX Service. Its only new product is an electronic mail service called EASYLINK. These products are in direct competition with each other. And, indeed, TELEX is slowly being nibbled away, not only by EASYLINK, but by all the other competitive electronic mail services. This situation is carried to its logical extreme by the final example.

The Osborn computer created, developed, and dominated the portable computer market. After a number of years, the firm designed an improved model which would make its initial offering obsolete. However, it made the mistake of announcing and advertising the new model before it was in production and before units were available for sale. With the announcement of the new model, sales of the initial unit dried up. Without income, the firm could not bring the new model to market. It filed under Chap. 11.

19. *Competitive responses.* This question requires serious consideration. Davids should not inadvertently take on Goliaths. BIC, Gillette-Papermate, and (while they were together at Allegheny) Scripto-Wilkinson were well enough financed to support a grand fight for dominance of the disposable razor, lighter, and ballpoint pen markets. Other firms may not be able to support such a struggle.

Over the years Cullinet Software had made an increasingly good living for itself by developing programs for IBM mainframes. Then IBM discovered that software was the interface between its customers and its hardware, the thing that made the hardware useful. It also discovered that software could be very profitable. With IBM as a new competitor, Cullinet went into a tailspin from which it has barely recovered.

21. *What should our strategies be?* Other strategies are available besides a head-on confrontation with the competition. One firm, for example, succeeded in introducing a number of new products and breaking into a number of new markets by the simple expedient of becoming an approved second source. Being a second source not only permitted higher prices, but accommodated a limited productive

capacity. Further, it allowed the firm to gain experience in those new markets and made it easier to introduce other new products to them. And, of course, the classic example is the Volkswagen Bug; it had *no* competition.

23. *What tests have been made?*   It is well known that if a toddler is left alone with a fistful of beans, more than a few will wind up in an ear or up a nostril. People who are experienced with children keep the beans out of reach. In the area of product test, the sins of omission are legion. For example, a well-regarded manufacturer of control equipment introduced a line of microprocessors to replace old-fashioned, but highly reliable, relay controls. The performance of the microprocessors was exceptional in all tests, and the product moved like hotcakes. Unfortunately, the new controls had never been tested in the hostile environment in which they would be used. Serious malfunctions resulted, and the firm is now nearly bankrupt.

Another firm developed a waterproofing compound for rain-coats. It did not affect the appearance or the hang of the garment and, more important, did not lose its effectiveness after repeated dry cleanings.The new product apparently satisfied the needs of the textile care (dry cleaning) industry. Unfortunately, no one had ever tested a raincoat treated with the new compound after exposure to several rainstorms. Each exposure caused the coat to shed a little bit of the compound. After several exposures the garment became less waterproof than an untreated coat.

Perhaps the supreme example of this involved the Commonwealth of Massachusetts and United Technologies' Hamilton Test Systems. The state had just required that automotive emissions be controlled; exhaust gases, therefore, had to be tested and analyzed. Two firms manufactured the necessary equipment which provided printed analysis by the date and hour of the test. Bear Manufacturing was one. Its equipment was expensive; it sold only 350 units. Hamilton was the other and was less expensive; it sold 1205 units at $7900 each.

During the first quarter of 1983 the machines were sold and installed and training was provided. The program started on the first of April. Things went well, and at the end of April the machines automatically kicked over into May. That month, too, went well. But at the end of the month all the Hamilton machines dropped dead. They had been programmed for April and May; June and beyond just didn't exist. The Bear machines worked just fine. The first week of June 1983 was an interesting one for Hamilton and for 1205 Official Inspection Stations of the Commonwealth.

26. *What will it cost to bring the product to market?*   This question and

its corollaries—payback and rate of return—are of course the nub of the matter. Simple mistakes and flaming disasters clutter the landscape. It is hard to tell miscalculations from ego-driven crash and burns.

The Hearst Corporation launched *Country Living* 8 years ago for about a quarter of a million dollars in total costs. It now has 1.6 million in circulation. In contrast, Time, Inc. required 11 years to make *Sports Illustrated* profitable, blew $47 million on TV-Cable Week, and is already $40 million into *Discover* with no return. *Discover* eventually was sold to the Family Media Group for beer money.

I have often wondered how many firms establish reserves for new-product development losses.

30. *How does it compare with our other new-product options?* The decision to develop and launch a new product will be more correct and certainly more comfortable if that product was selected from among several possibilities. And this doesn't mean crowding the field with a bunch of second-raters just to provide a little action. It is in this area that the 11 guidelines become extremely valuable. If all the contenders satisfy them, the decision on which to develop and launch can be made on the basis of the tactical considerations reflected in these 32 questions.

31. *Are our assumptions valid?* The assumptions made about a new product, its markets and its profitability, require very careful exploration. All of us, for example, assume, as the basis of our daily lives, that our paychecks will be there next time around and that our families will be waiting for us when we get home. Questioning such assumptions is very difficult even to contemplate.

Yet, when it comes to new products, we make equally basic assumptions which tend to be overlooked and go unquestioned. We project volume on the assumption that certain prospective users will consume "so much." We rarely check to make sure that their needs will continue or that the firms themselves will still be around to buy.

Milton Bradley, for example, dedicated a large portion of its production to supporting Texas Instrument's video game home computer efforts. When Texas Instrument abandoned the market after losses of nearly a quarter of a billion dollars, Milton Bradley nearly went down the tube. It was bought up by Hasbro, the manufacturer of G.I. Joe dolls.

We make similar assumptions about the availability of the materials we require. We assume that they will continue to be available at predictable costs. To illustrate: An organization, which eventually called itself the Disclosure Information Group, acquired a small firm whose business was photographing K-10s and 13-Ds and providing the Securities Exchange Commission (SEC) with microfiche copies. Its agreement with the SEC permitted it to sell this information for its own account. It developed quite a business doing this and throve. Then one day, at contract renewal time, it discovered that Bechtel Information Systems had, unknown to them, entered the picture. Bechtel made the SEC a better offer and secured the business.

We also assume that our tests of the new product have indeed been adequate. When it comes to new products, if we have made an assumption and have not questioned it, the marketplace will prove us wrong.

In the early eighties, faced with an unhappy combination of low, fixed-rate mortgages and high inflation, the home finance industry began pushing adjustable-rate mortgages (ARMs). By 1984, 60 percent of all new mortgages were ARMs. The typical sales tactic involved a *teaser* rate for the first year that was 2.5 percentage points below a comparable fixed-rate mortgage.

After the first year, payments, naturally, went up dramatically. The results were predictable. As one mortgage insurer put it, 25 percent of his premium income on fixed-rate mortgages went to cover losses. For ARMs, 80 percent of premium income was required to cover defaults and delinquencies.

To illustrate once more, in 1979 Exxon spent $1.2 billion to acquire the Reliance Electric Corporation so that it could have the Reliance Alternating-Current Synthesizer, a device purported to reduce the power requirements of electric motors. Exxon assumed that the product performance claims were valid and did not subject them to any kind of verification. Exxon's best return on this investment was about one-quarter of 1 percent. At the end of 1986 after 7 years of inflation, it sold Reliance for $1.35 billion.

32. *What is our decision?*   When made, the decision should be a clean one and without second guessing. If the decision is to develop and launch, then it should be implemented expeditiously. That is reasonable and generally what happens.

However, when the decision is to veto, a number of problems can arise. A major source of new-product ideas for any firm should be those products which were rejected at an earlier date. When a new-product idea is rejected, the file should not be jettisoned. Rather, an attempt should be made to summarize the conditions which ought to exist in order for the product to succeed. Tickler files should be established to bring that idea to the surface on a regular basis or when the right conditions exist.

When it comes to new products, Murphy's law applies in spades. Selecting new products to be developed and launched requires many things, but above all, it requires a kind of practical wisdom which grows with experience and which is also the same kind of practical wisdom required to manage a successful new-product launch. So, let's take a look at that process and see what's involved there.

Managing a Successful New Product Launch

Before we review what is involved in managing a successful new product launch, we probably should define what we mean by "success."

Defining Success

From any point of view, the product is a *success* when the breakeven point has been passed, the development costs have been recovered, and sales are being sustained at target levels or better with no more than normal effort. (See Fig. 11.2). Products are more or less successful, depending upon how quickly these things happen.

Engineering and manufacturing contribute to this situation by getting the cost curve to bottom out quickly and at as low a volume figure as

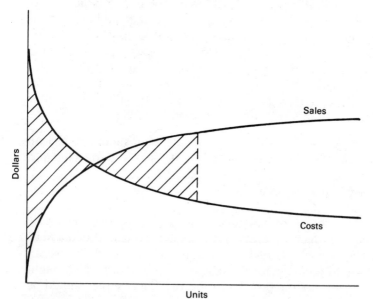

Figure 11.2. New product success.

possible. Marketing's contribution is to get the volume up through the breakeven point and into the range of profitability.

Competitive Responses

Unless we have made a horrible miscalculation about the product itself, the only thing we need fear is competitive responses. These can be merely annoying, or they can seem to be devastating. For example, General Mills tried to test-market a premium dog food called Speak. Consumer products, even in test markets, cannot be sold without advertising, and so everywhere that Speak was advertised, General Foods dropped the price of Gainesburgers. A satisfactory test was never completed, and the product was effectively sabotaged.

One wonders what there was about Speak that required a test. Perhaps if the front-end work had been properly done, no test would have been necessary; and, of course, the Gaines response would not have been so devastating.

In most instances, me-too consumer products do not require testing, merely sufficient resources to sustain the product as it builds share and becomes profitable. Diet Coke, for example, was introduced into a crowded market (at that time, over eighteen other kinds of cola drinks) because Coke had the resources to prevail. Even so, it succeeded by stealing volume from other Coke flavors whose sales declined by 35 percent. What happened with the new, old Coke and the old, new Coke is still too complicated for analysis. With a really new consumer product, it is a different ball game. The advantage lies with the prudent producer.

Industrial Products Are Different

Industrial products are not generally vulnerable to this kind of competitive response. We allow competition an opening only when we drag our feet and prolong a launch beyond a reasonable time. Naturally, if we drag our feet, we will also prolong the time it takes to reach breakeven and begin to show a profit.

However, industrial marketers can take advantage of two characteristics of industrial selling to avoid the situation entirely.

We know, for example, that roughly 80 percent of our volume will come from about 20 percent of our prospects. Further, since prudent new-product strategy calls for new products which tend to narrow the markets we serve, we should be fairly well aware who the key users of a new product will be.

We also know that very few industrial sales are made on impulse, like buying a second drink or a Hershey bar. Before a purchase is made, there is usually considerable deliberation, testing, and evaluation.

These two facts, the 80:20 rule and the need for testing, suggest that before we go public with a product, that is, before we advertise it and hand it over to the sales force, we should have it sold-in or, at the very least, under test with key potential users.

Initial Sales

Too frequently, those of us who have responsibility for developing new products have no responsibility for their sale. A new product is introduced to the sales force, its features and benefits demonstrated, its pricing explained, and its advertising and promotional support outlined. Yet, the most important attribute of a new product is not its features or its benefits, not its pricing, and surely not its advertising and promotional support. The most important attribute of a new product is its salability. This must be demonstrated.

New products should remain the responsibility of the new-product development people until the breakeven point has been reached or— and this is better—until all the development costs have been recovered.

Getting the new product sold-in or under test with key users may require selling at the executive level. But with only a handful of new products each year and a total new-product volume goal of from 3 to 10 percent of total volume, even the most distinguished CEOs should be willing to make a few sales calls on their opposite numbers with potential users.

Since salespeople do best with established products, and, in view of the high cost of having the sales force make sales calls, this, too, may be an idea whose time has come. The main men at Perdue Farms, Boeing, Remington Shavers, and Chrysler Motors have demonstrated that this is indeed so.

PART 3
Successful Pricing

*"There are two kinds of fools in any market.
One doesn't charge enough. The other
charges too much."* (RUSSIAN PROVERB)

Determining what people are willing to pay for something is a very complex business.

Under some circumstances, for example, a person will work for a day or more for a hot meal.

That's a question of *need.*

In another situation, someone else will pay $1.49 for a 12-oz box of Keebler Town House crackers.

That's a matter of *perceived value.*

The 12-oz box of Town House crackers is always displayed full-face on the grocer's shelf. The 16-oz package costs only $1.29, but all one sees of it is the narrow edge of the box. Even full-face, the heavier box appears smaller.

That is a matter of perceived value.

Still others will pay hundreds for a bottle of old claret. A 12-dollar bottle of California red goes as well with dinner.

That's a question of *status.* After all, as the girl in the L'Oréal Shampoo commercial says, "It costs more. But, I'm worth it."

All these factors—need, perceived value, and the desire for status—are involved in determining what a buyer will pay for something. It is, as we said, a complex business. But that complexity increases when we also have to consider our need to recover our costs and to optimize our earnings.

Simple complexity becomes very complex, indeed. So much so, in fact, that some claim successful pricing to be an *art*. Others say it is a matter of witchcraft; in fact, not so long ago prices for an entire industry were established by the phases of the moon.

This method for establishing prices turned out not to be astrology but a simple code to which the antitrust people took exception. Several high-priced executives, as a result, spent a lot of time in the pokey.

Successful pricing decisions do contain a large component of art or, if not art, at least sound judgment.

Even the most inspired pricing decisions, though, turn out to be not so much intuition as a shrewd weighing of costs against what the market can afford to pay.

It was, for example, no accident that Henry Ford's Model T was priced at $500 and just fitted America's pocketbook. Here, development began with a careful determination that most people could and would buy a car priced at $500. The car itself was then designed and built to meet this basic requirement. The inspiration here lay in first determining what the market could afford to pay.

This antique technique still works. Sippican Ocean Systems, for example, appears routinely to take defense business away from the likes of Raytheon, North American Rockwell, and Spartan by the simple means of determining a price which will give them the business and then designing and building to match that price. Most manufacturers design and build first; then they calculate the price needed to recover costs and generate a profit.

Establishing prices based upon what the market can afford to pay is just one way. There are others in common use.

Recently, for example, the publisher of a major paperback book house described the pricing procedure he followed. Ten or a dozen factors were considered in establishing cover prices. These included editorial costs; production costs; sales, marketing, and distribution costs; the sales prices of comparable titles; and so on. Ultimately, though, the cover price was based on a sense of "what the traffic would bear."

Others let competition establish their prices. In this situation, the assumption seems to be, "If they can sell at that price and make money, so can we." This justification cloaks a lot of assumptions. The principal one seems to be about the competitor's ability to make money at the price charged. The more prestigious the competitor, the surer people are that the assumption is correct.

Yet all around us is proof that such an assumption is rarely correct. For example, in the fall of 1985, General Motors, Ford, and Chrysler all offered to finance car sales at 7 or 8 percent. Banks at that time were charging 12 or 13 percent. The car manufacturers swallowed 5 percentage points—nearly half of the finance charges. That same quarter General Motors reported a $21 million loss on its car and truck business.

Yet, others follow traditional pricing formulas that have come to have the force of gospel—direct costs of labor and materials plus 40 percent; three times the cost of labor plus twice the cost of materials; twice all direct costs, plus many more. The principal weakness with such methods is knowing what all the costs are, and then making sure that all are covered. Chances are that they are not known and hence not covered.

We'll mention one more common method for establishing prices. Here a total for overhead and profits is added to the direct costs of production. This *burden* is divided among all products in proportion to the volume each product generates or in proportion to the distribution costs, the costs of getting the product to market. This is traditional *absorption accounting*. It is neat and tidy, but as we shall see, it makes it difficult to measure the true profitability of the products being sold.

Firms present themselves to the markets they serve in many ways. Chief among these are through its people, the products and services it provides, and its prices. Increasing amounts of corporate brains and capabilities are being invested to make sure that the people and the products and services are of increasing quality. Yet pricing, for the most part, is still carried out by methods which have never been accurate or satisfactory and which work best in inflationary times and in expanding markets where economies of scale tend to bring down costs. The combination ensures profits.

All this merely illustrates what we all know—that successful pricing is indeed a complex business and that people avoid the challenge. Unfortunately, nothing that follows will make it any less complex. However, by taking a view of pricing that may be a bit different from conventional views—indeed at one point we will literally stand conventional calculations on their head—we hope to provide a more realistic perspective on the process and to sort some of the complications into more manageable piles.

First, we will look at a few of the pricing challenges that arise from the nature of the markets we serve.

Next, we will get into the main business, calculating successful prices. Here we will do two things. We will define profits or acceptable earnings for any business in a realistic way. It will be a *nominal* definition, but better than none at all. And we will divide up the universe of possible prices for any product into three zones: One zone contains all those prices which guarantee a dead loss on sales regardless of the volume. The second zone contains all those prices which make a contribution to *overhead and profits*. These range from simple breakeven prices to fully profitable prices. The third zone is the land of milk and honey.

That done, we will review a few of the frequently overlooked causes of price and profit erosion and make a stab at establishing value. Finally, we will take a look at the options we have in competitive pricing situations.

Note: The examples in Chapter 12 have been calculated using a standard corporate tax rate of 50 percent. However, since the book went into production the maximum corporate rate has been confirmed at 34 percent. This change does not affect the argument and so has not been picked up. Besides, calculations based on 34 would be less clear than those based on 50.

12
Market-Centered Pricing Challenges

Each served market presents its own pricing challenges. Partly, challenges are established by the competition's advertising and pricing levels, partly by the expectations of the customers who make up the market, and always by our own need to design and manufacture products which can be sold profitably in the served markets.

In Chap. 2, we discussed the characteristics of seven familiar markets. From these discussions, the special pricing challenges of each market can be inferred. However, those discussions were many pages ago. So, let us now review briefly those special characteristics of each market which do seem to bear on pricing.

Consumer Packaged Goods

This is not a price-sensitive market. For, as we have seen, it permits retail price spreads of 50 to 100 percent between virtually identical products. Product positioning and advertising support such spreads. Nevertheless, there are some very real constraints.

The critical price in this market is that charged to the retailer. It must cover manufacturing costs, profit, and all the costs of getting the product into the hands of the consumer. The retailer will do very little beyond pricing the product for the customer, providing shelf space and an occasional display, and advertising it, provided there is a generous co-op program. There are exceptions, of course, "hot" products for which there is a large but short-lived demand. But hot products don't last forever and are hard to come by.

For preticketed merchandise, the spread between the ticketed price and the reseller's costs must be large enough to permit the reseller to offer occasional store specials and still come out ahead.

All the other burdens, however, fall back on the manufacturer. The spread between the manufacturing and packaging costs and the price to the reseller must be large enough to accommodate a host of additional costs, plus a profit. A glance at the Twenty-five Common Functional Responsibilities of Marketing will suggest what these will be. Chief among these will be the cost of protecting the reseller's markup and income when the market is slow or when the product itself is under competitive price pressure. In these situations extraordinary promotional efforts may be required, not the least of which would be rebates directly to the customer. Slotting allowances are usually added to the cost of the product, like packaging, while "spiffs" are handled as a sales expense.

Consumer Durables

In contrast to the packaged-goods market, the consumer durables market is extremely price-sensitive. From automobiles to white goods to coffee brewers, the price advertising of aggressive discounters conditions the market to what these things should cost.

Often such price promotions are supported by the manufacturer: A $6 rebate on a coffee machine, $700 to $1200 rebates on automobiles, or factory financing at 6 or 7 percentage points below local bank rates.

Because of all this, very few retailers have a clientele that willingly pays the list price. Except for the low-end appliances, price negotiations at the point of purchase are commonplace, with special concessions for individual customers. Reseller margins, as a consequence, tend to be slim, thus throwing many burdens back to the manufacturer.

The manufacturer's price to the reseller, therefore, must cover quite a bit. Among the essentials are benefit advertising and point-of-purchase material which distinguishes a product from competitive offerings and creates a preference. Often, this must supplement, if not completely replace personal contact and selling at the point of sale. The costs of full pipelines to the reseller must also be covered. And, of course, the costs of spare parts, service training, warranty and guaranty support, and customer service must be covered as well.

Occasionally, some of these support services may be farmed out to a contractor, such as an authorized factory service, or to the reseller if there is money to be made. The service departments of auto dealerships are examples.

Occasionally these support services can be made into a profit center, packaged and sold to the customer through a service contract. But as frequently, the cost of such support services must be carried by the manufacturer.

Once more, a look at the list of Twenty-five Common Functional Responsibilities of Marketing will suggest other items of cost which must be covered in either the price to the reseller or by special service contracts with the buyer.

Industrial Support-Consumables

The industrial support-consumables market corresponds closely to the consumer packaged-goods market. Since total purchases of individual products are small compared with other purchases, these are rarely budgeted. Purchases are, for the most part, made directly by the user and often not until the cupboard is bare. Price, therefore, is never as important as availability and familiarity with the item or its manufacturer.

Many products in this category can be sold by direct mail, and all respond well to promotional activities, especially premiums. Because most such sales are made in small volumes and immediate delivery is a requirement, these move best through local distributors.

The distributor's price, then, is critical, and the spread between the distributor's price and the going rate or the ticketed price must accommodate the distributor's profits and overhead as well as an occasional promotion.

Since these resellers are, typically, an undisciplined lot, they may and often do build their sales through deep price concessions or they may threaten to do so. Manufacturers are thus pressured into subsidizing or co-oping distributor promotions just to keep them whole. The spread between the manufacturer's costs and the distributor's costs must be wide enough to accommodate large promotional expenses and the cost of maintaining full pipelines.

Industrial Process-Consumables (Commodities)

For the most part, these are commodity products manufactured to standard specifications which many suppliers meet. Buying decisions are, therefore, based on some combination of price and availability.

A current supplier is hard to displace without cutting profits. The market itself is easily upset if a supplier wants to build sales by cutting prices.

The development of special, industrywide specifications—Mil Specs, for example—is occasionally a useful device for limiting competition to a few and for maintaining margins.

This is not a happy market to serve.

The most effective means of coping is through converting commodity products to proprietary or specialty products which justify higher prices and support wider margins.

Getting listed as a second source with a superior product at a higher price is frequently the key to this market.

Make-or-Buy Process-
Consumables

These are the bits and pieces or the major components used in building a product which the manufacturer decides are cheaper to acquire on the outside than to build in-house. The major competitor is the buyer's presumed capability to build in-house.

The costs to beat are the customer's own.

Success in this market comes through providing good products along with added values which the customer is unable to provide in-house or which have been overlooked in cost calculations. These range from engineering services to guaranty and warranty support and must include assurances of replacement availability long after the product has been sold and is still in use by the final customer. The list of Twenty-five Common Functional Responsibilities of Marketing will suggest other things that must be included in this added-value package. These must all be covered by the price, including the cost of maintaining inventory.

Capital Equipment

Except in rare emergency situations or in situations where new capital equipment will provide an immediate and clear economic or competitive advantage, purchases can and will be postponed through several budgeting cycles. The major pricing challenge in this market arises from the need to sustain a single selling effort over several years. And, along with the selling effort, the cost of idle inventory must be covered in the price or, what is quite similar for engineering-constructors, the cost of maintaining cadres of designers and engineers.

Some suppliers in this market attempt to cover such costs through the device of special charges for precontract engineering, a practice found among manufacturers of specially designed equipment and among architect-engineering firms and engineering-constructors. Where standard equipment is involved, the common device for covering the cost of a sustained sales effort is through the use of independent manufacturers' representatives. Here, sales costs are contingent and are covered by the representative's commission. The sales costs of the representative are spread out over all the products represented on the line card.

Beyond these special challenges are all the items suggested by the list of the twenty-five responsibilities.

Service Markets

A detailed discussion of pricing for service markets is outside the scope of this book. However, there are a couple of special challenges that all of us can recognize.

One arises from the nature and expectations of the customers being served. For a simple example, consider this: In Manhattan, the Blue Shield allowables for surgery and hospital care depend as much on neighborhood as on the nature of the procedure. The allowables for people living in certain better-off neighborhoods are much higher than those for people living in less affluent parts of the city, even though the skills required, their application, and the necessary aftercare are the same. This notion of value billing, in which the worth of the service rises or falls with the size of the fees charged, is important in service marketing.

The other challenge, one shared with those serving the capital equipment market, arises from the costs of maintaining personnel, equipment, and inventory during periods of downtime.

Beyond these special challenges, those in these service markets must cover and recover in their pricing all the other items suggested by the list of Twenty-five Common Functional Responsibilities of Marketing.

13

Establishing Prices
to Recover All the Costs

When we talk about "successful pricing," we simply mean that the prices for all products have been set so that when the sales of each product reach a reasonable target volume, the firm will have recovered all of its costs and will have made a healthy profit and that as sales continue to be made at these prices, they will continue to be profitable.

That's what we mean, and everybody *knows* what we mean. However, there is a problem, and that problem is the word *profit*.

A New View of Profits

When one speaks of "profit," the question always comes up, "How much is enough?" The general notion is that more is better and a lot more is a lot better.

The problem with profit as we understand the word is that it is merely a residue. It seems to happen by accident. After all, *profit* is a term meaning what's left over after all the bills have been paid. That's why it is called *the bottom line*.

What we need is a less chancy way of looking at things, and for that reason we are going to discuss successful pricing from another point of view.

We will speak of earnings and targeted earnings and we will start with the notion that the earnings of a firm must be large enough to cover all its costs including the cost of all the capital it uses. ROI will be the measure of success, not the conventional notions of profit. And the ROI required for success must be a targeted return on *all the capital employed*.

The shortfall will be a measure of the failure; the size of the overage, the measure of success.

Two Kinds of Capital

It is a curious fact that although most firms employ two kinds of capital—equity, what the stockholders and owners have invested, and debt, what's been borrowed—management seems to be conscious only of the cost of the borrowed funds. Management seems to have no notion that there might be or should be a cost associated with equity capital.

There is probably a good reason for this. Shares in a firm are bought and, mostly, sold as a speculation. Few equities seem to be bought solely because they throw off healthy dividends, that is, because they provide a good ROI. Indeed, the tax laws seem to support this view.

Suppliers of borrowed funds have an entirely different idea. They want to know what their *interest* will be, that is, what their return will be and how it will be protected. They want to know what assets will be pledged to ensure the repayment of principal and the payment of interest. The interest they charge and the security they require are measurements of their view of the risks involved.

Suppliers of equity capital have no such views and no such measure. Yet, as far as operations are concerned, all dollars are green. The source is unimportant. If a dollar of debt capital fetches a certain interest, the suppliers of equity should expect the same. In another area, this is the principle of equal pay for equal work.

It is a curious fact that over the years, the cost of borrowed capital for most industrial firms of normal risk comes close to 1.5 to 2.0 times the prime rate. For example, when the posted base rate, prime, was 9 percent, the going rate was around 12 or 13 percent. No matter that prime is a fiction and that most banks lend money to their best customers at well below prime. (When the First National Bank of Atlanta's posted prime was 12.25 percent, Coke was paying only 7.25 percent.) The prime rate, nevertheless, is still a useful measure.

ROI as Measure and Goal

The cost of borrowed funds over the last few years has been typically 18 to 20 percent. If prudent lenders have been getting this return, why shouldn't the same be paid for equity capital? Our goal, therefore, will be a 20 percent return on all capital employed, not just borrowed funds.

This is not a frivolous goal. Many multidivisional firms require their operating units to return at least at this level. Divisions cannot separate the money they use into borrowed funds and equity. Yet many do manage this ROI and sustain an annual compounded growth rate of 20 to 30 percent. (Few, however, use this ROI requirement in establishing their prices.)

Targeted earnings should produce a return on the total capital employed at least equal to the highest interest paid any long-term lender.

There is a danger here. Achievement of a targeted ROI is being proposed as a measuring tool and the basis for establishing prices. The business goal is different. It is to produce high-quality products which have long market lives and which make money and provide a competitive edge. The goal is a product line made up of Ivory Soaps, Campbell's Tomato Soups, Doublemint Gums, and Arm & Hammer Baking Sodas.

The means of measurement, ROI, must not become confused with the business goal which is the successful behavior of profitable products in the marketplace at prices which have been determined to return the required ROI.

Figure 13.1 provides an operating statement in typical bottom line format. It shows earnings after taxes of $500 for a return on total capital of 10 percent. There is an apparent shortfall here of $500. A 20 percent ROI would require $1000.

However, a complicating factor is at work here. According to the view we are expressing, interest payments become a distribution of profits before taxes. Consequently, an adjustment will be required in the bottom line to account for this. The after-tax, or net, cost of borrowed cap-

1. Net sales		10,000
2. Cost of goods sold		6,000
3. Gross profit		4,000
4. Sales and general expenses:		
Sales	500	
General and administrative	2,000	
Total		2,500
5. Operating profit		1,500
6. Cost of borrowed capital		500
7. Earnings before taxes		1,000
8. Income tax		500
9. Earnings after taxes		500
Capital employed:		
Borrowed	2,500	
Equity	2,500	
Total	5,000	
ROI	10%	

Figure 13.1. Operating statement—standard bottom-line format.

ital must be added back to bottom-line earnings. Line 10 of Fig. 13.2 shows this.

Real earnings become then $750 for a return on total capital of 15 percent. The shortfall is only $250 instead of $500.

This is a technical point, perhaps. But at the risk of making our calculations and examples more complicated, we will continue to include it in our illustrations.

However, regardless of any pretax distribution of profits, our goal remains a 20 percent rate of return on all the capital we employ. Pricing the products we sell is the most significant means we have for achieving these targeted earnings.

Figure 13.3, which inverts the standard operating statement format, shows this and compares actual performance with the required performance. An upward price adjustment to increase net sales by $500 seems necessary. This may not always be possible. The same 20 percent ROI goal may have to be achieved by other means. A reduction in costs or in the amount of capital employed are also possibilities. All may be necessary.

The leverage points are indicated by an asterisk. However, for purposes of the present discussion, we will assume that improving prices is

1. Net sales		10,000
2. Cost of goods sold		6,000
3. Gross profit		4,000
4. Sales and general expenses:		
Sales	500	
General and administrative	2,000	
Total		2,500
5. Operating profit		1,500
6. Cost of borrowed capital		500
7. Earnings before taxes		1,000
8. Income tax		500
9. Earnings after taxes		500
10. Net cost of borrowed capital		250
11. Real earnings		750
Capital employed:		
Borrowed	2,500	
Equity	2,500	
Total		5,000
Return on capital employed		15%
Cost of capital (20%)		1,000
Excess or (shortfall)		∂ 250 >

Figure 13.2. Standard bottom-line format, extended (net cost of borrowed capital added back).

	Required	Actual
*1. Capital employed	5,000	5,000
2. Targeted ROI	20%	15%
3. Earnings	1,000	750
4. Net cost of borrowed capital	250	250
5. Earnings after taxes	750	500
6. Income tax	750	500
7. Earnings before taxes	1,500	1,000
*8. Cost of borrowed capital	500	500
9. Operating profit	2,000	1,500
*10. Sales and general expenses	2,500	2,500
11. Gross profit	4,500	4,000
*12. Cost of goods sold	6,000	6,000
*13. Net sales	10,500	10,000

*Leverage points.

Figure 13.3. Operating statement—inverted ROI format (net cost of borrowed capital added back).

the only means we have for improving ROI. Later on, we will discuss the other options: reducing costs and reducing the capital employed.

Product Profitability and Improved Earnings

If our goal is to improve earnings by improving the prices of what we sell, we need to know how we fare in this regard. As a next step, an analysis of product or product-line profitability is required. Conventional accounting methods are not very helpful. Under standard, absorption accounting methods, all nondirect costs, generally thought of as *overhead and profits*, are charged against all products according to one of two common formulas.

One method allocates overhead and profits among products or product lines in proportion to the sales volume each generates. The other allocates overhead and profits in proportion to the costs of bringing those products to market, their distribution costs.

Each method reflects different assumptions about the way management is involved in running the business. Allocation of overhead and profits by volume is thought to work best for startups or for an operation with all new products. Here, clearly, management efforts do go toward building volume. With more mature operations, where getting the goods to market and keeping pipelines full is the major concern, the second means of allocation, according to distribution costs, is thought to be more appropriate.

Either way, the absorption method would be fine were there only one product. It might work well for the WD-40 Company whose only product is WD-40. Few companies, however, have just one product.

Standard Product Profitability

Figure 13.4 shows such a standard analysis of the profitability of three products. (The net cost of borrowed capital has not been added back.) Although it is conceivable that each may have the same percentage of gross profit, it seems unlikely that they will all require proportionately the same amount of management time and resources to move in the market place. This technique of expense and cost allocation forces a sameness on all products, whereas our goal should be to highlight the *differences* among them.

The absorption method of analysis suggests that an equal effort on all products will make up the shortfall or that a concerted effort behind *any* one of them (just pick one and push) may achieve the same results. We know in our bones that this is just not the way it is.

Direct Costing

What is actually required is a more accurate way of comparing the productivity of the three products. This comes through the application of the technique known as *direct costing* (see Fig. 13.5).

	Product A	Product B	Product C	Total
1. Net sales	3,000	2,000	5,000	10,000
2. Cost of goods sold	1,800	1,200	3,000	6,000
3. Gross profit	1,200	800	2,000	4,000
4. Gross profit as percent of sales	40%	40%	40%	40%
5. Sales and general expenses and cost of borrowed capital	900	600	1,500	3,000
6. Earnings before taxes	300	200	500	1,000
7. Income tax				500
8. Earnings after taxes				500
Total capital employed			5,000	
ROI			10%	

Figure 13.4. Product contribution—standard absorption accounting.

Direct costing takes a different view of both costs and assets. It views costs as consisting of three kinds.

There are those costs, principally labor and materials, which are charged directly to each product and which will vary up and down directly with the volume of product produced (line 4, Fig. 13.5). That's the commonsense traditional view.

Then, there are other more or less fixed costs also associated with each product. If the product didn't exist, the cost wouldn't either. Sales, advertising, and quality control might be typical of such costs for con-

	Product A	Product B	Product C	TOTAL
1. Gross sales	3,300	2,150	5,050	10,500
2. Adjustments	300	150	50	500
*3. Net sales	3,000	2,000	5,000	10,000
*4. Cost of goods sold	1,800	1,200	3,000	6,000
5. Gross profit	1,200	800	2,000	4,000
6. Gross profit as percent of sales	40%	40%	40%	40%
*7. Assigned fixed costs	100	200	700	1,000
8. Contribution	1,100	600	1,300	3,000
*9. Assets assigned:				
Inventory	150	100	250	500
Receivables	650	350	250	1,250
Tooling	—	—	250	250
Total	800	450	750	2,000
10. Turnover assigned assets	X3.8	X4.4	X6.7	X5
11. Contribution as return on assigned assets	138%	133%	173%	150%
*12. Unassigned fixed costs:				
Manufacturing				600
Sales & marketing				500
Engineering				150
Administration				250
Total				1,500
13. Operating profit				1,500
*14. Cost of borrowed capital				500
15. Earnings before taxes				1,000
16. Income tax				500
17. Earnings after taxes				500
18. Net cost of borrowed capital				250
19. Total earnings				750

Capital employed   5,000
ROI   15%

*Leverage points.

Figure 13.5. Product contribution—direct costing.

sumer packaged goods. (Packaging—that is, boxes, cartons, packing materials, etc.—no matter how elaborate, ought always to be a direct cost of manufacturing.) The special marketing and engineering services associated with make-or-buy industrial consumables would also be typical of such costs.

These costs remain more or less fixed for a period, and they increase or decrease by increments (as a salary, for example, is added or another advertising commitment made). (See line 7, Fig. 13.5.) Once more the listing of the Twenty-five Functional Responsibilities of Marketing (Chap. 4) will provide a useful checklist. It may suggest items of fixed costs which should be assigned to a specific product.

Finally, there are the ongoing costs of simply being in business—expenses like insurance, rent, and headquarters salaries—that would remain fixed for a period even if none of the products were sold or existed. These are the ongoing costs of keeping the doors open (line 12, Fig. 13.5). These ongoing costs are not associated with any product and should not be charged against any of them.

Direct costing also takes its own view of assets. It is concerned only with specifically productive assets, those associated with specific products. If the product were cancelled, the asset would be liquidated. These are the assets which make money for the firm (line 9, Fig. 13.5).

Included here among these assets are: raw materials, work in process, and finished goods inventories; special-purpose tooling and equipment; receivables; special distribution and storage equipment; and special sales tools such as samples, display equipment, demonstrators, and testing devices.

The other assets are, to a degree, unimportant and include everything else not specifically associated with a single product. They do not produce income.

According to this view of product profitability, the $2000 of productive assets of the firm, (those associated with the three products) return 150 percent, this enables the firm to cover all other costs and generate an ROI of 15 percent on total capital employed of $5000.

However, the goal is not 15 percent; it is 20 percent.

The question then becomes one of establishing the rate of return on the $2000 of productive assets to ensure a 20 percent return on total capital.

Figure 13.6 presents this analysis and shows that the productive assets of the firm must generate a return of 175 percent if the overall ROI goal of 20 percent is to be achieved.

Product C, with a return of 174 percent, comes close to doing so, but products A and B, with returns of only 138 and 133 percent, respectively, need attention. They must be repriced. (Remember, for the purpose of this discussion, we have eliminated the possibility of reducing costs or the amount of capital employed.)

	Required	Actual
1. Capital employed	5000	5000
2. Cost of borrowed capital	20%	15%
3. Earnings	1000	750
4. Net cost of borrowed capital	250	250
5. Earnings after taxes	750	500
6. Income tax	750	500
7. Earnings before taxes	1500	1000
8. Cost of borrowed capital	500	500
9. Operating profit	2000	1500
10. Unassigned fixed costs	1500	1500
11. Contribution	3500	3000
12. Assets assigned	2000	2000
13. Return on assigned assets	175%	150%

Figure 13.6. Required return—assets employed by product.

Pricing and Repricing

The procedure for repricing an existing product or for pricing a new product begins with a determination of the quantity that can be produced at various levels of capacity. Prudence suggests that a relaxed pace over one shift would be a better measure of capacity than all-out production for two or three shifts. With such variability possible, it is easy to see why pricing remains less of a science than an art.

At least five levels of capacity should be calculated. Our illustration uses 20 percent increments in capacity. (See line 1, Fig. 13.7 where product B is being repriced.) However, if a great deal of data is available, it may be possible to project productivity at 10 percent increments. Direct costs—labor and materials—are easily established and likely will remain constant across all levels of production.

Determining the assets assigned to a product requires considerable prudence. Just as capacity is perhaps best underestimated, receivables, inventory, special tooling, and similar items might be overestimated (line 3, Fig. 13.7).

The required rate of return, 175 percent, has already been calculated (Fig. 13.6), and the rest of the price determinations follow smoothly. Unit prices to ensure the 175 percent rate of return at various levels of capacity are easily calculated by dividing net sales by the number of units sold (line 9 ÷ line 1 = line 10).

However, this analysis will be much more useful if two simple ratios are calculated and a simple graph drawn. This usefulness will soon become apparent.

The first calculation involves determining the price to cost ratio at various levels of productivity for unit prices that give us the targeted

Capacity	20%	40%	60%	80%	100%
1. Units	2,000	4,000	6,000	8,000	10,000
2. Unit cost, direct	0.60	0.60	0.60	0.60	0.60
3. Assets assigned:					
Inventory	100	130	170	220	285
Receivables	350	385	424	466	513
Tooling	—	—	—	—	—
Total	450	515	594	686	798
4. Return required	175%	175%	175%	175%	175%
5. Contribution (line 4 × line 3)	788	901	1,040	1,200	1,397
6. Assigned fixed costs	200	200	200	200	200
7. Gross profit (line 5 + line 6)	988	1,101	1,240	1,400	1,597
8. Cost of goods sold (line 2 × line 1)	1,200	2,400	3,600	4,800	6,000
9. Net sales (line 7 + line 8)	2,188	3,501	4,840	6,200	7,597
10. Unit price (line 9 ÷ line 1)	1.09	0.88	0.81	0.78	0.76
11. Net sales ÷ cost of goods sold (line 9 ÷ line 8)	1.82	1.45	1.34	1.29	1.26
12. Breakeven ratio [(line 9 − line 5) ÷ line 8]	1.17	1.08	1.05	1.04	1.03

Figure 13.7. Pricing algorithm—Product B.

175 percent rate of return. This ratio is readily calculated by dividing net sales by the cost of goods sold (line 9 ÷ line 8 = line 11). These values are then plotted on a graph which has percent capacity as the abscissa and price to cost as the ordinate. When these values are plotted we have the upper curve of Fig. 13.8.

The second calculation involves determining the price-to-cost ratio at various levels of capacity for breakeven prices. By *breakeven prices,* I simply mean prices that cover direct variable and assigned fixed costs but which make no contribution beyond that. The calculation is simple: (line 9 − line 5) ÷ line 8 = line 12). When the value of these ratios are plotted we get the lower curve of Fig. 13.8.

These two curves, the 175 percent ROI curve and the breakeven curve, have divided all possible prices for product B into three zones.

Prices that would put us into the zone below the breakeven curve spell disaster. In spite of this, some firms use such prices to build volume and market share.

Prices that would put us into the zone between the curves will all result in a contribution, the range being from mere breakeven to our full, targeted 175 percent rate of return. And, of course, above the 175 percent ROI curve, it is all milk and honey.

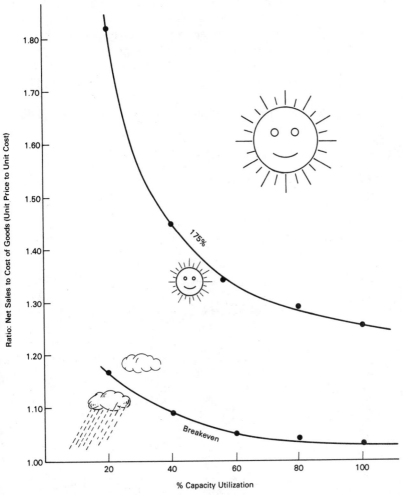

Figure 13.8. Three pricing zones—Product B.

Competitive Situations

The utility of these curves can be demonstrated in several ways. They are, for example, extremely useful in competitive situations.

Assume, for example, that a competitor offers a product identical to ours at a $0.78 unit price. A natural concern of ours would be to find out what effect matching that price would have on our earnings. All that's required is to divide that price by our own unit cost. The resulting ratio of price to cost 78/60 would be 1.30. This point is located on the ordinate and a horizontal line extended from it into the quadrant (product 1, Fig. 13.9). From this it is clear that at this price we would make money at any level of capacity and be assured of meeting our ROI goal at about 76 percent of capacity.

For another example, assume that a second competitor offered the same product at $0.66. Again, all that is required is to calculate the price-to-cost ratio and plot it on the chart: 66/60 = 1.10 (product 2, Fig. 13.9).

From this plot, we see that we would not hit breakeven until nearly 40

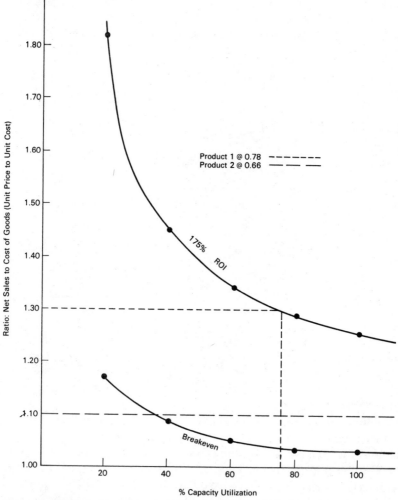

Figure 13.9. Three pricing zones—Product B and competitive offerings.

percent of capacity had been reached and that at 100 percent of capacity we would still be quite far from hitting our ROI goal.

In making this kind of competitive analysis, too many firms become concerned about competitive costs and spend considerable effort in speculation and pettyfogging espionage. Such knowledge is immaterial. What is important is that we know our own costs.

In thinking about the recent and sad Texas Instruments home computer fiasco, one is forced to wonder what kind of cost information its marketing people had to work with, and if the quarter of a billion writeoff of the whole line would have been necessary if the view of pricing presented here had been held. The Russian proverb with which we opened Part 3 may apply here.

Fortunately, such competitive situations are a rare phenomenon for most of us. Using these pricing curves as we have (Fig. 13.9) is a valuable aid in auditing competitive offerings. However, their greatest utility comes in guiding our own sales efforts, especially in negotiating large volume sales where guesswork often substitutes for certainty.

Once direct, as opposed to absorption, costing has been adopted, charts like these (Fig. 13.9) are readily prepared for all products or product families and easily kept up to date. Marketing & sales can then walk with certainty on the rocks and let the competition try to walk on water.

14

Trade Practices
as Occasional Causes
of Price and Profit Erosion

Tradition plays a large part in the way we do business. Often an entire industry does business in a certain way for no reason other than that is the way it has always been done. Trade practices and long-established policies need frequent examination. Occasionally, they can be the causes of serious price and profit erosion.

One illustration makes this point.

A mighty conglomerate got its start making heavy forgings: railroad wheels and axles and blanks for naval rifles. Its freight terms were FOB, point of origin. As this firm grew, it acquired other firms. One was a ladies' high-fashion house. Another was a manufacturer of electronic devices. The products of both acquisitions were light as a feather and always shipped prepaid via air freight. The added costs were minuscule and the competitive advantages of this policy great. However, tradition prevailed. The acquisitions were forced to conform to the policies of the new parent. The customers were suddenly forced to pick up the tab for freight. After some months of confusion, the market forced a reversion to the prepaid freight policy but not without some loss of market position. The conglomerate was eventually sold to the knackers.

There are a number of areas where the possibility of price and profit erosion are large. Figure 14.1 lists a few of them. They all need to be investigated. Sometimes they buy us more than they cost. As frequently, though, they are a serious and unnoticed drain. Evaluating them requires care and judgment.

1. Terms: 2 percent, 10 days; net, 30 days

2. Collection procedures

3. Freight policy

4. Volume discounts and rebates

5. Extended terms

6. Returns and allowances

7. Warranties

8. Trade discounts

Figure 14.1. Occasional causes of price and profit erosion.

1. Terms

The simple terms under which we sell need looking into: 2 percent, 10 days; net, 30 days seems harmless enough even though most customers will take the discount without earning it. Month to month, these terms may not seem like much, but in a year it adds up—a high cost for money 20 days early. Billing to recover the loss earns the vendor the reputation of being stingy.

2. Collection Procedures

Collection procedures are also either a source of profit and price gain or of erosion. If receivables are out 60 to 90 days on average, that, too, is a considerable penalty. Such increased costs should be built into the price structure. Charging interest on overdue accounts is a poor alternative.

3. Freight Policy

Freight policy is another area requiring a close look. Federal regulations used to require that common carriers be paid in 7 days. Perhaps they still do. If freight is prepaid, that's money out of the shipper's pocket and a considerable burden should the customer be slow in paying the vendor. However, if freight is FOB point of origin, the problem is eliminated. The burden is shifted to the customer. Further, if freight terms are FOB point of origin, that's where buyer takes title to the merchandise. The cost of insurance is therefore also shifted.

4. Rebates and Discounts

Volume rebates and discounts are a valuable selling aid if the discounts take the form of additional merchandise and not price concessions. For example, one case extra with every ten is effectively a 10 percent discount for the buyer. It is not, however, a 10 percent reduction in the money received. If costs are 40 percent of the selling price, then the buyer has a 10 percent discount, but it costs the vendor only 4 percent.

This is a simple point which many people, including clients, fail to understand. For example, the folks who do my dry cleaning promote with coupons that offer substantial cash discounts. Cleaning and pressing three suits costs me $10. But with the coupon, I pay only $6. I think the arrangement is wonderful. Yet, I would be just as happy to have four suits done for the price of three. The cleaner would take in two-thirds more money for one-third more work.

5. Dating and Extended Terms

Extended terms and dating are traditional in some lines of business and may be valuable sales aids, but they also may be the cause of serious erosion. The value of obtaining advanced bookings in this way—shipping in January and February for sales in April and May and collecting in June—must be weighed against the costs of maintaining an expanded inventory, and that inventory is at risk with the dealer.

6. Exchange and Returns

The policy covering exchanges and returns needs careful scrutiny. If there is a flaw in the system, it will be found. Obsolete merchandise will turn up for credit against current sales. For example, a firm which had added to its product line over the years through both development and acquisition decided to redesign its packaging to give everything a modern family look. Some packages dated from the late twenties, others from the early fifties. It declared a liberal exchange policy so that all dealers and distributors could have the new packages on their shelves. Some of the merchandise returned was nearly as old as the design of the package that held it.

7. Warranty Support

Warranty procedures also need careful evaluation. The volume of claims ought to be compared with the cost of administering them. Often it is cheaper and makes a better impression to replace without question than to maintain a system of paperwork and supervision.

8. Trade Discounts

Finally, discounts to dealers and distributors need to be looked into. Frequently, these discounts are deep enough to permit the reseller to undercut the factory on large order. This kind of direct in-house competition plays hob with established supply relationships.

Not all trade practices are hazardous to financial health, but they can be. Each should be evaluated periodically.

15

Pricing on Value: Nearly as Much as the Traffic Will Bear

This will not be a very long chapter since it merely pulls together a number of points that have been made explicitly and implicitly elsewhere. The points themselves are rather simple, and they add up to a simple story. Implementing them, however, is not so simple. Like "Go and sin no more," it's easier said than done.

Common Pricing Assumptions

Most discussions of pricing seem to be based upon a set of assumptions and preconceptions about the way things are and the way they have to be. For example, it is assumed that

Product design, manufacturing, sales & marketing, finance, and management are all natural adversaries and cannot work together on the same team.

If sales & marketing knows the true cost of products and services, the prices it sets will be based on what's been acceptable in the past and not upon what the marketplace will pay.

All products are, or soon will become, commodities with short life spans; the market price for them will always be set by the lowest-cost producer with the lowest overhead and smallest margins.

The quality and price of almost everything tends downward naturally and the decline cannot be averted.

The practice of increasing margins and, therefore, pricing flexibility by maintaining or improving quality and driving down costs is dirty pool, doubly so when practiced by foreigners, especially the Japanese.

Salespeople cannot handle—and are even incapable of handling—common pricing objections and just naturally give products and services away.

These assumptions have all the characteristics of self-fulfilling prophecies and, altogether, add up to a rather bleak picture. They put everybody's head in a vise and suggest that making money is wrong, impossible, or, simply, unnatural. Making money, of course, is merely difficult.

More-Hopeful Assumptions

Our view of the matter is a bit different. It seems to be shared by a number of successful firms who have been around for years and who are likely to be around for lots longer. There are not very many of these firms, however.

For us, the goal is to make pots and pots of money; it is necessary and natural. For only when this happens can a firm keep stockholders happy, employees productive, product lines fresh and profitable, and research & development effective.

This means earning as much money as possible from the markets and customers we serve through the quality of the products and services we provide. It means working from a set of assumptions and preconceptions that are a bit different from those above.

Product design, manufacturing, sales & marketing, and finance and management are a natural team whose goal is to make money by providing prospects and customers with superior products and services.

The cost to manufacture a product must be known to the people who price it otherwise cost and price cannot be kept as far apart as possible.

The life of a product becomes limited only when the producer begins to think of it solely in terms of its costs and physical specifications and ignores the functions it performs for its customers.

The decline in quality and price characteristics of specialty products which become commodities occurs when the producer loses control of the technology and contact with the customers.

The practice of widening margins and increasing pricing flexibility by maintaining or improving quality and driving down costs is simple prudence.

Salespeople who are thrown by price objections merely reflect a firm that is unsure of its product's quality and unfamiliar with the requirements of the customers it serves.

Avoiding Low-Price Traps

The pricing hang-ups of too many firms result from a general discomfort with the idea of knowing their costs and a lack of understanding of the markets they serve. Product costs and overhead costs are not properly segregated with the result that neither can be adequately controlled. Further, since market needs are never adequately explored, the focus shifts to beating the prices of apparently successful competitive products. The result is that margins begin to narrow as price and costs go down. Then, either the product or the firm fades away.

Parts 1, 2, and 3 of this work show many ways to avoid this.

Part 1 discusses (1) the way seven common markets work and the special sales problems each of them presents, (2) the effective ways in which each of them can be segmented to make them easier to know and manage, and (3) the twenty-five functional requirements to be satisfied in serving each of them, requirements that change in form and importance from market to market.

Part 2 shows how to use this knowledge to find opportunities for new products that will be superior to current market offerings. A current situation involving memory discs for computers illustrates this: optically recorded discs can hold 10 times the information stored on hard discs and 100 times that on floppy discs. The problem is, however, that there is no sure and economical way of erasing opticals. Here is where mastery of technology plays its role.

Every served market presents its own opportunities. Some even go so far as to suggest pricing parameters as the optical disc example clearly does: One erasable optical disc might cost as much as 10 hard discs or 100 floppies.

Part 3, of which this chapter is a part, discusses pricing. The significant points here are made in Chap. 13 where the techniques of direct costing are discussed. With this method, direct product costs are clearly separated from the costs of overhead and administration. The reduction of each can be controlled separately as the two sides of a knife blade are dressed during sharpening. Finally, breakeven prices are calculated at various volume levels, and separate prices are calculated to deliver a targeted ROI at the same volume levels.

Redefining Costs

Now, on the theory that one firm's price may be another firm's cost, I propose that firms begin thinking about the ROI price levels as the basic cost of a product and that they make sure that quality and service justify prices at and above these levels.

There is a caution here. Once a superior level of quality and service has been established, the prices should be set at nearly as much as the traffic will bear; nearly as much, but not quite all. Apparent margins that are too wide invite competition. The trick, of course, is to surround the product with enough support so that the product cannot be distinguished from its surrounds. Even so, competitors will still try to make a distinction and to beat the price. But the very wide margins will allow plenty of room to maneuver while costs are further reduced and the quality of the product and the services associated with it are increased with an appropriate increase in price.

I have discussed this approach to indexing costs and establishing prices on many occasions. Once in a while it has been hooted off the stage as being impractical. But, every time the notion of impracticality was explored, the discussion went in one of two directions.

One discussion usually boiled down to a "What's the use?" attitude. When explored further, it usually lead to a set of assumptions very much like those discussed at the beginning of this chapter.

Value Pricing

The other discussion usually wound up with the notion of value pricing. According to this idea, the price of a product or service should be based on the cost to the customer of the alternate solutions to the problem that the product or service aims to solve. This is an interesting idea, but it applies in very few situations.

Consider this: I have friends in Chicago with whom I like to talk once in a while. To do this, I could fly to Chicago or take Amtrak or some other form of ground transportation. On the other hand, I could use the telephone. According to this alternate-solutions value-pricing concept, the cost of the call to Chicago would be set by the cost of air or ground transport to Chicago. It is a nice idea, but the market won't buy it.

Here is a contrary situation: The discomfort caused by sunburn, mosquitoes, or a hot stove is easily reduced by the juice of the aloe vera, a plant that easily grows on a windowsill and costs next to nothing. Soda bicarbonate which costs just a bit more is nearly as effective. The alternatives are the sprays and ointments for sale at the local drugstore. If the prices for the drugstore palliatives were set by the cost of either aloe vera or soda bicarbonate, they wouldn't move at all. No one would buy them at that price. Even the people who run "pick your own" berry patches charge double or triple the going rates for freshness.

All of which is to say that a market has a sense of value which exists independently of the costs of alternate solutions. That sense of value results from a combination of things, mostly from the benefits that flow from the product itself and its surrounds—packaging, service, reputation, etc.

What we are proposing is an entirely different approach that involves developing a product in cooperation with the market that is to buy and use it (Chaps. 10 and 11). If a product so developed cannot be priced to deliver more than the targeted ROI, perhaps it should not be brought to market.

16

Rational Responses to Competitive Pricing Situations

There is a phenomenon, frequently encountered, in which all the suppliers to a market play follow the leader with prices. Once in a while prices go up. More usually, however, they go down, as firms, like lemmings, go to the edge of the cliff and jump off.

In the early eighties, for example, we saw the prices of home computers go down and down, mostly as a result of the liquidation of Texas Instrument's inventory. Then IBM entered the market with its PC Jr. at a relatively high price. The other major factors in this market halted their downward plunge, reversed themselves, and raised prices. Ironically, IBM, too, misjudged this market and has now liquidated its own inventory of home computers at fire sale prices.

Gasoline price wars are less common than they once were. But it is still possible to see three or four competitive service stations lower prices round-robin fashion until they are all selling at well below cost. Indeed, stories of a station filling a tank wagon at a competitor's pump are not all fabrications.

This kind of irrational response to a competitor's price reduction spells financial hardship or, even, doom. It never occurs with firms who understand the place their products have in the markets they serve and who also understand what it costs them to generate profitable sales. Two kinds of ongoing efforts are required: one focuses on each product-market combination, the other on overall corporate operations.

Ongoing Audits of Each Product-Market Combination

One characteristic of successful firms is that they maintain an ongoing effort aimed at (1) maintaining or improving the quality of existing products; (2) reducing the costs of producing them, (3) increasing the effectiveness of the sales & marketing efforts that support them, (4) improving their distribution, and (5) finding new markets and new product opportunities (see Fig. 16.1). As just one small example of part of this process, during its long and happy market life, Ivory Soap has been reformulated at least 70 times and more likely close to 80 times.

In fact, in most successful companies, as we have seen (Chap. 8), the bulk of the research and development expenditures are in support of these five activities, not toward the development of new products. These five activities are part and parcel of the continuing responsibilities of manufacturing and of sales & marketing, and all are market-centered. While improvements are measured against a firm's own past performance, there is always the acceptance and performance of competitive products in the served markets to supply a more objective standard against which to measure improvement.

Ongoing Audit of Corporate Operations

At the corporate level, there are analogous activities to be pursued. These involve determining what's required to generate profitable sales and take the form of calculating various operating ratios, watching them change over time, and comparing them with industry figures available from several sources. The objective is to find line items which are over- or underproductive. There surely must be some opportunities for improvement since business overhead seems to have increased from 20 percent of sales in the mid-fifties to 50 percent of sales in the eighties.

The operating ratios take the form of turnover rates or the percentage of sales for each operating line item. Turnover rates and percent-

---

1. Maintaining or improving product quality
2. Reducing production costs
3. Improving distribution
4. Increasing marketing & sales effectiveness
5. Identifying opportunities for new products and markets

Figure 16.1. Audit goals for each product-market combination.

ages to sales of major operating accounts for our example (the profit and price leverage points) are shown in Fig. 16.2.

Turnover rate is an alien notion to many. It derives, I think, from the idea of stock or inventory turns: To maintain sales at a particular volume, you must turn over your inventory five times. The turnover rate for inventory is simply the total annual net sales expressed in dollars divided by the dollar value of the average inventory for that year.

Turnover for any line item is calculated by dividing it into net sales.

	Total	Turnover	Percent of sales
1. Gross sales	10,500		
*2. Adjustments	500	20X	5 %
*3. Net sales	10,000	1X	100 %
*4. Cost of goods sold	6,000	1.6X	60 %
5. Gross profit	4,000		
6. Gross profit as percent of sales	40%		
*7. Assigned fixed costs	1,000	10X	10 %
8. Contribution	3,000		
*9. Assigned (productive) assets:			
Inventory	500		
Receivables	1,250		
Tooling	250		
Total	2,000	5X	20 %
10. Contribution as return on assigned assets	150%		
*11. Unassigned fixed costs:			
Manufacturing	600		
Sales & marketing	500		
Engineering	150		
Administration	250		
Total	1,500	6.7X	15 %
*12. Unassigned assets	3,000	3.3X	3.3%
13. Operating profit	1,500		
†14. Cost of borrowed capital	500	20X	5 %
15. Earnings before taxes	1,000		
16. Income tax	500		
17. Earnings after taxes	500		
18. Net cost of borrowed capital	250		
19. Total earnings	750		
*Leverage points			
†Capital employed	5,000		
		2X	
			50 %
	ROI 15%		

Figure 16.2. Critical operating ratios.

The percentage relationship is calculated by dividing net sales into the line item. The two ratios are, therefore, reciprocals of each other. This makes comparison with third-party figures easy.

"Standard Operating Ratios" for various kinds of businesses are available from Dun & Bradstreet. The Robert Morris Associates of Philadelphia, an association of commercial bank lending officers, publishes "Annual Statement Studies." The Federal Trade Commission publishes an annual *Line of Business Report* on 275, separate, four-digit SICs. And, many trade associations publish operating ratios based upon information supplied by their members.

Once a year, at least, a firm's own ratios should be compared with those furnished by third-party organizations. Significant differences between the homegrown ratios and the third-party ratios do not necessarily mean a problem. A difference may merely reflect another way of doing business or a different kind of organization—one that is more vertically or horizontally integrated, for example.

However, where such differences in operating ratios do exist, an effort should be made to find out *why* they exist. They should not be shrugged away. The results may lead to an improvement in one's own operations or to valuable insights into the way competitors organize and conduct their businesses.

Here is a simple example: A client, a compounder of materials used by the construction and manufacturing industries discovered that his direct costs for materials and labor were out of line with those of similar businesses. Since his labor costs were already minimal, he took a look at his costs of materials and his purchasing procedures. After a thorough review, which took a couple of months to complete, he was able to cut the costs of purchased materials by 23 percent. This of course dropped right to the bottom line.

All too frequently, however, no effort whatsoever is made to review costs as the following situation shows: The client was a well-established manufacturer of industrial process equipment, mostly standard products with some specially engineered items. When I first became acquainted with the firm, it had been operating at, or below, breakeven for a couple of years. Management thought that I might be able to do something about sales and, so, improve the situation.

I began by trying to identify the more profitable products. This, however, proved very difficult to do. Although a number of standard machines were produced each year, each new one was a bit different from the last. Gross profits ranged from 6 to 8 percent on the low end to a high of 39 percent. The gross *profit* on specials ranged from dead losses of 46 and 97 percent to a high of 40 percent. No one had taken a close look at manufacturing for nearly a decade. Given this situation, there was no point in doing anything about sales just yet. Bringing costs under control came first.

That was in 1982. A sharp, young engineer was found in the design and development group and, effectively, put in charge of manufacturing. Two years later, breakeven had dropped to 23 percent and gross profits were up on average to 39 percent. Further improvements are coming along all the time.

This kind of improvement happens often enough with manufacturing. It is not unusual. And the gain becomes profit and can be used to finance other activities.

That's not so with sales & marketing. Monies allocated to support sales & marketing activities are rarely subjected to cost-benefit analyses. They are either allocated as requested or chopped out, depending upon the economic health of the firm in question. Few firms keep track of the components of selling costs, making it hard to tighten up. Examples of the kind of gains in sales are difficult to find.

The usual effort is to increase volume and not look too hard at costs. This makes sense to a point. After all, one more order per week per sales representative does wonders for selling costs when they are expressed as a percentage of sales.

These activities which aim at cost control, the comparisons of operating ratios, and the five-part ongoing effort of manufacturing and sales & marketing, coupled with the direct costing techniques for pricing products, should make a firm quite sophisticated about its products and their movement in competitive marketplaces. Firms who carry out these activities continually need never be spooked by changes in a competitor's prices. Panic reactions can be avoided and competitor's pricing surprises can be met with rational reactions.

Common Causes of Competitive Price Reductions

The point here is that prices are only one form of competition, only one component in the competitive mix. The appropriate response to a reduction in a competitive price should not be a reflex reduction in the firm's own price.

It will not be, if management has the kind of sophisticated overview we recommend.

Overcapacity

For example, overcapacity, especially in capital-intensive, continuous process industries, is a frequent cause of price reductions. This was commonly encountered in traditional steel making, more recently in the conversion of atmospheric nitrogen to process- and fertilizer-grade ammonia, and more recently still in the silicon chip growing business. Usually, excess production is dumped overseas in order to avoid poisoning the domestic market. However, when such a reduction affects the at-home market, the move frequently is a prelude to the liquidation of a facility.

Inventory Liquidation

Occasionally, price reductions indicate inventory liquidations in the face of shrinking markets. Motor oil provides a good example. During 1983, 1984, and part of 1985, a quart of standard-weight motor oil, which still sells for $1.50 at service stations, could be purchased for 99 cents at auto stores and for less than 50 cents at discount chains. The reason: the gradual diminution in the crankcase capacities of the cars on American roads and the increasing interval between recommended oil changes. A few compounders who still process motor oils exclusively continue the price of 99 cents per quart through factory rebates to the consumer.

Dropping a Line

With other products, a price reduction may signify a liquidation prior to the dropping of a line. To illustrate: On the same day that full-page newspaper advertisements were announcing new, low prices for RCA video discs and video disc players, the business pages told why. After nearly a decade of effort and over half a billion dollars in losses, the line was being abandoned. Not all line liquidations are announced so publicly. Often there is just the price reduction.

It may also indicate an attempt to maintain share with an inferior product or with a product that has been overpriced. Or, it may indicate a need to generate cash by whatever means.

Rarely will a producer reduce prices out of charitable impulses. And it is just as rare for a manufacturer to poison the market by cutting prices voluntarily. Predatory pricing, to cut out or cripple competition, is much rarer than is supposed and even in monopoly situations—AT&T, for example—very hard to establish.

Reengineering

Occasionally, however, a market may discover that the specifications it has established for a product have been set too high. Therefore, in some situations the price reduction signals the replacement of an overengineered product with one that is equally serviceable but less costly. The substitution of idiot lights and digital readouts for analog meters and gages would be a simple illustration of this.

Handling Price Increases

More frequently, however, the problem is not a drop in a competitor's prices, but a necessary increase in one's own prices. A frequent response to this situation is to announce the price increases but to guarantee the old, lower prices for orders received before a specified future date. This is the reverse of a dealer loading or dating program. But, it puts vendors in competition with themselves.

A more rational response, if the increase will generate undue resistance, is to offset the increase with additional service or enhanced product surrounds or to add sufficiently to the product itself so that the increase is justified or not noticed. Since most buying decisions are based upon some combination of quality, availability, and price, any increase in price should be balanced by improvements in one or both of the other two factors.

In the face of rising costs, changes in the product packaging or the product surrounds are common devices for keeping prices within the range which people are used to paying. Ocean Spray Cranberries, for example, appears to be shifting its unrefrigerated single-strength juices from glass to paper containers. It even offers fresh concentrates in unrefrigerated paper containers. The new containers weigh considerably less than glass and thus have a positive effect on shipping costs. They cost less than glass and thus have a positive effect on packaging costs. Because the containers are sterile, a step in processing is eliminated. Further, empties are stored in a knocked-down state, thus freeing space for the storage of finished goods. The changeover appears to be proceeding cautiously because the consumer's reaction to buying unrefrigerated juice in paper is not completely known.

Heinz shifted the bulk of its ketchup from old-fashioned 12- and 14-oz bottles to 32- and 48-oz jugs. In so doing, it not only cloaked a price increase but increased its sales volume as well.

By reducing the amount of money available to spend, the recent recession effectively increased prices for all kinds of products. As a result, many producers changed the way their products were made available. Leasing programs or rental-purchasing plans became common where once there had been few. This permitted many industrial buyers to acquire new capital equipment from operating funds in the face of drastic cuts in capital budgets.

Segmenting an established market is another device for maintaining unit sales volume in the face of rising prices. Hard data is difficult to come by, but it appears likely that the White Letter tire market was created as much to cloak an increase as to capture a market opportunity in the face of a total market that was shrinking.

Incorporating a product into a system is another device frequently used to hide a price increase and maintain volume. The components of many home and personal computer systems and packaged stereo systems are assembled as frequently to protect prices as to ensure system performance.

Occasionally, one encounters firms that try to maintain or reduce prices by increasing their productive capacity. If the product is or is likely to become a staple or standard for the market it serves and that market is growing, the increase in productive capacity can be justified. However, buying equipment to support a product often has the effect of forcing prices downward.

Emphasis shifts from maintaining profitable sales to keeping capital equipment busy. The move is more readily justified if the new productive capacity—multipurpose machine tools, for example—can support several products and is not dedicated to just one.

Another device frequently used to control prices in the face of inevitable price increases is to eliminate the middle man. The idea here is that the net to the user can be maintained and the net back to the producer can be sweetened by eliminating the distributor and retaining the distributor's markup. The result is often to alienate all distributors, and other products suffer; further the producer must now establish and pay for other channels of distribution.

Of course, the reverse is true of Ma Bell. After the breakup, it lost its captive equipment market and has found replacement distribution at no apparent decrease in price through cooperative efforts with large chains like Sears.

Without profits, no firm can stay alive for long or become the preferred supplier for its customers or the good neighbor it would like to be. Its own pricing policies, therefore, must be under continuous examination. And those practices which can erode profits must be audited as carefully as the activities of competitors.

PART 4

About Salesmen

"Nothing happens until somebody sells something."   ARTHUR H. MOTLEY

Red Motley was right about this as he was right about so many important things. Everybody recognizes this truth about selling. Because we do, we turn a lot of salespeople loose without understanding very much about them or about what they do. Sometimes, what they do comes as a surprise.

Make no mistake about it, salespeople are different. And, in all but the most well-regulated firms, they do not share in what has come to be called the *corporate culture*.

Once, *salesmen* were popular heroes. During the thirties, for example, the adventures of Alexander Botts, chief salesman for Earthworm Tractor entertained the readers of the Saturday Evening Post. During the fifties and sixties, except for a few periods of recession, the sales force were largely ignored by others in an organization. The economy was growing; inflation covered cost increases and helped generate profits. Orders were plentiful.

Now, the economy is slow again and, for reasons discussed early in this book, orders are hard to come by and profits are slim. People are aware of the sales force once more. The TV performances of Kiam, Perdue, and Iacocca have restored its luster. But what salesmen do is still not very well understood. They are, somehow, responsible for bringing in business, but how they do it is a mystery.

Under capable sales management, they do very well. But the sales manager, too, is something of a mystery. The sales functions exist apart from the people and what goes on back at the factory or at the home office. The sales force has developed its own culture which further sets it apart from the rest.

17
The Sales Force and Corporate Culture

There are reasons why the sales force is outside the corporate culture.

To begin with, unlike others in a firm, salespeople work alone, and they work in a highly competitive atmosphere without much support. They rarely see their supervisors and have little chance to talk shop with colleagues.

In contrast, the people at the factory or at the home office do not work alone. There is always someone at the next machine, at the next bench, or at the next desk doing a comparable job or facing similar problems. Further, the supervisor is always just a few steps away and able to provide assistance when needed or upon request. And it is always possible to talk shop during lunch and coffee breaks, at the water cooler, or in the locker room or parking lot.

The sales force has none of this support.

To succeed in the environment in which they work, salespeople need special qualities of character and temperament. They need a high level of ego drive—the will to prevail—when face to face with a prospect. Additionally, since they deal primarily with people, they need the ability to empathize with customers and prospects. They need the ready ability to understand how customers and prospects *feel* and why they react as they do. They are trained in the skills and procedures that enhance these characteristics.

These traits need to be in balance, a balance dictated by the kind of markets they sell into. Otherwise the sales representative is ineffectual and unable to close, or overbearing and obnoxious. This balance is not always achieved. These traits are not commonly found among the people who work in finance, administration, engineering, or manufacturing. They are more commonly found among the human resources group, the people in industrial relations.

Selling: An Oral Tradition

Further, selling is a vocal art. The verbal and numerical skills of salespeople will be of a high order, but these skills will be expressed orally, rarely on paper. The traditions and mythology that surround the art of selling reinforce this. In contrast, back at the factory or at the home office, the emphasis is on the records, facts, and figures on paper or that can easily be punched up on a terminal display.

There is another consideration that separates the sales force from the rest of the organization, and that is the way they are paid. Most people who work for an organization can look for more money only if they survive an annual or semiannual performance review and a separate salary review. If times are good, maybe they'll get it.

Salespeople are in a different situation or, at least, are perceived to be so. With a sales-incentive program in place, they can earn more money. Often the added income is substantial.

Others, without the possibility of performance incentives, become resentful. Typically, rather than explain this situation to the others so that they can understand it, management tends to force an artificial separation of sales from the folks back at the home office or factory. This is one of the reasons some businesses sell their products through separate sales corporations. This has unfortunate consequences, especially at a time when the goal should be to transform business organizations into unified marketing machines.

A Disruptive Element

Going on, the condition of the markets in which they sell today causes the sales force to be disruptive of good order back at the factory or home office.

Finance, for example, wants standard price lists and standard terms. Today's customers don't go along with this. They don't want a vendor whose requirements they have to meet. They want a vendor to meet their requirements.

Manufacturing wants it all vanilla and in pints. Their tradition and training calls for long runs with standard products in order to control costs and quality more easily. The marketplace does not cooperate.

Administration wants complex forms carefully filled out. The market won't let the salespeople cooperate. Competition moves too fast.

Members of the sales force reflect all this and bring it back to the factory or home office, creating chaos and upsetting good order.

Finally, salespeople are still stereotyped in the tradition of the 3-B's: booze, broads, and bullshit. Occasionally, circumstantial evidence seems to support this view of them: company cars, expense accounts, entertainment, and travel. This view is further enhanced by senior marketing and sales management who unthinkingly talk about flying from Hilton Head to Camelback in search of a good meeting location and always, it would seem, with an obligatory stop in Houston for an evening at Caligula XXI.

The reality, of course, is much, much different, although there are some vestiges of the 3-B's in the sale of white goods in some metropolitan markets.

Assessing Integration

Water cooler conversation provides a good indicator of how salespeople are viewed within an organization. When finance, administrative, manufacturing, and personnel people meet and talk shop, the conversation usually shows a high degree of understanding about each other's problems and concerns. However, if the subject turns to the sales force or if a sales representative joins the group, the conversation becomes condescending or even childish. Too frequently, salespeople play along. The sales functions, clearly, do not receive the same understanding and support as the other corporate functions. These attitudes even creep up into the higher levels of management.

Even among firms where the role of *salesman* is understood, there are some problems of giving proper support and increasing effectiveness. For example, in recent years a major thrust in developing salespeople has been to train and equip them to take on a consultative role with their customers and prospects. Thus, in addition to basic sales skills and territory management procedures, they learn about pricing, unusual product applications, trouble shooting, and availability and delivery procedures.

They are trained to function independently and to build sales as if applications engineering, customer service, advertising, sales promotion, and other corporate functions were not available to them.

This is fine, and the efforts to provide this kind of training ought to continue. However, as sales costs continue to inch upward (currently $230 per call), a greater effort must be made to coordinate all sales & marketing functions so that the sales representative can once more become more of an order taker than a business developer. (Let others "prep" the patient so the *salesman* can operate.)

There are several traits common to firms that succeed in today's markets. One of the more significant, perhaps, is the fact that in a successful firm, sales functions are an integral part of the whole, and, to the extent possible, everyone understands these functions and supports them. This should extend all the way from the board room to the workers in the cafeteria.

One test of how well this integration has been achieved is when the senior management of any firm can answer the questions posed in Fig. 17.1 in a positive way, either because they themselves have been involved in those calls or because they know the sales force and have confidence that its activities are going forward on a very high level.

In the chapters that follow, we'll discuss the sales representative's job and what's required to ensure that performance of it continually improves.

18
What Salespeople Do

Ideally salespeople call on customers and prospects and sell goods and services in ever-increasing quantities with ever-increasing profits.

They succeed because they make an optimum number of calls each day, call on the right accounts and individuals, and make high-quality sales presentations to those people.

Their priorities are simple: to protect and increase revenues from current customers, to follow up and convert the qualified leads furnished by headquarters, and then to do a little prospecting on their own (see Fig. 18.1).

---

1. To protect and enhance revenues from current customers and products.
2. To follow up and convert leads furnished by headquarters.
3. To do a little prospecting on their own.

Figure 18.1. Priorities for salespeople.

They do all this guided by a few simple policies established by their employer, simple guidelines that help ensure their effectiveness and the company's follow-through on their activities.

That's the way it should be. That's the way it is with some firms. For most firms, however, the reality is far different.

In too many firms, salespeople cover their territories in a purely haphazard fashion, with no purpose except to pick up orders if they can find them. Others have likened them to unguided missiles or to loose cannons. The similes are apt.

First of all, if a sales representative is going to sell, to reach certain volume goals by making sales calls, he or she ought to know how many sales calls there are to "spend" in the time period given for making those goals. To *not* know this would be like doing the family marketing without knowing how much is in your pocket to spend. You wind up with the ice cream and beer nuts with nothing left for meat, potatoes, and laundry soap. Too many salespeople only get as far as the beer nuts.

Once a sales representative knows how many calls there are to spend, the next step is to know *how* to invest them, on whom they should be spent. When it comes to the quality of products and services and to the support of warranties and guaranties, all customers are equal. But when it comes to the investment of sales calls, they assuredly are not. Yet ask a sales representative to name six important accounts and when one of them was called on last—pick a name, any name—he or she will usually guess and be off by 6 weeks, 6 weeks on the near side of the actual date.

And, once a sales representative has worked out the call budget and has a fix on which accounts should get a lot of attention and which should get less, the representative next needs to know what to do. Far too many sales representatives think sales call planning means getting there on time.

Too many businesses allow their sales force to operate without this kind of knowledge and skills. Some, a lucky few, succeed not because of the effectiveness of their sales efforts but because their products and services are superior and widely known to be so.

Some industries recognize this situation and have compassion for the untrained, unprepared sales rep. In the soft-goods industries, the *rachmonis* order was a tradition—a small order handed to the "last dumb schnook who called at the end of the week, so he shouldn't cry."

Hyperbole? Of course. Off the mark? Yes, again. But not by far, the measurements are made in microns if not in angstroms.

Let's look at each of these areas and see what the requirements are. They are simpler than would appear.

Establishing a Sales Call Budget

Here, the problem is readily resolved. The worksheet in Fig. 18.2 illustrates it nicely.

Most customers and prospects work 5 days a week, and there are 52 weeks in the year. This would suggest that a sales representative has 260 days each year to make sales calls. However, not all that time can be spent in the territory making calls. There are holidays when all the ac-

	Illustration	Territory
1. Business days per year (5 days/week × 52 weeks/year)	260	_____
2. Nonselling business days		
Holidays — 10		_____
Vacation days — 15		_____
Trade shows, etc. — 10		_____
Sales meetings — 12		_____
Other — 2		_____
Total nonselling business days	49	_____
3. Total available selling days	211	_____
4. Twenty percent contingency allowance	× 0.8 (168.8)	× 0.8 ( )
5. Total plannable selling days	169	_____
6. Average calls per day	× 5	×
7. Yearly sales call budget	845	_____
8. Monthly sales call budget	12) 845	12)_____
	70	_____

Figure 18.2. Sales call budget worksheet.

counts are closed. There are vacations. Further, there are sales meetings and trade shows that take the rep from the territory.

The 260 days rapidly and predictably shrink to something just over 200 days.

As a realistic matter, not all this time can be spent making sales calls. Something always comes up: Show the boss around. Prepare a special report. Make an emergency delivery. Follow up a lead furnished by headquarters. An allowance must be made for contingencies. Twenty percent may be adequate for such things.

Thus the 260 days shrinks to about 170. And that's it; there ain't no more.

If a sales representative can make five effective calls a day—and that's a pretty fair load for a typical day—the total yearly budget is only 850 calls. It is not very much when the rep comes to think of it. It's only 70 calls a month. The sales rep should be *made* to think about it.

Obviously, there are all kinds of variations in the number of sales calls salespeople make. Some lines take longer to sell, and so fewer calls are possible. The preparation and presentations involved in selling some kinds of capital equipment may permit only one call a day or even one call every other day.

Some territories are compact metropolitan areas. In others, the accounts are spread out all over the back forty. In these, travel becomes a serious consumer of time.

However, the principles just described and illustrated in Fig. 18.2 hold. This worksheet and method of establishing a call budget may be no better than others I've seen. But, the point is that the entire sales force should be made to understand that time and, therefore, sales calls are a limited and limiting resource. They should not be squandered. Running through a drill like this periodically helps ensure that they will not be.

Allocating Sales Efforts

Since a sales representative's first priority is to protect the business from current customers and to make it grow, a method is needed for allocating calls among them (see Fig. 18.3). Clearly, they don't all require or deserve the same amount of attention. Therefore, some method of distinguishing the important few from the (relatively) unimportant many is needed.

The most practical means of doing this is through the application of a modified 80:20 rule.

If one ranks the buying accounts in a typical territory by volume, high to low, the numbers will not be continuous. There will be a discontinuity in the progression of numbers in two spots. The accounts clearly sepa-

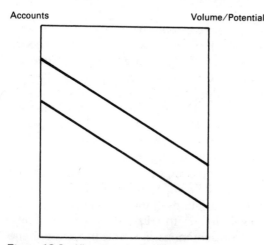

Figure 18.3. Allocation of sales effort.

rate themselves into three groups. Approximately 15 percent of the accounts will deliver 65 percent of the volume. Another 20 percent will provide 20 percent. And, fully 65 percent of the accounts will deliver only 15 percent of the sales volume. These breakpoints move around a bit from territory to territory, but they are fairly close to these numbers. I've found spreads as wide as 12 and 40 and as narrow as 17 and 32. The discontinuities are quite clear.

These three groupings provide an easy way for developing guidelines for the investment of time and sales calls.

The 15 percent, for example, might become A accounts and be called on once a month. The middle 20 percent might become B accounts to be called on once a quarter. And the 65 percent might become C accounts to be called on once a year.

Expressed as a formula, the monthly allocation of calls might look like this:

$$A + \frac{1}{3} B + \frac{1}{12} C = 70$$

The seventy is, of course, the monthly sales call budget.

At this point, all accounts can be located on a map and daily and weekly itineraries planned through the territory to minimize travel, to make it happen. It is a cut-and-try method, to be sure. Accounts may even have to be upgraded or downgraded to make it work out. Some accounts may even have to be transferred to another territory. Field supervisors need to be good at this.

Once this coverage pattern is established, it needs to be reviewed periodically. Accounts come and go. Big accounts become small accounts, and small ones grow. A quarterly review is usually sufficient to accommodate these changes as well as the changes due to seasonal buying patterns common to some industries.

There is a criticism of this scheme for classification and route planning. Some say that it downgrades salespeople by making them no more than an old-fashioned milkman or diaper-route salesman. But that is just the point. It provides a procedure to follow, and it provides order and regularity in what otherwise would be an ad hoc "what-will-I-do-today" nightmare.

Further, it solves another serious problem. A common complaint heard from purchasing agents and others is that they never see the "factory man" on a regular basis. For this reason, many prefer to work with manufacturers' reps who do show up regularly and who just happen to carry another line.

This method of classifying accounts in order to establish calling frequencies is based on the account's buying history. It is basic and especially useful for new sales representatives who are unfamiliar with territories and their accounts. There are other, more sophisticated methods. Some are based on the expected value of a forecast and others develop special programs of face-to-face, phone, and mail contacts with each account. These require great familiarity with territories and accounts. All aim at taking the guesswork out of itinerary planning and investing sales calls.

These milk run approaches to territory coverage work well for those who sell consumer goods, industrial supplies (support-consumables, as we have defined them in Chap. 2), process-consumables (commodities), make-or-buy process-consumables, and certain types of capital equipment where there is a continuing need for replacement units and spare parts.

On a much more attenuated scale, the procedure also works well for high-ticket, once-in-a-lifetime, capital equipment. The difference is that these salespeople call on prospects, not regular buying accounts.

If a sales representative selling standard products can receive adequate support from the inside—from the district or regional office or, even, from headquarters—some of the account load can be transferred to inside salespeople. In this way, the representative can be enabled to invest more calls on productive accounts or on accounts with great potential. This, unfortunately, is a dream situation. The problems of coordination and communications are enormous even with modern computer technology. However, where these problems have been solved, the results are astonishing.

Planning Sales Calls

The final item we need to be concerned with is the quality of the calls the sales force makes when it does reach the accounts it is scheduled to call on. This involves sales call planning. It is a discipline, a procedure everyone should be drilled in until it becomes second nature.

Further, it is a procedure that should be understood by anyone who works with salespeople or with customers. It makes intelligent, job-oriented conversation with the sales force possible thus eliminating the 3 B's orientation of most such small talk. It provides structure to the shoptalk salespeople indulge in on the rare occasions when they are able to get together. And, of course, it is essential for the field supervisor. It is the basis of the analysis of the calls observed, the criticism made, and the coaching provided.

The procedure (Fig. 18.4) which we will soon outline has significance far beyond its application to field sales situations. With only minor modifications, it is a procedure for developing any presentation which seeks

Figure 18.4. Sales call planner.

1. Account:_____

2. Calling on:_____ Title:_____

   _____ Title:_____

3. Key background/Long-range goals:_____

   _____

   _____

4. What's my objective for this call? (What do I want the prospect to do **as a** result of this call:)

   Primary objective:_____

   _____

   Fallback objective:_____

   _____

5. Opener/ice breaker (What do I say to get the prospect's attention, to arouse interest?):_____

   _____

6. Benefits (What's in it for them if I make my objective?):

Business benefits	How can I illustrate, prove, or dramatize it?
_____	_____
_____	_____
_____	_____
_____	_____
Personal benefits	
_____	_____
_____	_____
_____	_____

(Continued)

Figure 18.4. (*Continued*)

---

7. Objections (What kind of resistance might be offered?):

The resistance   My answer

_____   _____

_____   _____

_____   _____

_____   _____

8. Closing (What questions will I ask to take the prospect's "temperature," achieve my objective?):

   a._____

   b._____

   c._____

9. Follow-up (What's the next step if I achieve my objective, or if I don't?): If I do:_____

   _____

   _____

   If I don't:_____

   _____

   _____

---

to obtain action from another—recruiting another executive for the United Way or requesting a budget authorization from the board of directors.

Making effective sales calls can be likened to playing golf. And there are a large number of similarities. Each hole, for example, is just a little different from all the others. Customers and prospects are that way, too. Further, just as par changes from hole to hole, each sales call has its own goals and objectives. And, when par for two holes is the same or the objective for two sales calls is the same, the approach to each will be a bit different.

Before good golfers tee off on a new course, they walk it a couple of times. As they do so, they note the distance to the pin, the run of the fairway, the location of traps and hazards, and the condition of the rough. As they continue, they play each hole mentally in several different ways, selecting woods and irons for the requisite loft and distance from where an imaginary ball lies. If they are familiar with several different courses, they'll compare similar holes—Augusta's no. 9 with Fleetwood's no. 3, for example—and remember how they played them.

By the time they have walked the course a couple of times, not only do they have a plan for each hole, but they know what the *goal* for the course should be: to maintain handicap, to scratch, or to break par.

Making effective sales calls involves a similar process. Experienced sales representatives run through each call mentally and develop a plan before they even give a card to the receptionist. Planning an effective sales call (see Fig. 18.4) is a direct process involving:

Reviewing the status of the account and the long-range goals set for it.

Setting an appropriate goal or objective for the call.

Planning how to get the call started.

Organizing an effective benefit story.

Anticipating resistance and objections and planning how to handle them.

Working out appropriate closing questions. And,

Planning the necessary follow-up to the call.

Here's what's involved in accomplishing each of these.

Reviewing Account Status and Setting Long-Range Goals

An effective sales call begins with a quick review of what is known about the account and about the person to be called on. If the account is already a customer, this means reviewing what has been sold to identify areas of satisfaction or any cause of dissatisfaction. It also means recalling what happened on earlier calls and determining how close the situation is to achieving the long-range goals set for the account. If it is a new account, it means reviewing what is known about it and setting a tentative long-range goal or two. This means, based on what is known of this account and others like it, identifying the products and services to be sold when the occasion arises and the reasons they should be bought.

Planning the Opener or Ice Breaker

Talking about the weather, or the super bowl, or last night's TV special is an easy and innocuous means of getting a sales call started. It gets a conversation under way, but unfortunately it is the *wrong* conversation.

Talking about such easy subjects makes it more difficult to get down to business and to talk about the purpose of the call. A more effective gambit and one that really does convey some advantage is to begin the conversation by talking about the organization or the person being called on. The subject should be something complimentary.

The look of the offices or the building, the crowded parking lot, the efficiency of the receptionist, the professionalism of the switchboard operator, and the quality of its products are examples of the kinds of conversational gambits that break ice and open the sales call effectively. If such a worthy-of-comment situation doesn't come, then one can fall back on news about the company or the person, about the industry or its customers, or even about the economy or taxes.

An intelligent ice breaker makes it easy for both sales representative and prospect to get down to business.

Setting Sales Call Goals and Objectives

Calls must not be wasted. One way to avoid such waste is to set a clear-cut objective for each call. An effective objective is:

- Specific
- Ambitious but realistic
- Measurable
- Stated in terms of what the prospect will do

And, of course, the objective should move the situation closer to achieving the long-term goal established for the account.

Objectives must be specific: 20 cases, ship by Friday, FOB factory. When the goal is vague, it is hard to tell whether it has been achieved, and it's even harder to tell what has to be done to achieve it.

Objectives must be ambitious but realistic. If it is possible to accomplish the objective on one call, why drag it out over two or three calls? If it is possible to sell a tank car, why settle for a tank truck? However, goals must be realistic. If the goal is to supplant an existing supplier who has given good service for a number of years, it would be unrealistic to expect to do it on the first call.

The objective must be measurable. For example, the goal isn't merely to find out about something but to find out how much, at what cost, when, who, where, and so on. By using numbers in setting objectives, it's easy to know what has been accomplished and what's still left to do.

Finally, the goal must be stated in terms of what the prospect will do. To describe the objective in terms of what the sales rep will do is unproductive. If the objective is to tell the prospect about XYZ, it will almost always be accomplished. The rep has achieved the objective, and so the call is a success. That should not be the goal, however. The goal is to explain XYZ well enough so that the prospect tells how much XYZ might be used or—even better—gives a trial order. Getting the prospect to do something is the objective, not describing XYZ.

Stating call objectives in terms of what the prospect will do means making fewer successful sales calls. However, the rep will sign up more accounts and write more business, which is, after all, the real goal.

Once a primary goal or objective has been established for the call, it is good practice to establish a fallback objective, something to settle for if the primary objective is not achieved. Thus, getting a trial order might be the primary objective and learning how much is used might be the fallback objective.

Organizing Benefits

Once the call objective has been established, the next step is to figure out why the prospect should go along. This means determining and communicating what's in it for the prospect. This means organizing a benefit story.

The representative's knowledge of the account should tell what benefits will most likely be effective. If the call is on a new prospect, knowledge of similar organizations will provide clues about how to develop the benefit story that has the greatest chance of being effective.

There are two kinds of benefits to be concerned with: business benefits and personal benefits.

Business benefits quickly boil down to two things, reducing costs or increasing volume and profits. Of the two, benefits that increase revenue are the more powerful.

Personal benefits are a bit more elusive, but they are just as real. Personal benefits vary from person to person. They include such things as making the prospect's job easier, removing uncertainty, making the prospect look good in front of boss and colleagues, or enhancing the prospect's status within the organization or community.

A major problem in putting together an effective benefit story is that after a while benefits become old hat. The sales rep tells the story so many times that it gets boring; details begin to be left out. The tremendous trifles that are so significant to the prospect get dropped by the wayside. It may be boring to the salesperson, perhaps; but it's all new to the prospect.

Another problem which interferes with effective benefit presentation is this booby trap: The sales representative recites a list of features, characteristics of the product or service, and assumes that the prospect can figure out what they mean in terms of benefits. Sometimes this means demonstrating obvious benefits. This can be done without insulting the prospect by the use of phrases like "As you know,...."

Benefits answer this question, "What's in it for me and my organization?" If the prospect can respond to a presentation with a "So what?" then it's not a benefit presentation.

And in presenting benefits, the most effective method is to state the benefit first and then mention the feature that ensures the benefit as proof: "And you'll have it the next day because our automated C-23...."

There is one more point about benefits. A benefit doesn't have to be exclusive to be a benefit for the prospect. What prospects need to know is that if they do business with the sales representative, they'll have that benefit.

Anticipating Objections

It is a safe bet that the prospect isn't going to go belly-up and say "Take me!" as soon as the sales representative walks through the door. Some resistance can be expected—a few objections to whatever is proposed. The representative, in turn, can anticipate from experience what those resistances are most likely to be and plan how to handle them when they do arise.

There are a number of techniques available for handling objections.

- Ignore them and keep going
- Acknowledge them, but postpone the answer
- Offset them with benefits
- Convert them into questions being asked
- Cite third parties

Occasionally, when faced with a smooth, effective sales presentation, the prospect will resist and offer an objection, just to get into the act, just to have something to say. An experienced salesperson recognizes such objections for what they are worth and ignores them, but does not ignore the prospect.

More frequently, the resistance is real and must be handled. If the sales representative has planned to cover the point later on, the objection can be acknowledged and the answer postponed:

> That's a good point, Mr. Prospect. I plan to cover that in detail later on. But first, let me....

Occasionally, an objection can be handled effectively by offsetting it with benefits:

> On occasion that certainly does occur, Mr. Prospect. However, on the other side, there are these things to consider....

Since most resistance is merely the prospect's way of asking for more information, a useful way of handling some objections is to convert them into questions which the prospect is asking you:

> In other words, Mr. Prospect, you would be interested if I can show you how we....

Finally, it is possible to cite the experience of a third party who had a similar objection but whose experience proved it to be unfounded.

> The people at GPX wondered about the same thing. But when the system was up and running, they found that....

Resistances and objections need not be a barrier to a sale. In fact, when recognized as merely a way of asking for more information and properly handled, they can be a great aid to closing a sale.

Closing

Surprisingly to many salespeople, even the closing questions can be planned before the call is made. Then, when the time comes to close, these already formulated questions seem to pop right out. This is possible because prospects usually signal when they are ready to close.

As a general rule, it is time to close whenever you have handled a major objection to the satisfaction of a prospect. In the absence of such an occurrence, close whenever a prospect sends a buying signal.

Whenever the prospect seems to be thinking in terms of possessing or using what's proposed, it is time to close. And the close is always a *question*.

It may be an either/or question, a choice:

Shall we sign the papers here, or would you rather come downtown?

Or you may assume that you are going to get the go ahead, that an order will be forthcoming. Then, you may ask a more directing question:

The paperwork will be done on Tuesday. Shall we meet Wednesday morning at nine?

If there is any uncertainty as to how ready the prospect is to move, you can check the prospect's temperature with a trial close. Trial closes are easily formed by adding an *if* to the already formulated closing questions:

If you were to sign, would you prefer to do it here or would you like to come downtown?
If the paperwork can be finished on Tuesday, would you like to meet Wednesday morning at nine?

There is one more point about closing. Once the closing question has been asked, keep quiet. The one who speaks first *loses*.

Follow-up

The final step in the planning process is simply to figure out in advance what the follow-up will be if the objective is achieved or if it isn't. The representative must prepare for success with all the necessary materials and forms ready to go back at the office or factory. If the prospect is hot to trot, why go back to the barn?

On the other hand, objectives may not be achieved on all calls. In these cases also, the options can be figured out in advance. Then, when it is necessary to fall back to regroup, it won't be necessary to decide what the options are. All that will be needed is to select the one that is most appropriate: Send further information, make another call plan, reevaluate the account's need for what was being sold, etc.

Sales representatives come armed with their knowledge and skills and with the number of sales calls to be made. Knowledge and skills can be developed and increased, but nothing can be done about the number of sales calls. They are always in short supply. They cannot be wasted. And they will not be wasted if the sales representative knows how many calls there are to make, if those calls are properly allocated, and if they are all carefully planned.

19

What Salespeople Don't Do

What salespeople don't do is keep records. They don't write down where they are going, what they plan to accomplish, or what happened during the calls they make. They will not put down on paper who they call on, who else calls on them, who makes the buying decisions, or who influences those buying decisions.

Their sins of omission in this regard are legion.

They rely on memory and the spoken word. As a result, they make their own jobs difficult and the job of management more complex than it need be. Situations like these result:

When a sales representative leaves—moves to another job, moves to another company, or retires—almost all knowledge of the territory departs too. The new representative has to start from scratch. There may be an account list and, with luck, an order shipment history. But that's all. Even the field supervisor will have difficulty introducing new representative to the accounts.

Contrast this common situation with the following:

A superior sales representative resigned from a dying high-tech firm to accept a position with another high-tech firm whose future was more assured. The representative gave the former employer a generous four weeks notice. During the first weekend of the notice period, the representative met with the *new* regional manager. Together, they reviewed the account records for the territory the representative would soon take over. And together, they talked a history of each account with thumbnail sketches of the key players into a tape recorder: two 90-minute tapes, three and one-half sides. During the following weeks, as the sales representative completed rounds for the old employer, the tapes were played. When it came time to take over the new territory, the representative knew the accounts well. Such records and salespeople are blessed.

Here is another situation: a recent assignment of mine was with a major producer of industrial make-or-buy process-consumables. Our goal was to identify those product-customer combinations that had proved to be the most successful for the firm. Our notion was simple: If we could identify current and past successes and find out what caused the successes, then we could replicate them in other areas. This is a very effective market development procedure which eliminates reinventing the wheel or trying something new that carries a high risk.

The firm was highly computerized and took pride in its data banks. We all thought that this would be an easy job. What actually happened though, surprised us all. The complete *bill-to* information was available in a single file. And, with considerable effort, we were able to compile *ship-to* information. When it came time to identifying the buyers—the decision makers, the buying influences—at each account, however, we were up a stump.

"Take it easy," said management. "We'll ask the sales force." The stump grew higher immediately. In the final analysis, the salespeople were able to provide names that checked out for only about 8 percent of the accounts. The project finally changed direction when we installed a simple account record system for the salespeople.

Such stories are sad, and sadder still because there are so many. Here is another: the sales of one division of a prestigious firm had grown stagnant and remained so for a number of quarters; perhaps they had even begun to decline. New products and a snappy advertising program didn't seem to help. Even though the market had contracted a bit, it was still large enough to absorb all that the division could produce.

An audit of the situation disclosed that field supervision had become burdened with a number of meaningless administrative chores. It had gotten out of the habit of comparing itineraries and call reports with account records and forecasts. As a result, the sales force had fallen back into the habit of making the easy calls and was investing more and more effort with fewer and fewer accounts.

War stories like this are in endless supply. Sometimes they are even funny: The new president of a firm whose products were sold through building materials supply houses decided that he would like to call personally on a few accounts—some high producers, some low producers, and some nonbuyers. He selected a few names from the appropriate directories and asked his salespeople for a few more. Then he made his calls.

One account interested him particularly. It was an occasional buyer of very small amounts but it had a sizable potential. The sales representative had said that he called on the boss—no name, just "the boss." The president made the call and indeed saw the boss whom he had identified from a directory. The boss was pleased by the depth and quality of the line, surprised that no one had ever called on him before, and discouraged that his purchases had been so scant. Several blanket orders were negotiated as a result of the visit.

An investigation turned up these facts: Many years earlier, on his first call, the sales representative had asked to see the boss and as a joke had been introduced to the counter clerk. The representative looked no further. All subsequent calls were made on the counter clerk, who had some very limited buying authority in a few, well-defined out-of-stock situations.

If blame is to be laid in any of these situations, the fault lies with management. Record keeping for salespeople is an alien discipline. Getting them to put things on paper is like trying to get children to say "please" and "thank you," to pick up their rooms, and to close the back door. Some industries, in fact, couldn't exist if they didn't control their representative's itineraries and demand complete account records. Salespersons who call on supermarkets and other mass merchandisers, for example, have their itineraries programmed by computer and their computerized account records updated after each call.

Getting a sales force to keep records involves solving two problems. One problem stems from the simple fact that salespeople work in an oral culture. The spoken word is paramount. It is the major form of communication. The other problem is, perhaps, one of motivation (or, perhaps, understanding). Most salespeople view paperwork as an obstacle which cuts into valuable selling time. Some even have the feeling that doing paperwork costs them money.

Although they may have an intellectual grasp of how call reports, account profiles, itineraries, and other territory records may ease their jobs, their impulse is always to get to the next call and not complete the paperwork on the call just made. They need discipline and constant encouragement. Too many have neither.

Some CEOs permit this sad situation to continue because they are either ignorant of it or don't understand its significance. Some know about it and tolerate it. But others, and they are joys to work with, completely understand the aversion of the sales force to paperwork and yet take a completely pragmatic and hard-nosed attitude toward the situation.

They view the costs to operate a territory not as an item of expense—that view is for accountants and the IRS—but as an investment. (They view training in the same way.) Indeed, if McGraw-Hill is right, and individual sales calls cost upward of $230, then it doesn't take long for that investment to grow. Capitalized over 3 years—about the time it takes a new representative to really make the territory productive—the investment is considerable.

These CEOs don't want that investment to evaporate when the salespeople move on. They don't want the territory to dry up if all or part of their product lines become suddenly obsolete; silicon, for example, replaced germanium overnight.

They want to know, account by account, who to see before establishing the specifications for new products. They also know that it is easier to keep current customers happy than to sign up new ones. They want the key players identified—name, rank, and serial number.

To meet these goals, three kinds of reports and records seem to be required of all salespeople:

- Itineraries and call reports
- Account records—some call them *account profiles*
- Assessments of account potential—some call them *forecasts*

That's about it for sales representatives. Their supervisors, naturally, will have a few more. We haven't mentioned expense reports and written orders. We hope that most firms have these situations under control.

Itineraries and Call Reports

All agree that paperwork is a pain. However, one of the happy facts some managements have discovered is that a lot of paperwork is not necessary. This is especially true in the communications between sales representative and supervisor. When they talk about an account, what they say is easily reduced to a verbal-numerical shorthand. When they talk about people, that's another matter.

Once the possibility of this kind of shorthand is understood, the burden of preparing itineraries and call reports is greatly reduced.

Further, the existence of NCR paper in snapout sets eliminates making carbons or xerographic copies.

Fig. 19.1 shows a combination itinerary plan and call report. Commonly, it is a three-part NCR snapout. More sheets are possible, but they are rarely necessary.

It is a very easy form to use. At the end of every week, as the sales representative completes the necessary paperwork for the week just finished, the next week's itinerary is planned. The left-hand side of the form is filled out: the name of the hotel for the night before, the ac-

WEEKLY ITINERARY AND CALL REPORT							
WEEK OF_____ REP._____ TERRITORY_____							
ITINERARY AND PLAN		MADE	NOT MADE	WHAT HAPPENED — CALL REPORT		SEE SPECIAL REPORT
ACCOUNT & INDIVIDUALS	OBJECTIVE			RESULTS	NEXT STEP	

(Day blocks down the left side, each with EVE. IN / HOTEL / TEL. lines:)

- SUNDAY / MONDAY
- MONDAY / TUESDAY
- TUESDAY / WEDNESDAY
- WEDNESDAY / THURSDAY
- THURSDAY / FRIDAY

TOTALS

Figure 19.1. Weekly itinerary and call report.

counts and people to be called on each day, and the objective for each call:

> *Holiday Inn, Ames*
> PBF, Smith   Trial K34
> Metals, Inc., Henry   Reslts Tr K34/200 cs.

and so on for the week.

This should not be a tremendous task since all accounts have been classified as to frequency of calls and placed on a route (see Chap. 18).

When the week's plan is done, the second copy goes to the field supervisor who should have no trouble reading and understanding what it means: "I'll be at the Holiday Inn at Ames, Sunday night. My first call will be on the PBF Corporation. I'll be seeing Archie Smith and I hope to set up a trial for K34." If this kind of shoptalk shorthand cannot be understood, then there are other, more serious problems.

During the week, after each call has been made, a similar notation is made on the right side of the form detailing the call results and the necessary follow-up. The same shorthand is used:

> Sold 150   Must have by 10/26
> Stains Carb 20   Pete to fix Ph by 11th

In longhand this means that "Smith bought 150 cases of K34 which must be delivered by 10/26 and Henry at Metals, Inc., says K34 stains his carbon steel twenty. Pete should adjust the Ph before the eleventh of the month."

Most communications can be handled in this way through simple reports that are readily understood by others from the same firm. If anything unusual develops on a call, a separate special report can and should be prepared. Unfortunately, most reporting systems in use are structured to accommodate the extraordinary situations, not what normally happens.

At the end of the week, the copy of the completed report is snapped off and mailed to the field supervisor along with the itinerary plan for the next week. The completed original remains with the sales representative's records.

It is that simple. Nothing more is required. This form and procedure works well for those selling industrial support-consumables; industrial process-consumables (commodities); industrial process, make-or-buy consumables; some capital equipment; and some items to the retail trade.

For salespeople selling complex or sophisticated capital equipment or for sales representatives with long product lines calling on mass merchandisers, more comprehensive reports will be required, but the principle remains the same.

There is a common criticism of this method of itinerary planning and call reporting. It comes mostly from the management levels between the field supervisor and the top. These people feel cut out of the loop and otherwise deprived of essential information. They try continually to overlay a simple system with special procedures and special reports. Having watched this process in more than one firm, I get the feeling that these people either don't want to get their hands out of the cookie jar or don't trust the people they have made field supervisors.

Account Records

In addition to putting down on paper and using itinerary plans and call reports, salespeople also need to record what they learn about the accounts they call on. *Account profiles* or *account records* are the names commonly used to refer to such records. This means another form for the sales representative, and they groan—something they do very well. In any case, designing an account record form takes a bit of doing; it should accomplish four things:

1. It should give the sales rep a place to record the information needed about an account so that it can be managed along with the territory. Management has some obligation to make sure that the form actually does this.

2. It should be specific and complete enough so that anyone else can read it and understand the essentials of the account.

3. It should contain other information about the account which may be more important to the firm than to the sales reps—information which the salespeople may be asked to report from time to time.

4. It should force the sales rep to think "professionally" about the account.

Typically, a well-designed form will display this kind of information about an account:

- Location
- Key personnel
- Phone numbers

- Calling hours
- History of calls made
- History of purchases and product use
- Reason the account buys or doesn't
- Competitors
- Type of location: using, buying, or billing
- Credit rating
- Plans
- Product usage projections

This list gets longer or shorter, depending upon what market the sales representative works and what kind of product is being sold.

Such records must be market-oriented. A single profile form cannot be made to fit all customers or every sales force.

Figs. 19.2 through 19.4 show an account record maintained by field representatives whose job it is to secure the participation of supermarkets, convenience stores, and other mass merchandisers of food products in state-sponsored promotions for its agricultural products. Part of their job involves also measuring the increased product movement that results from participation in those promotions. The complexity of the form arises from the complexity of the task, not from the governmental sponsorship of the effort.

The information that the account records contain is the major evidence of the firm's investment in a territory. A territory account record book is equivalent to a certificate of deposit or a bond, the record of a major investment.

The records, essential parts of the job, must be complete, up-to-date, and available. They belong to the employer, not to the sales representative, and they must be returned like a company car, credit cards, cash advances, and other such vital property when the sales representative moves on. As a part of normal auditing procedures, they must be reviewed whenever the supervisor rides shotgun with the sales representative.

With the advent of xerographic copies, it is easy for the supervisor to maintain a personal copy of each sales representative's territory record book. It is, after all, the common point of reference for them both.

Installing such a record-keeping system gets to be a real pain. However, there are ways of making it easy. I usually have sales representatives bring to the meeting where the account record system is to be introduced whatever basic data they have on each of their accounts.

Account profile

DOC Rep _____

Dept: Frozen _____ Dairy _____ Grocery _____ Produce _____ Adv/Mdsg _____

Type: Chain _____ Vol/Co-op _____ Ind _____ Broker _____ Wholesaler _____ Distr. _____

        Other _____

Account _____

Contact _____

Title _____

Secretary _____ Phone _____

Address _____

City _____ State _____ Zip _____ Phone _____

Buying days   M   T   W   T   F   S   Appointment procedure: _____

Hours _____   _____

Total annual sales ($) $_____ $_____ $_____ $_____

Number of outlets   _____ _____ _____ _____

Florida Citrus volume (sizes & cases)

    FCOJ. . . . . 48/6 oz   _____ _____ _____ _____

                    48/6 multi   _____ _____ _____ _____

                    24/12   _____ _____ _____ _____

                    24/16   _____

                    12/32

    FCGFJ. . . . . 48/6 oz

                    24/12

                    12/6

    Chilled OJ

Account profile

Dept: Frozen
        Chain
Type: Other

    Account
    Contact
    Title
    Secretary
    Address
    City
    Buying days   M   T   W   T   F   S
    Hours

    (cartons)
    . . . . . . (cartons)

Figure 19.2. Account Record: account profile (courtesy Florida Citrus Commission).

Three-by-five-inch index cards are fine for this. Then a group of typists transfer this information to the new forms. This process usually runs

Promotional history

Account: _____

Dept.: _____

No. 1   Calls made (dates)   1. _____ 2. _____ 3. _____ 4. _____ 5. _____ 6. _____

Starting date _____ Closing date _____ $ _____

Description _____

_____

Result _____

Vol before promo _____ Peak vol _____ Post promo vol _____

No. 2   Calls made (dates)   1. _____ 2. _____ 3. _____ 4. _____ 5. _____ 6. _____

Starting date _____ Closing date _____ $ _____

Description _____

_____

Result _____

Vol before promo _____ Peak vol _____ Post promo vol _____

No. 3   Calls made (dates)   1. _____ 2. _____ 3. _____ 4. _____ 5. _____ 6. _____

Starting date _____ Closing date _____ $ _____

Description _____

_____

Result _____

Vol before promo _____ Peak vol _____ Post promo vol _____

No. 4   Calls made (dates)   1. _____ 2. _____ 3. _____ 4. _____ 5. _____ 6. _____

Starting date _____ Closing date _____ $ _____

Description _____

_____

Result _____

Vol before promo _____ Peak vol _____ Post promo vol _____

No. 5   Calls made (dates)   1. _____ 2. _____ 3. _____ 4. _____ 5. _____ 6. _____

Starting date _____ Closing date _____ $ _____

Description _____

_____

Result _____

Vol before promo _____ Peak vol _____ Post promo vol _____

Figure 19.3. Account Record: call record (courtesy Florida Citrus Commission).

well into the wee hours of the morning, but the result is that each account record book gets a good start. The basic data on each account is finally on paper. The other information can be provided later on.

Call record

DATE	Objective _____
_____	Results _____
DATE	Objective _____
_____	Results _____
DATE	Objective _____
_____	Results _____
DATE	Objective _____
_____	Results _____
DATE	Objective _____
_____	Results _____
DATE	Objective _____
_____	Results _____
DATE	Objective _____
_____	Results _____
DATE	Objective _____
_____	Results _____
DATE	Objective _____
_____	Results _____
DATE	Objective _____
_____	Results _____
DATE	Objective _____
_____	Results _____

Figure 19.4. Account Record: account profile (courtesy Florida Citrus Commission).

There is no use to kidding around on this subject. Getting the sales force to maintain up-to-date account records, an up-to-date territory account book, will be a test of wills. Although keeping account records is not quite as important as cashing-out procedures are to a retailer, it comes close. If management sees the need for such a system and installs it, it must be maintained. Management cannot flinch on this matter.

Many claims have been made in recent years that, with modern computer technology, pencil and paper account records are no longer necessary. I wish that were true. It may be so when a sales representative can pull over to the side of the road, plug a terminal into the cigarette lighter outlet, and punch up an account record. Until that time comes, however, the paperwork will have to do.

Forecasts: Assessments of Account Potentials

Finally, we come to the last essential record. Once a quarter, every six months, or annually—the more frequently the better—each salesperson ought to assess the buying potential of each account for each of the major products or product lines. This is a forecasting exercise. However, there is something unforgiving about forecasts. They are viewed as a firm commitment to an uncertain future. Forecasting spooks senior managers as well as salespeople.

In most sales forces, forecasts are a big deal. Sales representatives panic, and their supervisors become tyrants. Everything comes to a halt as the numbers get filled in. Asking for a best-guess assessment of what each account *will* buy and of what each account *could* buy is better than a formal forecast for getting sales representatives to review their accounts in terms of future sales.

Assessing the potential of territory accounts need not be such a trauma. Formidable forms and enormous pressure are unnecessary.

Fig. 19.5 shows a form which is quite innocuous in its appearance. It has teeth in it, however, since it requires sales representatives to estimate by product what they are going to sell to each account in their territories.

There are two goals to be achieved in having the sales force complete this form. One goal is, hopefully, to provide management with useful information, information valuable in its planning. Many firms, however strongly they require these numbers, base their forecasts on entirely separate inputs because they lack confidence in field-generated figures. Occasionally it's because field data contradicts management's preconceptions.

The second goal is, therefore, the more important of the two. The forecasting exercise helps the sales force to view a territory as any manager must look at a market. Whether anyone else uses their assessments of territory po-

Account	Projected sales by product group for quarter beginning ______								Total
Totals									

Figure 19.5. Quarterly forecast and sales planning form.

tential, the sales rep needs them for planning purposes. The stress, therefore, ought to be on how the sales rep will use this information. And the sooner each representative begins to develop information which is useful in managing the territory, the sooner management will begin receiving forecasts which will be reliable and useful for its own purposes.

Reality and reality checks, of course, are critical in establishing the usefulness of forecast figures.

The form itself (Fig. 19.3) with its account product grid provides one reality test of the numbers. There is, however, another reality check; it requires the calculation of *expected value*.

Most forecast figures are based on (1) what the account says it will buy (and if the account doesn't say, the representative is obliged to ask), (2) the past purchasing history of the account (what it has actually bought), and (3) the representative's evaluation of the situation based on hunches and the observation of many things. The process for calculating expected value merely regularizes and proceduralizes the representative's subjective evaluation of account potential. If the evaluation is wrong, the source of the error can be more readily found. If the evaluation is correct, the reasons why are easily spotted. If the procedure needs to be discussed with another, that, too, is easily accomplished.

Regardless of what the account says about future purchases and regardless of what the past buying history shows, the representative should take nothing at face value. If the account says 100 and past history says 100, the representative commits to 100 at great personal peril. Actually, about the best that should be hoped for is 80; that's an expected value of 80 percent under the best of circumstances.

Many factors have to come together to ensure the best of conditions. These factors range from the way the numbers do conform to past buying practices at one end to the absence of threats to the customer's business at the other. In most selling situations, the following seem to be the most significant indicators of expected value:

- *The projection conforms to established buying patterns.* Many sales representatives are content to consider only this indicator, but it is readily modified by other considerations.

- *The same personnel provides the buying information.* Continuity among the people with whom the representative does business is a very positive indicator.

- *No negative changes in the customer's business.* If the customer predicts that sales will continue at historical levels, then the customer's supply requirements should not change.

• *No increase in the price of the products being sold.* Price increases cause all customers to reconsider all supply relationships and to look for alternatives.

• *No increase in competitive activity.* Prudent accounts will always consider a business proposition from another supplier. They may not go for it, but it will be considered.

• *No decrease in the health of the customer's industry.* A particular customer may not yet be in trouble, but if the industry as a whole is threatened, the entire market could be drying up.

• *No change in the customer's management.* New management often means new supply relationships. That change, however, may be delayed until the new management feels secure.

• *No threats on the horizon.* Anything may be a threat. The range is from strikes and shutdowns at other suppliers to strong predictions of a slow Christmas buying season.

Moving from these indicators to expected value can be done like this. If the indicator applies to the situation with no qualification, let it have a value of 10 percent; if there is doubt, give it a value of 5 percent; and if there is no way in which it applies, let it have a value of *zero*. Thus, one gets expected value indicators like this:

	Application		
Expected Value Indicators	Applies	Can't be sure	No way
Conforms to established buying patterns	10%	5%	0%
Same personnel provided inputs as before	10%	5%	0%
No negative changes in customer's business	10%	5%	0%
No increase in the price of the product	10%	5%	0%
No increase in competitive activity	10%	5%	0%
No decrease in the health of customer's industry	10%	5%	0%
No change in customer's management	10%	5%	0%
No threats on the horizon	10%	5%	0%
Total Expected Values	80%	40%	0%

There is one small complication here. This procedure may suggest that the representative has to calculate expected value for each product that is sold to each account. If the line is a long one, the prospect of all that paperwork can be very discouraging—enough to turn anyone off to the idea of calculating expected value.

However, most product lines can readily be divided into three classes of product:

1. *New proprietary products* where complete acceptance within a market has not been secured and on which the profits are high.
2. *Standard products* for which broad acceptance has been secured and on which the profits are moderate.
3. *Commodity products* which meet well-established specifications and which are sold on the basis of some combination of price and availability. These are the most vulnerable to competitive activity.

The chances of selling products in any of these groups will be about the same for all products within that group. This means that it isn't necessary to calculate expected value for each product with each account. Three calculations, one for each class will be enough. And, very likely, the same probabilities will apply to many, if not to all, accounts. Thus, for every account, the probabilities might look like this:

- New products, 60 percent
- Standard products, 80 percent
- Commodity products, 50 percent

And the expected value of product sales might look like this:

Account	Product	Projection		Probability		Expected value
S&D	Stainless 30s	10,000	×	60%	=	$ 6,000
	Stainless 45s	6,000	×	60%	=	$ 3,600
	Stainless 60s	4,000	×	60%	=	$ 2,400
	Alum 30s	20,000	×	80%	=	$16,000
	Alum 45s	10,000	×	80%	=	$ 8,000
	Alum 60s	7,000	×	80%	=	$ 5,600
	Galv 30s	10,000	×	50%	=	$ 5,000
		$67,000				$46,000

Of course, the expected value figures are what would go into the forecasting form.

20

Converting Leads into Customers: Using the Telephone to Sell

If McGraw-Hill is only half right and a single sales call costs only something over $115 rather than $230, it still makes sense to use the telephone to sell. We are not talking about *telemarketing*. That may have been a promising idea once, but it is now much debased. All the telemarketing efforts I have encountered in the past few years have been frivolous, offensive, and ineffectual, or more important, separate from normal selling activities.

In what follows, we'll take a close look at a process for converting leads into happy customers who willingly refer business to us. Leads, of course, are people who identify themselves by name and firm and who say "Tell me about your products and services." What we will review is a lead conversion procedure used by manufacturers of capital equipment—industrial process equipment—ranging in price from $4500 to upward of half a million dollars per unit. The sale of this equipment is rather complex and the conversion process quite thorough and complete. It will serve as a model for those who may have a less complex sale.

What's significant about this process is that it is used by people who sell high-cost capital equipment entirely by telephone and mail. Not a dime is spent for travel until the sale is virtually assured. And then, under many circumstances, it is the prospect, the potential customer, who does the traveling.

The process must be followed from start to finish regardless of how sales are made—in person, by phone, or by mail. Omitting steps is a major cause of sales ineffectiveness. Fragmenting it, assigning bits and pieces to several people with no overall supervision, is equally disasterous. Lead conversion is, after all, a prime sales management responsibility.

Figures. 20.1 through 20.11 outline the procedure. It starts with the receipt of a lead or inquiry, regardless of its source. It ends with a happy customer who can be asked for endorsements and referrals.

Identifying Leads

The first step in the process identifies the inquirer, records the source of the lead so that it may be evaluated as a guide to planning future lead-generating activities, and requires an initial evaluation of the lead itself (see Fig. 20.1).

All leads must be responded to promptly; for all practical purposes, an old lead is a dead lead. Turnaround time for a lead should be as close to zero as possible. What throws most people, preventing a rapid response and causing leads to wither and die, is not having thought through the possible levels of response and figuring out when each should be applied.

Levels of Response

Three levels of response are possible:

1. The information requested along with a thank-you-for-your-interest acknowledgement, or *buck-slip*, should go out immediately. The buck-slip should identify someone to write to or to call for further information. Since the inquiry may be from a competitor, the material sent out should not compromise either the firm or its products. Prompt response terrorizes competitors and causes them to wonder how promptly the leads they receive are followed up.

2. Some inquiries require a telephone call "just to make sure that we send you the most useful information." Something about the name, title, or firm will suggest that the inquiry is not a frivolous one. A telephone call is quicker and cheaper than a face-to-face call. It may be more effective.

3. Some inquiries may require an immediate, personal visit. The combination of title, firm, and level of interest expressed may indicate a situation far enough along to require a face-to-face meeting with the inquirer. This, of course, would be arranged by telephone.

I. *Lead—Inquirer identification*

Name_____—

Title_____—

Company_____—

Address_____—

_____

Telephone( )_____—

SIC Code_____—

A. *Source:*

_____ Bingo card

_____ Phone

_____ Letter

_____ Personal contact

_____ Customer

_____ Former prospect

B. *Evaluation/Disposition:*

_____ Buck-slip and literature

_____ Phone

_____ Visit

Figure 20.1. Conversion procedure: lead to satisfied customer and referral source.

This simple triage procedure is required for the initial screening of leads. With experience, whoever does this acquires great skills. Screening, therefore, should not be assigned to whoever has free time. Literature collectors and competitors are quickly separated from those who might be real prospects. Since knowing for sure which is which, is difficult, be sure that all get a response. Those not worth a telephone call get the minimal response by mail. These inquiries go into a hold file. The rest get a telephone response and are added to the mailing list.

Converting Inquirer to Prospect

In Fig. 20.2 the process begins for determining whether the inquiry is indeed from a bona fide prospect. The information outlined here can be developed either by a telephone call or during a face-to-face visit. To get it all, one or more telephone calls or visits may be required.

Failure at this stage occurs because the people handling the lead follow-up don't know the questions to ask or are a little diffident about asking those questions. The one that throws most people is IIC, which asks about money. The answers here, of course, are the surest indicators of how serious such inquirers are and how close to moving they may be.

Item IIE, in Fig. 20.3, covers inquiries about the technical requirements the prospect is trying to meet.

These answers are also important in deciding whether the inquirer is really a competitor or a prospect and for determining what the next step should be. This information is often not developed because the sales representative doesn't know what to ask or is uncomfortable about asking.

This first screen begins the accumulation of information about the firm on whose behalf the inquiry is made. One of the important things to learn about the inquiring firm is its Standard Industrial Classification (SIC) code. You can expect most inquiries to come from firms within just a few SICs. However, occasionally another SIC turns up and may indicate that another market is forming or that special equipment may be required. Sometimes it is possible to get this SIC information early in the conversion process. Generally, it will be picked up later in the process. But, early or late, the SIC of the inquirer should be determined.

The questions in Fig. 20.4 complete this phase of the process. On the basis of all the information developed for Items IIA through IIK (which may be incomplete at this stage), the lead must be evaluated and the appropriate next step decided upon.

Levels of Response

The options at this stage increase by one. The inquiry may, after all, turn out to be of no consequence. If this is so, as before, literature and a buck-slip are sent out.

II. *Inquirer to prospect—Qualification* (in person_____; by phone_____)

A. *Type of inquiry:*

_____ General information

_____ Budget (ballpark estimate)

_____ Action imminent

_____ Update old quote

_____ Competitive probe

B. *Intended use:*

_____ Production

_____ Pilot plant

_____ Lab

C. *Project status:*

_____ Developing technical specifications

_____ Developing budget

_____ RFQ/RFP

_____ Funded

_____ Expenditures authorized

D. *Reason for action:*

_____ Process evaluation

_____ Cost reduction

_____ Quality improvement

_____ Government requirement: OSHA, EPA, contract requirement

_____ Nice to have

Figure 20.2. Inquirer to prospect—identification.

However, enough information may have been developed to warrant sending out ballpark or order-of-magnitude figures on costs, plus more detailed literature. Many, or even most, inquiries qualified in person or by telephone will fall into this group.

II. Inquirer to Prospect (Continued)

   E. *Technical requirements:*

      Process:_____

      _____

      _____

      Quantity/volume (current and target):_____

      _____

      _____

      Quality (current and target):_____

      _____

      _____

      Cost (current and target):_____

      _____

      _____

   F. *Feasibility* (samples and test requirements):

      Ours:_____

      _____

      Theirs:_____

      _____

Figure 20.3. Inquirer to prospect—identification (*Continued*).

Bona Fide Prospects

With some prospects, however, events may move along far enough so that a hard quote, specification, and supporting literature—a proposal—are in order.

Once more, the final option is a personal visit and a formal sales presentation—a go-for-an-order effort.

Figure 20.5 outlines the first three response options.

Figure 20.4. Inquirer to prospect—identification (*Continued*).

II. Inquirer to Prospect (Continued)

  G. *Identifiable competition:*

    _____ The prospect may make no change, continue as is

    _____ Other technologies:_____

    _____

    _____ Direct competitors:

Firm	Make and Model	Price
_____	_____	____
_____	_____	____
_____	_____	____

  H. *Decision-making process:*

    Decision maker_____

    Engineering influence_____

    Manufacturing influence_____

    Purchasing influence_____

  I. *Likely timetable:*

               Date

    Evaluation   _____

    Decision   _____

    Purchase order   _____

    Installation   _____

    Operation   _____

  J. *Contingencies leading to:*

    Postponement:_____

    Acceleration:_____

    Cancellation:_____

Figure 20.4. Inquirer to prospect—identification (*Continued*)

II. Inquirer to Prospect (Concluded)

   K. *Probable customer for:*

      Standard unit(s)_____

          Options_____

      Modified standard units_____

      Special unit(s)_____

                              Evaluation/disposition:

                      _____ Literature and buck-slip

                      _____ Ballpark estimates and literature

                      _____ Hard quote and literature (proposal)

                      _____ Visit and presentation

Once the prospect has been furnished the appropriate information, follow-up is necessary. Figure 20.6 details what's involved in the necessary follow-up. Usually, this is a very poorly executed part of selling endeavors. Either there is no follow-up whatsoever or the follow-up is done so long after the initial response that the prospect will have trouble remembering it and discussing it. Follow-up calls should be made within a week or 10 days after the response, certainly no later.

During this initial follow-up, the missing information for section II is gathered. Here, too, the general cost estimates and general performance data which have been supplied are converted to a formal proposal. Then the follow-up sequence begins once more.

After the initial follow-up has been made, contact with the prospect must be maintained until the situation is officially dead or a sale is made. Figure 20.7 outlines a few of the options open at this point. In view of the fact that this procedure was developed for the capital-goods market, two or even three budgeting cycles may be completed before action becomes imminent. Follow-up at reasonable intervals becomes important.

Signs of Trouble

During this long period, the person doing the follow-up should be alert to signs of trouble. The situation is like a failing romance. Item IVB-5,

III. *Prospect to purchase order (level of response)*

  A. *Literature and buck-slip—No follow-up required*

    1. *Literature:* General benefits of the house, the technology, the equipment. No price information or specs. Nothing of significance to competition.

    2. *Buck-slip:* Whom to call or write for more information. Response to be used when:_____

    _____

    3. *Do not add to mailing list.*

  B. *Ballpark estimates and literature:*

    1. *Literature:* Features and benefits plus performance and equipment specifications. Items of special interest highlighted. Available options listed.

    2. *Letter:* Ballpark estimates plus specific benefits pitch based upon section II, Fig. 20.2, above. Response to be used when:_____

    _____

    3. *Add to mailing list.*

  C. *Firm quote and literature—Follow-up required*

    1. *Literature:* Features and benefits plus performance and equipment specifications. Items of special interest highlighted. Available options listed.

    2. *Letter:* Recommended equipment and options described. Specific benefits presented. Firm prices quoted. Terms and conditions stated. Necessary lead times presented. Special ordering, testing, acceptance, shipping, installation, startup and training procedures described. Countersignature block included for ready approval and acceptance.
       Response to be used when:_____

    _____

    3. *Add to mailing list.*

General cautions: Hold back on literature sent to prospect at this stage. Don't spend it all. Keep some in reserve for follow-up. Carefully document how prices were arrived at: labor, engineering, materials, special testing, etc.

Figure 20.5. Prospect to purchase order—level of response.

in Fig. 20.7, suggests a few of these signs. Some of these signs are not serious but might become so, and some are quite serious. For inexperienced people, these signs tend to go unrecognized.

Figure 20.6. Follow-up.

IV. *Follow-up*

    A. *Initial follow-up to III (2) and (3) above:* Date _____,
        by phone _____, in person _____,

        1. *Proposal/quote received* _____ *read* _____.

        2. *Review proposal.* As appropriate, clarify prospect's understanding of:

             _____ recommended equipment

             _____ recommended options

             _____ benefits presented

             _____ ordering procedure

             _____ testing procedure

             _____ acceptance procedure

             _____ shipping

             _____ installation

             _____ start-up

             _____ training

             _____ prices

             _____ terms and conditions

             _____ warranty and guaranty

       3. *Prospect's questions:*

          Asked   Answers provided

          _____   _____

          _____   _____

          _____   _____

      4. *Complete/up-date information required in Part II.*

(Continued)

    At some point in the continuing discussion, the prospect may begin talking about owning the equipment, about problems of using the equipment, or about delivery or general availability. Or some of the other things listed in

Figure 20.6. (Continued)

---

5. *Determine prospect's next step:*

_____ Secure other approvals; whose?

_____ Budget status change: funded _____,

authorized _____,   released _____.

_____ Supply samples for test; what, when?

_____ Check references; who?

_____ Visit installation; where?

_____ Issue PO; number, date?

6. *Our next step:*

_____ Supply additional information; what?

_____ Provide reference list.

_____ Arrange installation visit; where? when?

_____ Arrange visit to our plant; when?

_____ Test samples; what? when?

_____ Make visit and presentation; where? when?

_____ Supply firm quote.

7. *Agreed upon next follow-up date:* _____.

With whom_____?   By phone_____,

In person_____.

Fig. 20.8 may come to pass. When any of these things happen, it is time to make a trial close and, if the response is favorable, to actually close.

Lost-Business Reports

Once the closing effort has been made and it is clear from the response that nothing further will happen, a lost-business report must be prepared. Lost-business reports are, of course, admissions of failure and an awful stigma is usually attached to having to prepare one. It is hard to determine which makes salespeople more apprehensive, forecasts or lost-business reports.

However, honest lost-business reports may be the best tool there is for improving sales performance. Their preparation should be encouraged

IV. Follow-up (Continued)

   B. Continuing follow-up: In person_____; by phone_____.

     1. Complete or update section II information (Figs. 20.2 to 20.4).

     2. Expand follow-up to others beyond initial contact.

     _____ Manufacturing influence

     _____ Engineering influence

     _____ Purchasing influence

     _____ Decision maker

     3. Repeat follow-up procedure (Item IVA, Fig. 20.6, above) with each.

     4. Combine follow-up with continued promotion (good news about firm, equipment, process, etc.):

     _____ New, additional literature

     _____ New installations, customers

     _____ New or refined performance or cost-effectiveness data

     _____ Additional case histories

     _____ New applications

     _____ New options, modifications

     5. Watch for signs of potential trouble

     _____ Change in contact's manner

     _____ Nitpicking of details

     _____ Evasive answers

     _____ Changes in scheduled dates

     _____ Resistance to additional probes

     _____ Holdups in scheduling tests, sending samples, etc.

     _____ New names in approval loop

     _____ Shifts in project goals, specifications

     _____ Requests for additional, new detailed information

     _____ Names of competitors loom large in discussions

Figure 20.7. Continuing follow-up.

V. *Closing: Prospect to customer trial close; Close*

  A.

    When:

      _____ The prospect begins to discuss owning or using the equipment.

      _____ There is an opening in our production schedule.

      _____ There may be a price break (economies of scale) due to similar unit going into production.

      _____ A price hike is to be announced.

      _____ Samples run/tests completed satisfactorily.

      _____ Installation visits went well.

      _____ All approvals and endorsements secured.

  B.

    How:

      _____ Ask for purchase order, billing number.

      _____ Ask for countersigned proposal.

      _____ Work backward to purchase order from agreed upon delivery, installation, startup, or on-line dates.

Figure 20.8. Closing: prospect to customer trial close; close.

and no stigma attached to having to prepare one.

If a good relationship has been established between the prospect and the salesperson—whether by telephone or in person—the information necessary to prepare an effective lost-business report should be easy to develop. Item IV A, in Fig. 20.9, lists a few of the possibilities.

New Customer

The more likely event, however, is that a purchase order or its equivalent will be issued by the prospect. Too many firms, under pressure to build volume or simply starved for business, blow themselves out of the water at this point. They do not compare what the customer has ordered with what they have specified in their proposal.

Purchase Order Review

The purchase order or its equivalent must be carefully compared with the proposal and any discrepancies identified. Before any formal, legally binding

VI. *Purchase order to satisfied customer and referral source*

   A. *Lost-business report*

      1. Prime contact had no authority to act.

      2. Project cancelled or postponed.

         _____ Lost budget

         _____ Pressure off (EPA, OSHA, etc.)

         _____ Contract not received (DoD, etc.)

         _____ Operation/production line scrapped

         _____ Next follow-up: How? When?

      3. Awarded to competitor based on

         _____ Price

         _____ Availability

         _____ Operating/maintenance/installation requirements

         _____ Terms

         _____ Warranty/guaranty

         _____ Better reputation/financial stability

         _____ Equipment capacity

         _____ Quality of equipment or its output

Figure 20.9. Lost business report.

acceptance of the purchase order is issued, all changes must be reviewed by engineering, manufacturing, and finance. If necessary, there must be a renegotiation with the prospect before a formal acceptance is issued. Once in a while it may even be necessary to turn down an order just to prevent future trouble. Figure 20.10 reviews the problems and booby traps in this area.

Continued Sales Involvement

When the acceptance has been issued and the project has been brought in-house, there is a tendency for salespeople to bow out of the picture and to let someone else see the project through to delivery, startup, and acceptance by the customer. That is the way of folly. However, salespeo-

VI. Purchase order to satisfied customer (Continued)

  B. *Edit purchase order*

    1. Compare purchase order with original order or quote

      _____ Model/parts numbers

      _____ Modifications

      _____ Options

      _____ Terms (up-front money)

      _____ Packing, shipping, delivery

      _____ Test and acceptance procedures

      _____ Installation, startup, training

      _____ Process, equipment guaranty and warranty

    2. Look for

      _____ New terms and conditions

      _____ New names for approvals, acceptances, authorizations for payment

      _____ Special requirements: spare parts, manuals, packaging, OSHA, EPA, etc.

      _____ Basic changes in capacity, design, quality, quantity, etc.

  C. *Determine conditions for acceptance*

    1. Review all changes with engineering, manufacturing, and finance. Determine effect on

      _____ Quantity

      _____ Quality

      _____ Delivery

      _____ Cost

      _____ Price

    2. Negotiate changes in price and delivery, etc., with customer.

    3. Issue formal acceptance, initial invoice.

Figure 20.10. Editing purchase order.

ple can't be totally involved in the project either.

Therefore, part of the handoff process from sales to manufacturing must involve an agreement on when and how the sales representative will remain involved and when the account returns to sales.

Figure 20.11 reviews this matter and lists those steps where sales must

VI. Purchase order to satisfied customer (Concluded)

   D. *Handoff to manufacturing, engineering, and finance*

      1. Review, secure acknowledgement of all aspects of agreement. If nonstandard products involved, furnish details of cost base for materials, labor, engineering, and special purchases.

      2. Establish or confirm ongoing customer contact procedures: Who does what and when.

      3. Determine sales follow-up dates for:

         _____ In-house testing

         _____ Customer tests and acceptance

         _____ Shipment

         _____ Delivery

         _____ Installation

         _____ Startup

         _____ Training

         _____ Handoff to customer

   E. *Ongoing follow-up*

      1. Supervise/monitor project per Item D3 above.

      2. After startup and hand off, maintain follow-up to:

         a. Monitor performance or equipment after installation and startup

         b. Sell modifications/additional equipment

         c. Identify opportunitites for new products/applications/modifications.

         d. Secure endorsements/referrals

Figure 20.11. Handoff to manufacturing.

be involved. Of course, once the customer has accepted delivery and everything is running well, the ball goes back to the salespeople.

As we said earlier, this detailed procedure was developed to help the manufacturers of capital equipment sell by telephone. It is successful only when one person assumes responsibility for seeing the process through to completion for each lead that comes in-house. Others may become involved and handle pieces of the process. But over them, one person must have total and personal responsibility for the conversion process.

21

Motivating the Sales Force Without Spending Money

Motivation is at least a three-dimensional problem. It involves individual salespeople, various motivational techniques and our own company's needs, and the improved sales goals we want to achieve. All these dimensions (see Fig. 21.1) must be taken into account together to find our answers, motivators that work.

We tend to look at motivation two dimensions at a time, ignoring the third. Frequently, we try to attain sales goals with motivators selected because they are traditional or because we can afford them, not because of their probable effect on the individual sales representatives involved. Or we plan a contest and select prizes because we know the prizes will appeal to the sales force; often, we do this without considering whether a contest would further the goals we'd really like to achieve.

Barry's First Law

To illustrate: Not so long ago a client was considering using an incentive compensation program for his sales force. To help him decide, I made a survey among his competitors to determine how they compensated their sales forces and what the range of incomes were.

The results tended to confirm the client's hunch; all but one of his identifiable competitors paid some form of incentive—either salary plus a performance bonus or a guarantee against commission. Only one competitor paid straight salary only.

However, we also had fairly reliable share-of-market figures, and so we decided to see what relationship, if any, existed between the methods of compensation and the sales results. Since the products in this company's field are highly engineered with the sales representatives of-

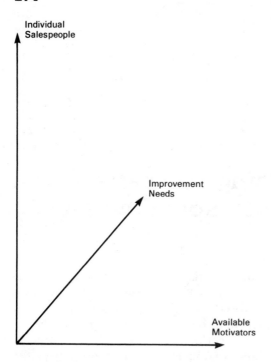

Figure 21.1. Motivation: a three-dimensional problem.

ten acting as engineer for the client, results can safely be attributed to the sales representative's effectiveness, or lack of it. The results shown in Fig. 21.2 astonished the client. Like many others, he had always believed that incentive compensation was the essential means to motivate sales performance. Yet here was the market leader with a growing 28 percent share of the business, paying no incentives whatever and offering salaries that averaged no higher than the rest of the industry.

Clients are sometimes surprised to learn that there are many ways to motivate improved performance, ways that do not involve more money, ways that are often more effective than just more money. Ways that, for the moment, we can sum up under the term *good management.*

Indeed, this is a prime example of what some of us in the trade have come to call *Barry's first law* after the sales incentive compensation expert, John W. Barry, who first propounded it in our time. We quote Barry's first law in full:

Barry's First Law: *Money is no substitute for good management.*

Oddly enough, in his experience and my own, this seems to be a difficult notion for many managements to accept. In good times with grow-

Company	Salary Only	Salary Plus Bonus	Commission	Share of Market
A		X		10% flat
B			X	8% +
C		X		9% +
D		X		11% flat
E	X			28% +
F			X	7% -
G			X	5% -
H		● X		12% -
Others		X		10% flat

+, Increasing Market Share; - , Declining Share

Figure 21.2. Compensation versus productivity.

ing markets, good products from reputable manufacturers seem to sell themselves. In hard times, when product movement is sluggish, the typical response seems to be to beef up the sales force and to increase the performance bonuses.

In the spring of 1985, when the minicomputer market fell apart, the general response of this industry seems to have been to expand the sales force—20 to 25 percent increases were common—and to lay on the incentives. Not much, however, seems to have been done about the quality or the quantity of either sales management or field sales supervision. The real problem was not addressed—too much stress on technology and not enough attention to customer benefits.

Nonfinancial Motivators

One important part of good management is knowing the sales force well enough to be able to predict what they will respond to with greater effort, what motivational techniques will be more effective than mere money. First, however, we need to identify the kind of performance improvement required.

Identifying Required Improvements

There are, as we can see from Fig. 21.3, a number of quantifiable sales functions, functions where performance can be measured and specific

QUANTIFIABLE SALES FUNCTIONS						
Selling — Volume						
Size of Order						
Number of Orders						
Calls per Order						
Managing Time: Calls per Day						
Expenses: Cost per Call						
Products Under Test						
New Accounts						
Implementing Promotions						
Controlling Receivables						
OTHER SALES FUNCTIONS						
Planning Territory Coverage						
Forecasting — Products						
Customers						
Developing Resellers						
Communications						
Record Keeping						
Handling Complaints						

Figure 21.3. Areas for performance improvement by salespeople.

improvement goals and targets can be set for each salesperson. We can measure the effectiveness of individual selling efforts by dollar or unit size of orders written, number of orders, number of calls per order, etc. (see Chap. 24). We can measure how well each sales representative invests time and controls expenses. We can easily measure how well new accounts are opened, how new promotions get off the ground, and, in some situations, how receivables are controlled. And, in all these areas where performance can be measured, improved performance can be easily targeted. Similarly, there are a number of other sales functions that may not be so easily quantified, but where qualitative performance improvement goals can still be set by or through the judgments of the field supervisor.

Once we have identified the kinds of performance improvement required, we must relate these goals to the performance of each sales representative. Obviously, not all salespeople will perform equally well in all these areas, and not all will have the same potential for improvement. Motivating salespeople should begin with a realistic appraisal, person by person, of strengths, weaknesses, and areas where a little improvement will pay off the most.

Motivators to Fit the Salesperson

Once we have identified our needs on a rep by rep basis, we can begin relating these needs to the kinds of motivators available to us—we can begin by identifying each person's hot button, as it were. To help us do so, let's take a look at some of the ways of motivating sales representatives and their supervisors, or anyone else, to perform at higher levels of proficiency—ways that need not cost more money.

Before we explore the motivational techniques available to us (Fig. 21.4), however, we should recall a few things about the sales force as people and about the jobs we ask them to do.

Pride

Pride in doing a good job is a very strong motivator. When the sales rep believes that he or she is a leader on a winning team, the rep will strive to perform at increasingly higher levels just to maintain that status.

Self-Confidence

Self-confidence is another very strong motivator, and management can do a great deal to build a sales rep's self-confidence. Knowing that he or she is well-trained, and can answer the questions the customer throws, helps provide that necessary degree of assurance. Knowing that a supervisor is available to help in tight situations will encourage stretching, trying something new. Knowing that the company will answer questions, meet promised delivery schedules, maintain quality, and be flexible in handling unusual situations—all these effects of good management enable the sales rep to step forward and do a first-rate job of

MOTIVATORS					
Two-way Communications					
Self-Scoring Achievements					
Procedures					
Job Enrichment Recognition					
Challenge					
Increased Responsibility					
One-time Awards					
Bonuses or Commissions					

Figure 21.4. Motivators by salesperson.

selling, secure in the knowledge of representing the best. Nothing enhances the ability to sell more than the knowledge that there is complete support from "home"—the certainty of being backed up by fine products in every sense of that term.

Both pride and self-confidence will follow if everything we discuss here is implemented.

Two-Way Communications

This leads to our first motivator. Open, easy two-way communications between sales force and the office is essential in creating this kind of motivational atmosphere.

Recognizing that salespeople are human beings and treating them accordingly is essential to good motivation. We can recognize the importance of this when we remember that the sales representative's job is a very lonely one. For "outside" salespeople there is no one at the next desk with whom to compare notes and no roving supervisor to turn to for advice.

Self-Scoring Achievements

A sales representative may go for long periods of time without personal contact with either supervisor or colleagues. During that time there may not even be an order. It may even be unreasonable to expect to write an order. The potential for discouragement is large. Management can help by defining a "good job," so that at the end of each day or each week, the representative can know and not wonder about performance. It can also help with immediate approval for a job well done.

What's required here is a series of *self-scoring achievements* which will tell the salespeople, in the absence of written orders, that they have indeed done a good job.

Procedures to Follow

Frequently, and especially with mature sales forces, we find situations in which the older, more experienced people perform at significantly higher levels than those who are newer and less experienced. The newer people seem never able to catch up.

Through years of experience in the territory, the old hands have developed complete mastery of all the simple, but essentially basic, skills—how to pack a briefcase, how to plan itineraries to minimize travel time, how to establish an expected value for an account and use it as a guide to investing limited sales calls.

Not understanding these seemingly simple basics or how the command of them eases the way of the older people and allows them to concentrate on the actual selling job, the younger salespeople can and do become discouraged. They become *de*motivated and increasingly less effective.

In situations like this, it is often possible to develop a few simple procedures for the younger salespeople to follow. These procedures can then be explained casually or taught formally, depending on the size of sales force and the nature of the procedures. In either case, the results will be better performance.

Job Enrichment

Often, through simple job enrichment, we can motivate sales representatives to sustain high levels of performance and to strive for even higher levels. Recognition is one form of job enrichment that pays off handsomely. Sales Representative of the Year awards and President's Clubs are formalized ways of providing such recognition.

But many times, a simple word of appreciation at a sales meeting or a handwritten note offering congratulations for a good job will work even better.

Challenge is another form of job enrichment with a large payoff. Being assigned a tough new account to crack or being asked to help get a new product off the ground in record time are typical of the kind of challenges salespeople respond to. The sales representative who meets these challenges earns the respect of colleagues. And that is one of the most powerful motivators there is.

Increased responsibility is another powerful motivator. We can make one or more of the superior performers responsible for simplifying our training program undertake special market research, or participate in department planning.

Asking sales representatives to accept increased responsibility is also a good way of assessing their potential for management positions. We must recognize, however, that not all superior salespeople aspire to management activities or positions. In fact, most want and expect to remain salesreps. Our job is to keep them happy being superior producers. They are more likely to stay happy if they know that management values the contributions they have made and will continue to make.

Contests

Then there are contests and other one-time awards. Properly used, they can be powerful motivators that also produce the added benefit of a permanent improvement in overall performance.

For example, let's assume that for the past few quarters your best producers have reached a plateau and sell at an $800,000-per-year rate. The problem: How to get them off the plateau and back climbing the mountain? One possible way: Offer a substantial award to the sales representative who sells $250,000 in a single quarter. If the award is interesting enough, the entire sales force will go after it. In the course of the contest, the sales of a significant number of salespeople will improve, and several may even reach the target.

You may have to provide more than one award, but you will have the satisfaction of having raised everyone's level of performance. Although there will surely be some slackening of effort once the contest ends, sales should not fall to the previous level. You will have achieved a permanent improvement in the total performance of the entire sales force.

However, there are dangers in using one-time awards and contests. Those who are less scrupulous may manipulate sales for contest purposes; for example, they may delay turning in sales made just prior to the beginning of the contest period or hurry a client into a sale that would normally be made just after the end of the contest, thus increasing contest-time sales without adding anything to overall sales.

Product managers often use contests and other one-time awards to compete for the attention and for the time of the sales force without regard for overall sales goals or for the realities of the marketplace. This could lead to demotivation.

These dangers can be guarded against by careful formulation of contest rules and close supervision of the contest itself. Management's reward for the effort this takes is to have the satisfaction of producing a permanent improvement in levels of sales performance.

The final option, of course, is a completely revised compensation program which includes some form of salary-based bonuses. This is, however, another matter entirely, which we will discuss later on.

As we have seen, it is possible for a firm to lead the pack without any incentive compensation plans. The primary requirement is simply smart management.

The point of all this is simple: There are many ways to motivate a sales force to improved performance. As managers, we should be aware of them all. We should not let our vision be limited by past practices or by what the competition does.

If we know our salespeople and if we have a realistic fix on what it is we want them to accomplish, then we can select from the many possible motivators the ones that will produce the performance improvements we want.

The matrix shown in Fig. Fig. 21.5 will enable us to match our needs with our motivational options.

QUANTIFIABLE SALES FUNCTIONS	Communications	Self-scoring Achievements	Procedures	Job Enrichment	One-time Awards	Bonuses or Commissions
Selling Volume						
Size of Order						
Number of Orders						
Calls per Order						
Managing Time: Calls per Day						
Expenses: Cost per Call						
Products Under Test						
New Accounts						
Implementing Promotions						
Controlling Receivables						
OTHER SALES FUNCTIONS						
Forecasting Products						
Customers						
Developing Resellers						
Communications						
Record Keeping						
Handling Complaints						

Figure 21.5. Needs versus available motivators.

Field Supervision

As we have suggested above, the way to effective motivation is field supervision. This is where everything comes together or where everything falls apart.

Neither the Patriots nor the Bears got to the Super Bowl through the efforts of the players alone. There were coaches involved. Coaches who charted and measured the performance of individual players. Coaches who spotted and reinforced the strengths of individuals. Coaches who spotted weaknesses and suggested better ways and who planned and provided the training exercises necessary to make sure that those better ways were adopted and became second nature. It was the coaches who decided when individuals couldn't and wouldn't measure up and had to be replaced. These are coaches whose full-time responsibilities are to coach, not to play.

We have the same need in managing a field sales effort. Our coaches are field supervisors, district managers, division managers, area managers, or regional managers. Without them, our jobs become difficult, if not impossible. Playing coaches are better than no coaches at all, but we should aim at having full-time coaches with no responsibility beyond that of improving the performance of our salespeople.

It is for this reason that if an experienced sales trainer were forced to decide between training new sales representatives or training first-line supervisors, the decision would be to train the managers. The leverage is so much greater. A study of sales representatives' performance under good and poor managers shows that salespeople of middling abilities do as well or even better under good field supervisors as *good* salespeople under poor managers. Although the study is several years old, nothing has happened since then to make the conclusions invalid today. Details of the study are given in *Field Sales Managers* by Robert T. Davis. The book is listed in the appendix.

Ideally, we should shoot for a situation in which our field supervisors spend 80 percent of their time working with sales representatives measuring performance, reinforcing those actions that are done well, suggesting better ways in those areas where improvement is necessary and possible, and encouraging them to attempt challenging situations.

The balance of the field supervisor's time, up to 20 percent, should be available for planning, paperwork, and other administrative chores.

Too frequently, however, we load down field supervisors with administration and find ourselves with field coaches who spend only 20 percent of their time working with individual salespeople and 80 percent of their time handling unproductive administrative work which is either best-handled by others or is even unnecessary.

In addition to not giving our field supervisors enough time to supervise, we may also be asking them to supervise too many people. We may be asking them to work with too broad a span of control. For most industrial sales forces, the ideal is one full-time supervisor—that is, someone with no direct account responsibility, for every eight to ten full-time salespeople. If the sale is complicated and the ticket high, five or six is plenty. When salespeople call on mass marketers, the span can be increased to ten or twelve.

However, in this area of field supervision, we all operate under some very real constraints and often have to settle for something less than the ideal. Often we have to settle for playing coaches—field managers with both selling responsibilities and supervisory responsibilities. When this happens, we should aim at one playing coach for every three or four full-time sales representatives. And the supervisor's account load should be small enough so that at least one-third of the time and possibly even one-half of the time can be spent working with salespeople.

Monetary Incentives

In spite of what we said earlier, monetary incentives have their place. In fact, in some industries they are traditional and it becomes difficult to recruit good sales help without them. They do have their attractions for both management and the sales force.

They reduce the fixed cost of the selling effort since some portion of the total selling expense is not incurred until a high level of sales has been achieved. The payout is based upon sales above that level. For the sales force, monetary incentives provide extra rewards for above-average performance and, hopefully, encourage more of it.

For cash incentives to work, careful planning and administration are required. A lot of work is involved. There are pitfalls and booby traps aplenty for the unwary.

Booby Traps

Many firms, without much thought, establish incentive plans which pay off on total volume a percentage of the increase above a predetermined level. Such plans encourage the sales force to go for the quantity of sales without regard for the quality of them. People go for the easy sale; they avoid the more difficult products, which are often the most profitable or newer products not yet generally accepted.

Typically, the payoffs are calculated as a percentage of total sales without regard for an upper limit on payoffs. Runaway situations and large windfalls are not uncommon. Caps are required. Sometimes they are in place before the event. More usually, they are established after the windfall. However, caps on money incentives are demotivators and tend to shut off extra effort once the caps have been reached. Therefore, as a general rule, it is often better to shrink the territory rather than to cap the incentive. This means that a sales representative will have to dig deeper, to work harder to achieve the same income.

Since salespeople expect their territories to be reduced, it is less bothersome and less demotivating than to place an obvious cap on possible incentive payoffs. This idea of shrinking the territory not the incentives is often called *Barry's second law.*

Similarly, firms pay off yearly on total annual sales. Sometimes annual payoffs are prompted by simple greed. Good quarters tend to balance poor quarters, and at the end of the year there may not be much to pay out. But there is a more significant problem. Since the awards are months away, when they are received, salespeople will have forgotten the specifics of what they did during a good quarter to cause their superior performance. There is no built-in encouragement to repeat success.

Further, many programs now in operation have remained the same from year to year, even though the firm's needs have changed. Such programs are taken for granted by all and really have no motivating effect whatsoever.

Finally, many programs fail simply because the sales representatives don't understand where they stand with respect to potential payoffs. The program doesn't tell them where extra effort will produce a larger payoff.

Since the goals of any program to motivate a sales force ought to be to reduce management's supervisory burden and to build profitable sales, it is surprising that so many firms continue to pay out under ineffective programs.

Many of the problems inherent in monetary incentive programs are readily solved. Some, as we shall see, require a bit more effort than others.

Basis for Payoffs

Total sales volume need not be the only basis for payoff. Provided there is enough money on the table, the plan can be as complicated as need be. The limiting factor is not the sales representative's ability to comprehend. Salespeople as a group can understand anything they have to understand. Rather, ease of administration is the limiting concern.

Good plans need a threshold beyond which the plan begins to operate. Typically the threshold would be some high percentage of the past year's performance, but not 100 percent. This eases the sales force into the plan's payoff area and encourages increased effort. Having to beat last year's total performance, especially if last year was a good one, can be discouraging—a definite demotivator. In establishing this triggering level, some consideration must be given to any adjustments that may be required to accommodate inflation, price increases, and similar concerns.

Beyond this volume trigger point, payoffs can be based on many things: the sale of individual products, product mix, acquisition of new accounts, controlling sales expense (expressed, of course, as a percent of sales rather than as a simple dollar figure), and many other things which may be important to the firm during the incentive period.

Payoffs need not be calculated as a percentage of sales. Salary-based programs in which the payoff is a percentage of salary have many advantages, not the least of which is a built-in but not so obvious cap on payouts. In this connection, one consideration is frequently overlooked: Salary is paid because a sales rep performs at a certain minimum level of accomplishment. If this level cannot be achieved and maintained, some kind of coaching and training may be required. If this is not successful, the sales rep must be replaced. As performance levels increase, salary levels should increase also. Incentives should be paid only for performance which exceeds these minimum levels of expected performance.

Windfall situations are readily solved with a little forethought. Since the type of program we suggest pays off for performance that beats the past year's, few salespeople would want a windfall folded into next year's quota. Nevertheless, some recognition must be given to the event. Credits can be established against future years' quotas. The most usual solution is a salary increase large enough to be significant.

The contrary problem must also be anticipated. What happens in a general market turndown? Or, how should you react when a reliable, superior producer, who had been expected to *win well*, doesn't do so because the territory has dried up. In these uncertain times, good accounts can go belly up, often without warning. When this happens, the effective response is to cut quotas for the entire sales force or for that individual and to increase territory size or otherwise find replacement potential.

Frequent Payoffs

As with any incentive program, incentive compensation for salespeople is a ring-the-bell, win-a-cigar proposition. Annual payoffs to the sales force, except in very unusual situations, thwart this imperative. More frequent quarterly awards, although they may seem to increase the administrative burden, solve this problem. They also permit the sales rep to fold the incentive payoffs into normal spending patterns. Thus there is an added motivation to sustain performance at a high level. Annual payoffs are treated as a windfall.

Since the firm's needs change from year to year, the compensation plan should change, too. Some plans make this difficult to accomplish. The only way a purely volume-based plan or a commission plan can change is through fiddling with the quotas, changing the commission rates, or redefining the territory. However, if incentives are awarded for several separate activities, changes are easily made by adjusting a portion of the plan, not the whole thing. Good plans change as needed, often quarterly.

Finally, a plan which pays off frequently for performance in a number of discrete areas considerably reduces administrative chores. Indeed, the plan can almost be self-administering. The sales force itself can keep track of its own progress toward achieving each of its goals. The supervisor will have an easier time making sure that it does. Problem performance areas will be highlighted, and the reason for improvement will be spelled out in dollars and cents.

Figure 21.6 illustrates such a plan. Here payoffs are for sales by product, individually and in total; for new account acquisition; and for controlling sales expenses. This plan is presented only as an example of

Figure 21.6. Incentive plan for territory sales representatives.

INCENTIVE COMPENSATION PLAN FOR
TERRITORY SALES REPRESENTATIVE—19 ____
(To be revised for _____ 19 ____)

Plan becomes effective only if territory sales for the quarter reach 90 percent of one-quarter of last year's total sales adjusted for inflation and price changes.

For sales performance:
- When total quarterly
  sales reach $_____ .... 5% of quarterly salary
Additionally:
- When product line A achieves
  its quarterly goal .... 2½% of quarterly salary
- When product line B achieves
  its quarterly goal .... 2½% of quarterly salary
- When product line C achieves
  its quarterly goal ....2½% of quarterly salary
- When product line D achieves
  its quarterly goal .... 2½% of quarterly salary
Further:
- When any three product lines
  achieve their quarterly goals,
  in addition to any of the above,
  an extra .... 5% of quarterly salary
- When all four product lines achieve
  their quarterly goals, in addition
  to the above, an extra............................10% of quarterly salary
- When the targeted product mix is
  achieved, in addition to the
  above, an extra............................20% of quarterly salary
- *Maximum bonus opportunity for
  Sales Performance*.................................50% of quarterly salary
For Administrative Performance:
- If five new accounts billing at
  least $20,000 quarterly are
  signed up, an additional............................5% of quarterly salary
- And for each additional new
  account billing at least
  $20,000 quarterly, an
  additional.................................2% of quarterly salary

(Continued)

what's possible. Developing such a plan for any firm requires careful analysis of past performances and testing under likely future situations.

However, a plan for sales reps is not enough.

No matter how good it may be, the sales rep's plan should be com-

Figure 21.6. (Continued)

INCENTIVE COMPENSATION PLAN FOR
TERRITORY SALES REPRESENTATIVE

And:
- If territory selling expenses
  (as a percent of sales) remain at
  or below last year's average
  for company as a whole, an
  additional..5% of quarterly salary
- And for each 1 percent territory
  selling expenses (as percent of sales)
  drop below last year's average,
  an additional ....1% of quarterly salary

---

plemented and reinforced by the plan for the supervisor, the district manager. Payoffs for the supervisor need not be as frequent. The district manager's salary should be considerably better than that of the typical sales representative. The need for more frequent payoffs isn't as keen. Response to management activity is always a little slower the further up the management ladder one moves. Under normal circumstances, the effectiveness of a sales representative is more quickly seen and measured than that of a supervisor.

Figure 21.7 illustrates a plan for field supervisors. It is an annual plan and complements the plan shown for territory sales representatives. Again, this is presented just to illustrate the possibilities. It is not something to be adopted and implemented without a close look at the situation it is to improve.

PROPOSED INCENTIVE COMPENSATION PLAN FOR
DISTRICT SALES MANAGER 19____
(To be revised for_____19____)
Plan becomes effective only when total sales for the year reach 90 percent of
last year's sales adjusted for inflation and price changes.

For Sales Performance
- When total sales reach $_____...5% of salary
Additionally:
- When four territories each achieve
three product goals for each quarter,
an additional..10% of salary
- When, in addition, a fifth territory
also achieves three product goals
for each quarter, an additional...15% of salary
- When, in addition, a sixth territory
also achieves three product goals
for each quarter, an additional...20% of salary
- Finally, when all seven territories
achieve three product goals for
each quarter, an additional..25% of salary
- *Maximum Bonus Opportunity for*
  Sales Performance...75% of salary

For Administrative Performance
Further:
- If contribution from district
sales is_____% or better,
an additional...5% of salary
- And for each percentage point district
contribution rises above_____%,
an additional...2% of salary
And:
- If district selling expenses (as a
percent of sales) remain at or below last
year's average for the company as a
whole..5% of salary
- And for each percentage point district selling
expenses (as a percent of sales) drop below
last year's average, an additional...1% of salary

Figure 21.7. Incentive plan for district managers.

PART 5

Measuring Marketing Effectiveness and Productivity

"We cannot solve one doubt without creating several new ones."   J. PRIESTLEY

Over the past few years, measuring the effectiveness and productivity of a sales & marketing effort has become an unnecessarily complicated issue. At times, it has been quite controversial. The complexity and the controversy arise from a few basic misunderstandings, a confusion of means and ends.

The cause of the present confusion seems to be this: there are two separate and distinct reasons for measuring sales & marketing effectiveness and productivity. One aims at giving line management operational control of the day-to-day income-producing efforts, especially selling. The other aims at assisting top management in evaluating the entire marketing process so that it can allocate resources and set goals. Each of these requirements has its own separate measurements and measuring techniques, and each has its own goals and needs.

Line sales management's concerns are primarily short-term, tactical in nature. Whatever else sales management may be asked to do, its most important task is to generate orders. To this end, it is concerned with deploying, developing, and utilizing individual salespeople to achieve the goals it has received from, or negotiated with, top management. Managers of the other functional responsibilities of marketing have other, similar concerns.

Top management's concerns, in contrast, are primarily long-range. It is concerned with the allocation of resources, the setting of long-range goals and targets, and the establishment of policies to guide the achievement of those goals.

These separate roles and interests have become confused. And as long as these two separate families of measurements and those two separate sets of needs and objectives are confused, measuring sales & marketing effectiveness and productivity will remain a complex and controversial issue. This confusion will continue to make for lively arguments. But it won't do much to relieve a situation which has become critical and which requires resolution.

This resolution is required by quite real and pressing needs. The economy is uncertain. Growth is exceedingly slow. Inflation is temporarily under control, and the costs of doing business may be stabilized. But sales costs themselves grow continually. For example, according to McGraw-Hill, during the 2-year period from 1977 to 1979, the cost of making a single sales call on an industrial customer rose by 42 percent, from $96.79 in 1977 to $137.02 in 1979. This is the largest single increase since 1942 when McGraw-Hill began keeping track of these costs. (Then it cost only $9 and change to make one call.) In the 4-year period from 1979 to 1983, the increase was nearly as large, 40 percent. Costs went from $137.02 to $205.40. By 1985 the cost had risen to $230.00 per call. Indications are that the increase beyond the 1987 figures, available in June of '88, will be a bit smaller. Further, McGraw-Hill also shows that today, five calls are required to close a typical sale; thus the cost of a field sales-generated order runs about $1150.

Studies of other types of selling confirm these trends and costs. Faced with this situation, the top management of many organizations has become concerned with the effectiveness of their marketing and selling efforts, perhaps for the first time. Chief executive officers, chief financial officers, and boards of directors want assurances that the corporate resources tied up in sales & marketing are providing an adequate and acceptable return.

Sales management, for its part, is increasingly concerned with maintaining operating control of the sales effort and giving it direction in the face of an economy and a marketplace which have changed. General sales managers, regional sales managers, zone managers, area managers, district managers, and even salespeople need assurances that they are doing what is required to meet the challenges and opportunities of the marketplace as well as to reach the sales goals and targets set for them by management. Measurement of the other twenty-two functional responsibilities of marketing is a sometime thing.

During the past few years, in an effort to put a handle on this situation, a number of powerful measurements have been proposed for determining the effectiveness and productivity of marketing & sales operations. As each new measure has been proposed, it comes with the suggestion, sometimes even the insistence, that it alone is the single, most important measure of productivity and effectiveness. And when applied, the results are often more Procrustean than effective or revealing.

Thus we have seen such measures as *return on capital employed* or *return on assets managed, closing ratios,* and *share of market* come into vogue, only to be replaced in time by another measure, another buzzword. The pendulum swings back and forth, reflecting alternately the concerns of top management and then the concerns of line management—and the real needs of neither.

The problem with each of these proposed measures of sales & marketing productivity and effectiveness is that each is concerned with only one aspect of the process and then from only one point of view. And, while every one of these proposed measures is indeed valid and necessary, none of them alone is sufficient.

What is required, of course, is not a single measure of productivity and effectiveness but a system of measurements which takes into account the entire marketing & selling process from the points of view of both top management and line management. Further, both levels of management need to understand the complete system. Top management must understand the kinds of measures necessary to achieve and maintain operational control of the many marketing functions. Line management must understand the measures required to enable top management to assess the entire marketing & sales process as a suitable investment for corporate resources. Anything less than this mutual understanding will lead not only to merely incomplete measurements, but to costly and mistaken efforts as well.

Here is a not-unusual case history that illustrates what can happen in the absence of such understanding. It concerns a major division of a very large consumer-products firm. Through aggressive salesmanship, clever promotions, very attractive deals, and the occasional acquisition of a competitor, the division came as close to dominating its market as the law would allow.

However, inflation had steadily eroded the division's contribution to corporate profits. Further, there was evidence that too much of the division's volume was being bought through cents-off deals of one kind or another. To correct the situation, it was decided to reorganize the sales force. Field sales managers, who until the reorganization had functioned primarily as key account salespeople, were relieved of all selling responsibility and asked to become real managers.

It was hoped that, by moving decision making and operational control of the sales effort into the field and turning the supersalespeople into managers, total volume might increase a bit and off-deal volume would increase considerably.

The reorganization was not accomplished overnight. New operating procedures had to be developed, and quite a bit of retraining was required to convert the key account salespeople into effective field managers. After about a year, the retraining had been completed, and the new operating procedures were in place and working well.

At this point, top management increased the volume and profitability goals it expected the division to achieve. However, preoccupied as it was with its new methods and procedures and its new ways of doing business, the division appeared slow in responding to the new demands. After about 6 months of impatient waiting, management scrapped the reorganization and reverted to previous ways. Yet, at the time this reversal was ordered, all regions had shown a steady increase in the number of sales calls made each day, a steady growth in the size of the orders being written on each call, and a steady increase in off-deal volume. Further, all the regions but one had shown a steady *decrease* in the costs of making sales calls.

Obviously, the situation just described is a classic case of misunderstanding and noncommunication. Situations like this happen all too frequently. Perhaps now the climate is right to make certain that they do not happen again.

What follows, therefore, is a review of all the requirements for measuring marketing and sales effectiveness and productivity.

First, we will take a look at the marketing & sales effort as a process with inputs and outputs.

Second, we will take a brief look at the kind of measures available for evaluating total sales effectiveness and productivity.

Third, we will review in some detail the kinds of measurements that line management should make of the selling process to secure operational control of it.

Fourth, we will take a look at the kinds of measures top management should use in its evaluation of the entire sales & marketing process.

Fifth, we will propose and review a few measurements of the incremental contributions made by each of the Twenty-five Common Functional Responsibilities of Marketing (see Chap. 4). Many of these are rarely, if ever, measured, and where measurement is attempted, there are few agreed-upon ways of doing so.

22

The Sales & Marketing Effort as a Measurable Process

A useful way of beginning our discussion of the marketing and selling operation as a measurable process is to draw an analogy between it and manufacturing. Like all analogies, this one can be misleading if it is pursued too far, but if viewed within some limits, it will be useful for clarifying a few aspects of the sales & marketing operation which are frequently misunderstood.

Most of us understand that manufacturing is a process that converts raw materials into merchantable products. Materials and labor are the basic *inputs*. Tangible products, meeting certain standards of acceptability, are the *outputs*. Similarly, it is generally understood that the job of manufacturing management is to optimize the productivity of the process. It is concerned with individual production units, their number and quality.

Top management's role is a little less well understood. It is concerned with aggregate numbers, and its role is to evaluate the entire manufacturing process along with its inputs and outputs to determine if it is a suitable investment for corporate resources. This is the continual *make-or-buy* decision of management. To this end, it sets certain goals and targets for manufacturing management to achieve, and it establishes policies to ensure that those goals and targets are achieved.

To be effective and to achieve its goals, manufacturing management must continually monitor, measure, and adjust its processes. To accomplish this, it provides close supervision and establishes programs for quality assurance, materials management, production control, value engineering, and so on—all aimed at increasing productivity, improving quality, and decreasing costs. For manufacturing management, measurement is a continuing endeavor.

Top management, however, needs to perform its evaluations only periodically. The frequency of these evaluations may be monthly, quarterly, semiannually, or annually—as often as significant information accumulates, but not so often as to interfere with either the process or the management of it. The more manufacturing management and top management understand each other's interests in, and methods for, measuring and evaluation, the easier it will be to achieve the goals and targets that have been established. Where such mutual understanding does not exist, we find such situations as the following:

This story concerns a major manufacturer of electronic equipment. One of its product lines, a major income producer, was an important component for equipment which others manufactured and sold. The market for the product line was healthy and growing, and the profits were good. After a while, a whole plant was devoted to making the product line. First only one shift was needed to meet the demand. Then two shifts were required.

Unfortunately, the manufacturing process itself was not very efficient. Only 60 percent of the output met the established standards for the product line. Fully 40 percent of the output had to be sold as scrap for whatever salvage value it could fetch.

However, the market for the product line continued to grow, and soon a third shift had to be added to keep up with demand. The third shift, however, was barely able to maintain the established ratio of marketable products to scrap material.

The outcome, of course, was predictable. Another manufacturer developed a similar product line, the output of a more efficient manufacturing process. Its reject rate was quite low, just above 7 percent. Since it did not have such high manufacturing costs, it could and did offer its product line at a much lower price while at the same time guaranteeing comparable or better performance than the original manufacturer. In due course, the newer firm took over the market, and the first firm had to abandon a major manufacturing facility and what had once been a very profitable product line.

People view this situation with astonishment and freely comment on the ineptitude of both top management and manufacturing management. Yet when similar things happen in a selling operation—territories abandoned, distribution centers closed, sales forces discharged—people shrug and comment philosophically about the nature of selling and the fickleness of the marketplace. Recently, for example, a major manufacturer suddenly discharged its entire sales force and turned the sale of its products over to manufacturers' representatives. The industry trade press hailed this as a shrewd move. What had happened was that management for the first time became aware of the costs of its sales operations and panicked.

The sales & marketing operation, too, is a process like manufacturing. Its inputs are many and varied as we shall see. Its outputs are sales that hopefully meet certain standards of acceptability. It is the task of line sales management to monitor, measure, and adjust just one part of the entire marketing process, *selling*, in order to optimize its productivity and effectiveness. In contrast, it is the task of top management to evaluate the entire marketing & sales effort—inputs, outputs, and process. And therein lies the root of the problem.

Line sales management is concerned with only one part of the entire sales & marketing process: sales calls, individually and in the aggregate. To be effective, its monitoring and measuring efforts must be continuous.

Top management, on the other hand, takes a broader view and is concerned with the entire sales & marketing process, the total contributions of all 25 functional responsibilities discussed in Chap. 4. As with all top-management measurements, unless there is an emergency situation, the evaluations of top management need only be performed periodically. Again, as with manufacturing, the frequency of these evaluations may be monthly, quarterly, semiannually, or annually—as often as significant data accumulates, but not so often as to interfere with the selling process or the management of it.

Corporate Inputs to the Selling Operation

There are two kinds of inputs into the sales process. One originates outside the sales department. These inputs originate, for example, from corporate management, from manufacturing, and, of course, from the other 22 functional responsibilities. As far as line sales management is concerned, these are the givens in the selling situation. Typically, they include most or all the items shown in Figure 22.1.

These are the givens in the day-to-day selling situation, and few line sales managers have any authority to change or adjust any of them. Making a change in any of them requires considerable justification and negotiation. A convincing case based upon need, opportunity, or expected return must be made before any of these inputs can be changed or adjusted.

Sales Department Inputs into the Sales Process

There are, however, other inputs into the process over which line sales management does have control. These are the inputs contributed by the salespeople themselves:

* Products
* Packaging
* Prices
* Delivery schedule
* Operating policies
* Marketing strategy
* Equipment
* Operating funds
* Customer service
* Goals and targets
* Advertising & sales promotion
* Leads and inquiries
* Warehouses and distribution facilities
* Dedicated inventories

Figure 22.1. Corporate inputs to the selling effort.

* Number of sales calls
* Allocation of sales calls
* Quality of sales calls

The sales department's basic inputs into the total marketing effort are sales calls. It is these which require monitoring, measuring, and adjusting. Sales management needs to be concerned with the number of calls being made, on whom they are being made, and the quality of those calls. Sales calls are the incremental inputs to the sales & marketing process just as a screw or a washer or an hour of machine time is an incremental input to the manufacturing process.

Sales calls are in very limited supply. Each salesperson has very few to convert into sales. People selling capital equipment and some types of services may, for example, be able to make only one or two calls a day. Industrial salesreps typically make only four or five per day— potentially, 1000 to 1200 calls per year. Those calling on certain kinds of retailers (supermarkets, for example) may have more, 10 to 15 per day—2000 to 3750 per year. Door-to-door canvassers may have more still. Some door-to-door salespeople—those selling kitchenware or cosmetics, for example, hold parties so that 15 or 20 prospects can be called on in the time it would take to call on several individuals.

In any case, the stock of available sales calls is finite. Further, unlike the sheet steel or the nuts and bolts of manufacturing, it is a time-sensitive inventory. Like airplane seats, berths on a cruise ship, or hotel rooms, once the day has passed, its supply of calls evaporates. Additionally, unlike material processed by manufacturing, unacceptable sales calls have no salvage value. They cannot be sold as scrap. A call either achieves its objective or it does not. Consequently, sales management (that is, the monitoring, measuring, and adjusting of sales calls) is, relatively, a much more critical activity than is manufacturing management.

Standards for acceptable sales calls must be established and each call made measured against those standards. This means standards for the number of sales calls made each day, standards for the allocation of those calls—how many to be invested with customers and with prospects of various types—and, finally, standards for the quality of each call. Then, through direct observation and the analysis of various records, appropriate adjustments can be made through training, coaching, redeployment, and the other control devices available to line sales management. Selling, however, is just part of the marketing process. We need to look at it all.

Available Measures of Total Marketing Productivity and Effectiveness

Over the years, four powerful measures have evolved for gauging the effectiveness of the total marketing process. Taken together, they give an accurate assessment of how well the total marketing effort pays off. Here is the traditional but somewhat nearsighted explanation of their significance.

Volume

Volume, of course, is the traditional measure of sales & marketing productivity. It is a rare sales manager or marketing vice president, who is not under constant pressure to get the volume up. Volume is the first figure in the annual report. Management keeps track of orders booked, orders shipped, and backlog. Major changes in the volume figures are the cause of all kinds of publicity about a firm.

Volume, even after all adjustments have been made for credits and returns, is merely a measure of the quantity of sales. Reliance on it as the sole measure of productivity and effectiveness leads to all the hazards of *single-fact* analysis. In addition to knowing about the quantity of sales, one needs to know a great deal about the quality of those sales. Additional measures are required.

Contribution to Profits

Contribution to profits is the next measure of productivity and effectiveness to be considered. We need to know that, when all the costs of bringing products to market have been attended to, there is something left over for overhead, reinvestment, and the shareholders.

Therefore, we measure contribution to profits by product and product lines, by customers of various types, by sales territories, districts, and regions, and even by various channels of distribution. Measured in these ways, contribution to profits shows where to direct the sales & marketing efforts. However, we could be enjoying both a healthy volume and a substantial contribution to profits and still not know enough about the quality of sales. Competition could still be beating our brains out in the marketplace.

Share of Market

Share of market data, therefore, becomes a very important measure of effectiveness and productivity. Many studies have shown that beneficial things follow from an increase in share of market. A firm's return on investment (ROI) seems to rise in direct proportion to a growth in share of market. The pioneering study of this relationship, the PIMS Study, showed that firms whose share of market was 7 percent or less had an average ROI of about 9 percent; while firms whose share of market topped 36 percent enjoyed an ROI upward of 30 percent.

Like Jack and Jill, market share and ROI go up the hill together. However, as its share of market increases, a firm becomes increasingly vulnerable to competitive activity. Maintaining market share becomes increasingly difficult. Further, if the market share becomes too large, the government gets involved and there is the risk of antitrust litigation.

If the importance of share requires any demonstration, the following illustration will do. The domestic cigarette market is around $18 billion. Reynolds and Phillip Morris each have more than a 30 percent share; of the other players, Brown & Williamson has 11 percent, Lorillard and American 8 or 9 percent, and Liggett about 6 percent. With a share point being worth $180 million, a small shift in sales performance can be significant.

For all these reasons, share of market is a critical measure of total effectiveness and productivity. However, even with volume, contribution to profits, and share-of-market figures, we still do not have a complete picture.

Return on Capital Employed

Return on capital employed, or return on assets managed (ROAM), as it is sometimes called, is the final measure. Every marketing and sales effort, no matter how small, involves the commitment of a portion of a firm's assets. Accounts receivable immediately come to mind. But there are other ways in which the marketing & sales process ties down capital. Warehouses, dedicated inventories, and distribution facilities require capital. The tools and equipment used by salespeople, their automobiles, demonstrators, samples, and the testing equipment they use also tie up capital. The advances paid to the sales force to cover expenses tie up additional capital. The list goes on. Further, every time a new sales territory is added, another increment of the firm's capital is added to the investment.

Funds deposited in an ordinary passbook account return from 5 to 7 percent annually. The same funds invested in money market certificates fetch a little more. Top management, therefore, is increasingly calculating the return on the capital employed in the sales & marketing effort. Calculations are being made for each sales territory, district, and region. Some firms calculate the return by product or product line and even by class of customer and channels of distribution. Based on such analyses, the marketing and sales effort is either restricted or expanded.

Absolute measures of marketing and sales effectiveness and productivity are:

- Volume

- Contribution to profits

- Share of market

- Return on capital employed

Taken together, these four measures provide an absolute assessment of sales & marketing effectiveness and productivity. However, as with all such definitive measures, it takes a long time to assemble the data and put it into a form that can be evaluated. Often, the time required to do so makes these measures useless to line sales managers for guiding the day-to-day selling efforts. Further, since these are all measures of the total sales & marketing efforts, they are, perhaps, irrelevant to the problems of managing the sales effort. Line sales management must look elsewhere for the information it needs. Fortunately, it doesn't have far to go.

Sales Control Ratios

Every sales force does or should generate on a daily or weekly basis all the information needed to control its activities, predict the outcome of its activities, and provide an early warning of developing changes in the marketplace. The sales force itself can or should generate the kind of ongoing feedback information which sales management needs for operational control of the selling effort.

Salespeople file weekly itineraries, call reports, expense reports, and written orders. They should also work against a list of customers and prospects, a sales call budget, a monthly or quarterly sales forecast, and a plan for achieving that forecast (see Chap. 19).

From the information contained in these reports, sales management can develop a number of measures—sales control ratios—which will provide reasonable current feedback on the performance of individual salespeople, sales districts, and sales regions. With this information in hand, a sales manager is able to make the necessary adjustments in the selling process to ensure that the optimum number of sales calls are being made, that they are being made on the right buying accounts and prospects, and that they are producing the desired results.

When this is done on a weekly and monthly basis, sales management will have all the information it needs for good control of the sales effort. And, just as important, when sales management does get its official volume figures, contribution-to-profits figures, share-of-market figure, and return-on-assets-managed figures, it will already know what they mean and why they are as they are.

Let's look at all this in detail.

23
Measuring Marketing Effectiveness to Establish Policy and Allocate Resources

As we have seen from the foregoing, line sales management is concerned with measuring sales effectiveness and productivity in order to achieve and maintain operational control over the day-to-day selling effort. Its goal is to achieve the objectives and targets which have been set for it or which have been negotiated. It is a goal to be achieved increment by increment.

Top management, in contrast, has another and broader interest in overall marketing effectiveness and productivity. It is concerned with the utilization of corporate resources and the allocation of them among several corporate functions. When considering marketing, top management is concerned with the development of new products or the abandonment of older products, with the development of new markets or the expansion or restriction of existing markets, and with the investment in new channels of distribution or the liquidation of existing channels of distribution. It measures marketing productivity with a view to allocating resources and establishing policy to guide the day-to-day marketing effort. Its concerns are long-range and strategic, whereas those of line management are short-term and tactical.

Even though both top management and line management begin their considerations with the same thing—volume—they soon diverge. The four complementary measures of marketing effectiveness—volume, contribution to profits, share of market, and return on capital employed—taken together, are long-term considerations. It is not in the nature of things that they become tactical considerations.

These four measures may, however, influence day-to-day decisions. Contribution to profit figures may dictate an optimum product mix for line management to strive for. Similarly, share of market data may influence the way the sales effort is deployed. But these decisions are made at the top and come to the sales force by way of policy guidelines.

Following is a review of each of these traditional measures of sales & marketing effectiveness and productivity and a discussion of how and why they are necessarily strategic, and not tactical, considerations.

Net Volume

What is of concern here is net volume, which equals total sales less returns and credits of one kind or another.

This is the official volume figure with which a firm goes public, the first number in its annual report.

Net volume figures are hard to come by on any kind of current basis. By the time the value of credits and returns for a period have been calculated and subtracted from the sales for that period, weeks and even months will have passed. Because of the work involved, net volume figures are calculated only infrequently: quarterly, semiannually, or annually. Since aggregate numbers are what is important here, not day-to-day trends, more frequent calculations are unnecessary.

Net volume figures should be calculated by product or product lines (some firms use the term *product families*), customer classification, territory, and channel of distribution. Depending upon the industry, such a breakdown by channels of distribution might be as follows: direct versus distributor sales; grocery, drug, variety, or discount stores might be another channel; and even department, specialty, or discount stores yet another. Knowing the difference between sales and net sales is critical information, but it comes too late to guide the day-to-day selling effort.

Contribution to Profits

Net volume figures by product or product lines and by customer type, territory, and channels of distribution are only the beginning. We need to know how profitable those sales are.

Contribution to profit figures show which products to sell and which to drop, downplay, or reformulate. These figures show which customers to go after and which to avoid, which territories are in trouble and which are thriving, and which channels of distribution to develop and which to abandon or improve.

Fig. 23.1 provides a worksheet for calculating contribution from whatever area is required: product, territory, channel, and so on. The

Contribution Work Sheet—Direct Costing
(Calculate by product, by customer type, by territory, etc.)

				Total
1. Gross sales	—	—	—	—
2. Adjustments	—	—	—	—
3. Net sales	—	—	—	—
4. Cost of goods sold	—	—	—	—
5. Gross margin	—	—	—	—
6. Gross margin as percent of net sales	—	—	—	—
7. Assigned fixed costs:	—	—	—	—
Manufacturing	—	—	—	—
Marketing	—	—	—	—
Other	—	—	—	—
Total assigned fixed costs	—	—	—	—
8. Contribution	—	—	—	—
9. Contribution as percent of net sales	—	—	—	—
10. Assets assigned:				
Manufacturing	—	—	—	—
Marketing	—	—	—	—
Other	—	—	—	—
Total assets assigned	—	—	—	—
11. Turnover of assigned assets	—	—	—	—
12. Contribution as percent of assigned assets	—	—	—	—
13. Unassigned fixed costs				—
14. Operating profit				—
15. Cost of borrowed capital				—
16. Earnings before taxes				—
17. Income tax				—
18. Earnings after taxes				—
19. Net cost of borrowed capital				—
20. Total earnings				—

      Total capital employed _____
      ROI   _____

Figure 23.1. Contributions worksheet—direct costing.

methods to be used are those discussed in the chapters on pricing (see, especially, Chap. 13).

From the foregoing, it should be clear that establishing a procedure for determining contribution to profits will take a bit of doing. However, once the procedure has been established, modern EDP technology should make the calculations relatively simple. Such reports should be available quarterly or semiannually and within months of the end of a sales period.

Share of Market

Share-of-market data adds a considerable dimension to the view of sales & marketing performance. This information tells not only how one is doing in relationship to the market's potential for absorbing what is produced and sold, but it tells how one is doing in relationship to competitors.

Unfortunately, accurate share-of-market data is hard to come by, especially share-of-market data that is reasonably current.

Only the automobile industry has reasonably accurate and current share-of-market data. R, L. Polk and Wards see to that for cars and trucks. It is interesting to note that even though the PIMS study had long since demonstrated the relationship between ROI and market share, Detroit watched its market share decline week in and week out for several years before making any adjustments in its offerings. Thus, the single industry with the most accurate and current share-of-market data made little use of it. The quality of this industry's share-of-market data may be illustrated by the fact that on January 7, 1986, complete figures for the year 1985 were reported on the business pages of the daily press. Figures for later years were not so available.

A few other industries are reasonably well served in this regard. The Industrial Truck Association provides reasonably accurate and almost current data on some kinds of materials handling equipment. Neilsen and Towne-Oller give the grocery trades reasonably accurate share-of-market data about 3 months after the close of a quarter. And some segments of the engineering-construction industry have reasonably accurate share-of-market data thanks to McGraw-Hill's *Dodge Reports.*

Occasionally, special situations not only provide complete figures on the size of the market but make share figures easy to calculate. For example, not long ago, the EPA identified the 50 fossil-fuel power plants that contributed most to the acid rain problem. Also identified were the handful of engineering-constructors qualified to design and install the required scrubbers. Not only was the market defined but the players identified. Share-of-market figures become immediately obvious as each retrofitting contract is signed.

Most firms rely on share-of-market data laboriously gathered. It is never very accurate, and it is available only well after the fact. If a company has the previous year's figures by the following June, it considers itself to be very lucky indeed. When firms get whatever information they can, it comes too late to be of any value in guiding day-to-day selling activities.

Although the demonstrated relationship between share of market and ROI provides an interesting historical perspective, and such information may be useful for setting long-term goals and for establishing policy, this data proves of little use in guiding a day-to-day marketing effort.

A more useful concept at the sales management level is *share of customer's potential.* This is a much looser measure, to be sure, but more useful in expanding customer usage and, ultimately, in increasing market share. It requires that field sales representatives estimate the potential of *each* customer to absorb their products (see Chap. 19). These estimates are then used to establish sales goals for each account and to measure account penetration.

Return on Capital Employed, Return on Assets Managed (ROAM)

The final measure of sales & marketing effectiveness measures the rate of return on corporate assets tied up in sales & marketing activities. It allows one to compare the productivity of these funds with the productivity of other funds tied up in other corporate activities. More importantly, however, by calculating a rate of return on assets allocated by products, customer type, territory, and channels of distribution, management has a very precise means of comparing their productivity. This yields a sure guide to eliminating or strengthening the less productive aspects of the sales & marketing operation and to extending and expanding those which are most productive.

Identifying the assets tied up in the sales & marketing operation is not always easy; determining their value is often difficult. Some are readily identified and their value established—receivables, for example, are easy to pin down. Others are more difficult since some are unsegregated and others are expensed off.

A typical sales & marketing operation will tie up corporate funds in many of the ways shown in Fig. 23.2. Determining which investments

* Receivables
* Dedicated inventories (consignments)
* Warehousing and distribution facilities
* Offices' leasehold improvements
* Special equipment (office, test, demonstration, etc.)
* Automobiles
* Expense advances

Figure 23.2. Typical sales & marketing capital accounts.

are to be assigned to sales & marketing can become a problem. Generally, if the investment would have been made had there been no sales & marketing operation, it shouldn't be allocated to sales & marketing. Packaging materials and equipment are, for example, chargeable to manufacturing the cost of goods.

Although there are many ways to calculate the return on the capital employed in marketing operation, the method shown in Fig. 23.3 is preferred. This is a truncated form of the procedure outlined in Chap. 13.

It permits a direct comparison of all the items that go into the calculation and makes it easy to locate the causes of significant variations.

	Region 1	Region 2	Region 3	Total
1. Sales (net volume)	$100,000	$100,000	$100,000	$300,000
2. Cost of goods	45,000	45,000	45,000	135,000
3. Gross profit	55,000	55,000	55,000	165,000
4. Fixed costs	25,000	25,000	25,000	75,000
5. Contribution to profits	$ 30,000	$ 30,000	$ 30,000	$ 90,000
6. Assets assigned	$ 12,000	$ 18,000	$ 24,000	$ 54,000
Inventory	30,000	12,000	3,000	45,000
Display equipment	8,000	5,000	1,000	14,000
Assets assigned	$ 50,000	$ 35,000	$ 28,000	$113,000
7. Contribution as a percent of sales (line 5 divided by line 1)	30%	30%	30%	30%
8. Turnover of assigned assets (line 1 divided by line 6)	2X	2.9X	3.6X	2.6X
9. Return on assigned assets (line 7 multiplied by line 8).	60%	87%	108%	78%

Figure 23.3. Return on capital employed.

This method requires the calculation of *turnover of assigned assets,* a critical point of comparison.

The situation presented in Fig. 23.3 is based on the experience of a manufacturer who achieved his distribution by placing goods on consignment with distributors. The firm supports sales through heavy advertising. The figures, much simplified, show the performance for one quarter of three regions which make up a zone. From this analysis of the three regions, it is obvious that while the regional manager's contribution seem identical, there is little similarity beyond that.

Region 1 uses $50,000 of company assets and returns 60 percent; region 2 uses $35,000 and returns 87 percent; while region 3 uses only $28,000 and returns 108 percent. From this it would appear that region 3 is the most productive for the firm. However, a glance at how this region generates its return raises a number of questions. Its receivables nearly equal the contribution it generates and its inventory can support little more than 2 days' sales. Although at first region 3 seems to be the most attractive, closer examination shows that it is operating too close to the edge. If the receivables turn sour or if a delivery is missed, there will be serious trouble.

In contrast, region 1 seems to be too conservatively managed. It maintains nearly a month's inventory; it has the largest number of displays out, but the lowest receivables. On balance, region 2 seems to be the one to emulate. What management must do to bring the other regions into line is clear.

Analyses like this are readily made using modern computer technology. Data is usually available. Once a procedure has been established for identifying and allocating capital accounts by product, customer type, territory, and channels of distribution, results are easy to come by. The problem seems to be to determine when such analyses are justified and necessary. Although the value of such analyses has been demonstrated in one situation, not all sales forces place so much at risk.

Until a firm gets accustomed to using this method of measurement, such an analysis should be made each year by major product groups, major customer classification—territory or district, and channels of distribution. Then, depending upon what such analyses have shown, attention can be focused on one area or another, and more frequent analyses can made. It should be pointed out that such measurements will be available only weeks or months after the fact. They will, therefore, be useless for guiding the day-to-day sales activities.

24

Measuring Sales Effectiveness for Operational Control

From the information supplied each week by the field, sales management is able to calculate a number of control ratios. How these ratios compare with each other and how they vary over time gives line management all the information it needs to control the day-to-day selling activities of the field force, to predict the outcome of those efforts, and to make whatever adjustments are required.

Control Ratios

The list given in Fig. 24.1 suggests a few of the kinds of control ratios that may be calculated. However, there are a great many other ratios that can also be derived from field-generated data. These additional ratios will suggest themselves as sales management gets used to this kind of measuring and control. No two sales forces will have the same list, and no sales force will continue to track the same ratios all the time.

Special Ratios

The need for tracking special ratios is easily illustrated. For firms which manufacture process-consumables or make-or-buy consumables, it will be important to keep track of the number of initial tests or pilot plant tests of their products that are in progress and of the number of product approvals. Tests per territory will be a significant ratio to track, since such data are critical indicators of future business.

Here is another illustration of the kinds of special ratios possible. Firms which sell through manufacturers' representatives will be unable to keep track of the three basic ratios. Managing the sales effort is, of

1. Calls per day
2. Sales per call
3. Costs per call
4. Calls per order
5. Sales to costs
6. Leads converted to leads supplied
7. Sales per account
8. Selling time to nonselling time
9. Entertainment costs to sales
10. Prospect calls to total calls
11. Scheduled calls to nonscheduled calls
12. Territory sales to total sales
13. Sales to quota
14. Calls on buying influences to calls on decision makers

Figure 24.1. Sales control ratios.

course, the responsibility of the representing firm. The principal can, however, keep track of such ratios as performance against quota or forecast, conversion of leads furnished to RFQs, and the conversion of RFQs to purchase orders.

When distributors and manufacturer's representatives are involved, the sales management problems are theirs, not the principal's. In most situations, however, it is necessary for sales management to keep track of the first three ratios shown in Fig. 24.1 plus a few more.

Three Basic Ratios

Let us take a close look at how the first three ratios in Fig. 24.1 provide the basic information needed to guide the sales effort. As we become familiar with these three ratios, we will also begin to see which of the other possible control ratios may be required to provide the additional information needed for control.

Calls Per Day

The first ratio is, of course, calls per day. This is where the action begins. Nothing happens until the seller and the buyer get together, nothing happens unless the salesperson calls on the prospect.

It is axiomatic in selling that the more calls a salesperson makes, the more will be sold. It is sales management's goal, therefore, to pressure and encourage salespeople to increase the number of calls they make each day and each week. If a sales representative now makes four calls per day, the goal should be to increase that number to five. If the average is now five calls per day, sales management's objective should be to increase that number to six. The pressure and the encouragement should be applied continually.

Expectations, however, must be restrained by reason. There is a limit to the number of effective calls a salesperson can make. At some number of calls per day, the law of diminishing returns begins to take over, and each call becomes less productive. That point varies from one salesperson to another and from one situation to another. Further, the number of effective sales calls that can be made each day varies with the type of business and the complexity of the sale. A door-to-door canvasser (the Fuller Brush man) can make many more calls per day than a salesperson whose goal is to sell a turnkey construction project for a new plant.

Sale per Call

Thus, while it is very important to calculate and monitor the calls-per-day ratio, one must also calculate and monitor the second ratio on the list, the sales-per-call ratio. There is no use getting salespeople to make more calls per day if those additional calls do not add a respectable increment to sales.

The sales-per-call ratio can be calculated in a number of ways. The total dollar value for the orders written during a week can be determined and divided by the number of sales calls made. Dollars of sales per sales call is the most common form this ratio takes. However, some sales operations find it more convenient instead to keep track of production units sold. This is especially true where manufacturing capability is limited and shop loading is critical. Some men's clothing manufacturers, for example, keep track of sales units, with a suit being two units and a jacket or a pair of trousers as one unit each. Management's goal should be to keep increasing the value of this ratio.

Costs Per Call

Finally, we need to calculate and monitor the third of the basic ratios, the cost-per-call ratio. Here we are concerned with only those costs over which the salesperson has control, the costs reported on the weekly expense report. These costs include such things as travel, entertainment, telephone charges, postage, and in some cases, samples. This ratio, cost per call, is rarely calculated, even though it provides sales management with key leverage for increasing the contribution to profits of the sales effort. Cost control is an accepted part of manufacturing management; few sales operations, however, seem as concerned. Obviously, management's goal here is to force this ratio down without lessening effectiveness.

Reading Results

Figure 24.2 presents a set of hypothetical ratios and an average for each ratio. At first glance, one might be tempted to draw what seem to be obvious conclusions; for example, that Territory B was in trouble. To do so, however, would be misleading. There may be good and sufficient reason for such a spread in these performance indicators. For example, territory A might be a mature metropolitan market. Territory B might be a missionary territory. And territory C might be a mature rural-suburban territory.

These numbers are significant only when one observes how they change over time, when one sees how they vary and compares the variations with other inputs to the sales & marketing process. However, if the variations cannot be accounted for in this way, one should begin to find out the reason for it.

Perspectives, norms, and trends develop over a period of weeks and/or months. It is for this reason that when such a system of measurement and control is instituted, it is helpful to use available company data and calculate a few historical averages to provide a reference for the current data.

The point here is that after a few weeks, a database will be established and norms and trends will become obvious. Then and only then will management be able to use the information provided to guide the day-to-day sales effort.

	Calls per day	Sales per call	Costs per call
Territory A	6	$660	$ 90
Territory B	7	400	102
Territory C	4	580	195
Average	5	530	120

Figure 24.2. Basic ratios—initial calculations.

Graphic Displays

When displayed in graphic form, data on the three basic ratios gathered over several weeks or months might appear as shown in Fig. 24.3. Here we see costs per call rising rather rapidly, sales per call rising only modestly, and calls per day remaining quite constant. Each of these trends may be significant. Certainly, each requires a little analysis and investigation.

Just looking at this graphic display prompts certain questions:

- Why are the costs of making sales calls rising so rapidly?
- Why are sales per call rising only modestly, barely keeping up with inflation or growth targets?
- Why is the number of calls per day remaining constant?

It is here that other ratios come into play.

To gain insight into the causes of the rising costs of making sales calls, we could calculate such ratios as these:

- Entertainment costs to sales
- Scheduled calls to nonscheduled calls
- Calls on buying influences to calls on decision makers

We may get some insight into the reasons why sales per call are increasing only modestly by calculating such ratios as

- Calls per order
- Prospect calls to total calls

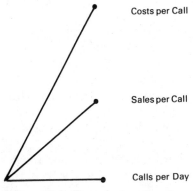

Figure 24.3. Three basic ratios over time.

• Sales per account

And to help us understand why there have been no improvements in the calls-per-day ratio, we might calculate such ratios as:

• Selling time to nonselling time
• Prospect calls to total calls
• Scheduled calls to nonscheduled calls

Alternatively, we could also calculate these same basic ratios by region, district, or territory, and, in this way, try to locate variations and the causes of these trends.

A situation like that shown in Fig. 24.3 may spell trouble. However, it could also indicate that things are going according to plan. For example, suppose that the sales force, whose performance is depicted here, is introducing a major new product, one that requires considerable lead time to the first sale, that requires time to sell its concept, more time to sell its benefits, and, then, more time to write the orders. Suppose further, that selling the product involves reaching other departments than those usually called on and requires taking two or three people to lunch rather than just one.

Under such circumstances, management would expect to see the cost-per-call ratio increase and would be pleased to see only a modest increase in regular sales. A management could even be surprised that the calls-per-day ratio had not decreased somewhat.

Under such circumstances management would not be alarmed by what the chart shows but would eagerly await signs that the effort was beginning to pay off. And as the payoff came, one would expect to see a decline in the costs per call, an increase in the sales per call, and maybe even an increase in the number of calls per day, as shown in Fig. 24.4.

The point of all this is a simple one. These methods of ratio analysis, based upon information which the sales force itself generates each day and each week, give sales management current feedback on what is happening in the marketplace and hence managerial control of it. There really is no need to wait for the more traditional measures of performance which are generated by others, which arrive too late to reflect current conditions, and which, in any case, may be irrelevant to the day-to-day problems of sales management.

Beyond this, however, there are a number of other advantages for everyone. These considerably extend and broaden the method's usefulness. The techniques themselves are simple.

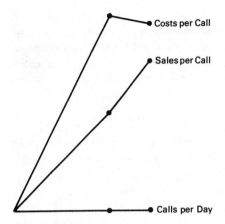

Figure 24.4. Three basic ratios over time—
payoffs begin.

Using Results

Once the key ratios have been identified, individual salespeople can keep track of their own performance. And once norms and trends have been established for regions, districts, and individuals, performance standards and improvement goals are easily established, and performance evaluations are simple to manage.

Additionally, this method of charting and keeping track of performance has a number of advantages for first-line supervision. By keeping track of the performance of individuals as well as averages for the group, the district manager has a ready-made series of goals for the salespeople to achieve. The district manager knows who needs assistance, the kind of assistance that is needed, and how to adjust territory boundaries to equalize work load and opportunity.

The same kinds of benefits accrue at each higher level of management. Regional managers have a ready means of evaluating the performance of both districts and district managers. Specific goals are easy to establish and performance evaluations can be made continuously and on a current basis.

One example will serve to illustrate the usefulness of these measures. Assume that through this kind of ongoing analysis it is discovered that the sales force does, on average, require 4.5 sales calls before writing an order. The McGraw-Hill studies suggest that this would be typical in industrial selling. A normal sales management goal would be to try to bring this ratio down to 4.0 or to 3.5, or even to 3.0. Now that it has identified a goal, it must plan how to achieve it. There are many options.

A direct-mail advertising campaign to customers and prospects might get the benefit story across to them independently of the direct effort of the salespeople. Thus, individual salespeople would not be required to spend so much face-to-face selling time conveying that story. The calls-per-order ratio should go down. Experience shows that a carefully coordinated program of direct-mail advertising and face-to-face sales calls does indeed accomplish this goal.

Another option is to equip all salespeople with an organized sales presentation (a pitch book) and train them in its use. In this way, each field person is guided in what is presented to customers and prospects. Nothing is left to chance. By improving the quality of each sales call, as this approach does, fewer calls will be required to make a sale.

Figure 24.5 summarizes a few of the options available to sales management for improving the basic cost and control ratios. The skill of the first-line supervisors makes the difference here.

Implementing the Ratio Analysis Method of Control

Although the advantages to sales force management of this approach are obvious, there are a number of practical problems to be solved in

Ratio	Objective	Possibilities
Calls per day	Increase	• Routing, better planning of territory coverage • Reducing length of calls • Reducing paperwork and administrative chores
Sales per call	Increase	• Improving quality of calls • Providing better advertising support • Better selection of accounts called on
Cost per call	Decrease	• Routing, better planning of territory coverage • Coordinating advertising with calling effort • Reducing length of calls

Figure 24.5. Improving field sales performance.

getting such a system of managerial controls up and running. The biggest problems involve time, discipline, and the management of accumulated data. These are not as formidable as they might seem at first.

Time is required to accumulate sufficient data so that norms and trends emerge at all reporting levels. This is, at most, a matter of weeks or months. However, it may take a couple of years for any seasonal variations in the selling process to become apparent; assuming, of course, a stable market.

Discipline is the second practical consideration. The requirement here is not the imposition of a new record-keeping burden on the field salespeople, merely the insistence that they do what they should be doing under any circumstance.

Assembling Data

In most sales forces, it is customary for salespeople to check in by telephone with their supervisors at least once a week. This is usually done at the end of the week, after all reports and records of the week's activities have been completed and brought up to date. This oral review of the past week's activities and the plans for the next week's activities is a critical part of management's control. It is a simple matter to build into this weekly review process the reporting of a few simple numbers that summarize key aspects of the past week's activities.

Figure 24.6 shows a simple data assembly form which can be used for this purpose. The same basic form can be used by individual salespeople in reporting to a district manager, by a district manager in reporting to a regional supervisor, and so on up the line. Since, with possibly one exception, the information required is already shown on one report or another, the only extra effort required is assembling it and relaying it by phone.

The possible exception concerns time utilization. Very few firms keep track of how their field people utilize available time. Doing so is, however, common practice in a number of industries. Many grocery product and health and beauty aids salespeople, for example, are required to keep track of and report such information.

With the information suggested in Fig. 24.6 reported weekly by salespeople to their district managers, the basic ratios for the district can be readily calculated. When the district managers, in turn, make their weekly telephone reports to their supervisors, they have the basic data for their districts. And so it goes up the line. By Monday afternoon or Tuesday morning at the latest, the general sales manager would have a complete and accurate picture of both the past week's activities and of the results they have produced.

As far as accuracy is concerned, simple audit procedures are easily es-

Orders written:

Number of orders   —————

Total dollars (units)   —————

Sales calls:

Total calls made   —————

Scheduled calls   —————

Nonscheduled calls   —————

Sales costs:

Total expenses   —————

Entertainment   —————

Mileage   —————

Time utilization:

Total hours worked   —————

Sales time   —————

Travel time   —————

Administrative time   —————

Quota performance:

Quota   —————

Achievement to date   —————

Figure 24.6. Data assembly reporting form.

tablished. These procedures are readily added to the regular review of the written reports submitted and to the normal review of records that takes place whenever a district manager spends time with a salesperson or a regional manager makes periodic visits with the district managers.

Managing Accumulated Data

This leaves just one practical consideration to discuss: the management of the enormous amount of data accumulated over time. There are only a couple of points to be made here. Since this is the age of computers, many managers may be tempted to store the basic data in a computer for use at some future date. Modern computer technology makes all this quite possible. However, there are a couple of important cautions.

The first is that the process of logging data onto tapes or disks should not get in the way of making the basic information available to management in a timely fashion. Perhaps an illustration might help prove this point. A large, well-known firm has an elaborate system for capturing and analyzing the type of information under discussion. Salespeople record this relevant information on special forms which can be read by optical scanners. These forms are mailed weekly from all over the country to a central processing unit. There, a gigantic computer processes all the data and issues comprehensive, seemingly useful reports. These reports are sent back to the district, regional, and zone offices where the data originated, and a summary report is sent to headquarters.

Unfortunately, these magnificent reports arrive 5 or 6 weeks after the close of the period being analyzed, making them interesting historical documents but useless management tools. In the process of taking advantage of computer technology, what had been a simple and useful telephone reporting system was converted into another useless pile of zebra sheets.

So the caution here is: computerize if you must but make sure that the computerized system of analysis and reporting remains an *adjunct* or *supplement* to the basic telephone reporting system described above. Immediacy is just one advantage of such telephone reporting. The chance to discuss data as it is reported is an even bigger advantage.

The second caution concerns the way the basic information is entered into the computer. Make sure that the person doing the initial programming establishes a true database. Every piece of information entered into the computer should be retrievable as entered. Further, each piece of information should have the capability of being compared with, added to, multiplied by, subtracted from and divided by every other piece of information. To let a straitjacketing program limit access to and use of stored information will defeat the purpose of computerization.

As a general rule, if management has confidence in the information being reported by telephone and in the written records and graphs generated from it, independent computerization is unnecessary. Prudence may require separate working and file copies, but more than this is rarely required. After all, the objective is managerial not archival.

25

Measuring the Performance of the 25 Functional Marketing Responsibilities

As the foregoing has suggested, the most common measures of marketing effectiveness are applied to either the major sales effort—outside salespeople for most of us—or to the entire marketing effort. For the most part, these measures are used as part of a system of rewards and penalties. Less so as planning tools. The other 22 or 23 marketing functions are not subjected to any measurement.

There are reasons for this situation. In part, it results from the fact that until recently these many and varied responsibilities have rarely seemed important enough to require measurement. After all, a growing market hides many inefficiencies even if the growth is provided by inflation. In part, the situation also occurs because it is fairly hard to figure out appropriate measures for many of these functions, let alone discover suitable ways of applying them.

However, in an era when significant breakthroughs are rare and profit growth from the sales of superior products and services is hard to come by, one has to look for contributions wherever they can be found. These can come only from incremental improvements in each of the 25 functional responsibilities of marketing.

Although the goal is to optimize the contribution from each of the 25, the real challenge is to develop reasonable performance measures for each of them—objective and well-understood measures based upon data available to both management and the people whose efforts are being measured. The difficulty in developing these measures is compounded by the fact that they will change from served market to served market.

In what follows, we'll take a look at each of the common marketing functions and suggest a few measurements that may be appropriate. As we do, we should bear in mind that in addition to measuring the performance of people in specific markets against specific criteria, we are also measuring the performance of products and of markets and of product-market combination. As we do, we will accumulate information about high performers, average performers, and poor performers. The high performers show us what is possible. The mediocre and poor performers will show where improvements are necessary and possible. Discovering the reasons for superior performance will provide us with the clues necessary for improving the performance of others.

The list of functions to be discussed is a long one, and it may be a drag getting through them all. I could shorten the effort considerably by leaving out those where there are no generally accepted measures of effectiveness and productivity. But while each of these functions may not be important in every served market, each of them will be important in some served markets.

1. Product Design and Development

Product design and development is concerned with a mix of products, some new, some established, and some being reengineered or reformulated for reduced costs and improved quality.

Many studies have shown that successful firms generate about 10 percent of their volume from products that have been on the market for less than 3 years. These are truly new products, not merely established products in a new color or new size. Some firms have higher expectations than 10 percent in this area because a new-product orientation is built into the way they do things. For most of us, however, new products can represent a serious distraction from core business. A more modest goal—the 10 percent figure—for new-product contributions to revenue is recommended.

For all products—established products, new products, and those being reengineered and reformulated—the goal ought to be longevity in the marketplace. Thinking about product life cycles is dangerous and counterproductive. The life cycle idea produces a built-in bias toward cheaper products of inferior quality which eventually will be sold at price alone. Rather than this, the goal should be high-quality products with long lives which become the staples of the markets they serve: They should become our own Scotch Tape, Ivory Soap, Campbell's Tomato Soup, Swingline Staples, or Kodacolor Film.

The measures here are product longevity, volume growth, and new-product volume. Market-share measurements are also most useful if we are able to assemble the data and trust its reliability.

2. Market Identification and Development

Market identification and development is concerned with the quality of the markets served, not the quality of the products serving them. Our concern should be as much with the overall market as with the customers that make it up. Several aspects of growth become important: growth in volume, growth in the number of customers, growth in the number of identifiable prospects, and, unfortunately, growth in competitive activity.

Other measures here are also important. They range from contribution, as discussed in Chap. 23, to the amount of trouble it takes to sell and service these markets.

Most of us would like to reduce the amount of paperwork associated with a transaction to a minimum. The federal government and especially the Department of Defense seem to have opposite views. Procurement procedures and contract administration place enormous burdens on the vendor. This is an essential characteristic of these markets. Many potential vendors cannot afford to become involved or do not care to become involved, with such burdens, and so they avoid these markets.

Homogeneity of a market is important. The greater the similarity of problems and needs, the more focused and effective the marketing effort can be. Even credit worthiness of customers making up a market segment is a measurable consideration.

3. Strategy, Positioning, and Product Surrounds

Except in very subjective ways, direct measurement of the immediate effectiveness of strategy and positioning is difficult. However, volume growth at the most profitable end of the line plus product advertising that cannot be mistaken for that of a competitor may be useful measures. Certainly, in the longer term, measures of market share, the capture and holding of important accounts, and penetration of new accounts in targeted markets are useful.

4. Packaging

With packaging measurement is growth in volume and in the number of new customers—customers whose profile is significantly different from that of customers currently being served. Performance vis-à-vis the competition in limited markets, acquisition of shelf space in retail channels, and in-store placements may all relate to the quality of packaging.

The basic rules of packaging—protection during shipment and prolonging shelf life—should not be overlooked.

5. Pricing

The goal for pricing is to identify those product-market combinations which permit the firm to realize its targeted rate-of-return on all the capital employed. The requirement here is for direct, not absorption, costing and for the identification of those product-market combinations which permit full markups. Those which do not may indicate situations that require repositioning and repackaging to support wider margins, or redesign or reformulation to reduce costs or even abandonment.

6. Advertising

When we discuss advertising, we are talking about using the media to create a preference in an identifiable market for a specific product or service. One measure, although a somewhat subjective one, is the observable difference between one's own advertisements and those of the competition. There should be no confusion between theirs and ours. Rosser Reeves referred to this difference as a unique selling proposition. More useful measures, however, are to be found when advertisements to support a particular product in a specific market are given definite jobs to do—increase order size, reduce the number of sales calls to an order, or speed the acceptance of a new product. Measures can then be established and data analyzed to determine whether desired results are being obtained.

7. Sales Promotion

Since the purpose of sales promotion is to get action in a particular market on behalf of a specific product, measurements are easy to come by. Such measurements include increased product movement, a permanent gain in the rate of sales, and the costs of the increase, to name but a few.

8. Lead Generation

The goal of lead generation is to have people say, "Tell me more." The cost of leads is high. We want as low a cost per lead as possible consistent with a high conversion rate. We need to know by product and market the number of leads generated by source, their costs, the organization level reached by the effort, the number of casual inquirers versus prospects, the conversion rate, and the time intervals between the effort, the receipt of the inquiry, and the action.

9. Physical Distribution

The goal of physical distribution is to prevent a customer from gaining experience with a competitive product or from interrupting a favorable buying habit. Either of these developments may occur when our product is not available when the customer is ready to buy. The prime measures of this activity are changes in traditional buying patterns, out-of-stock reports, lost-business reports, and forecast versus sales figures.

10. Outside Sales

The measures of outside sales are many and varied and should be selected by market to reflect the number of calls, the quality of calls, and the allocation of calls. These measures will take the form of control ratios of one sort or another which by themselves sales representatives can compute and which district, regional, and national sales managers can compute from itineraries and call reports.

Typical of such ratios are calls per day, calls per order, total selling time per order or per dollar, dollars or units per order, cost per call, and the conversion rates of prospects to customers.

In some kinds of selling, trial orders and samples undergoing tests are important indicators of future business and must be tracked.

For a fuller discussion of outside sales, see Chap. 24.

11. Inside Sales

Inside sales require the same kinds of measures with some adjustments for the type of sales effort. If the inside sales effort takes the form of responses to inquiries by other means, additional measures will be required (as in Item 8 above). These measures will aim at evaluating the lead sources. Other inside sales activities actively solicit business from customers and accounts of known creditworthiness. Standard products and fill-in goods may be sold this way. These efforts are measured as in Item 10 above.

12. Direct Response Selling

Telephone, television, radio, and direct mail, are all used to generate sales on a direct-response basis. The major problem with such sales is creditworthiness, a problem solved in some markets by credit cards. Measurements aim at list or audience evaluation, as well as the bottom-line productivity.

13. Key Account Management and Sales

Since key accounts are of three types—volume buyers, trend setters, and technological leaders—and are mostly handled by specialized managerial sales efforts, both subjective and objective measures of productivity will be important. Among the objective measures are continuity and share of purchases, price maintenance, and the number of products out for trial and evaluation.

More difficult to measure, but equally important, are such factors as the number of levels on which sales relationships are maintained and the number of ideas generated for new products or product modifications, etc. Performance records should be kept by market and by the responsible senior managers.

14. Controlling Product Mix

The direct measurements for controlling product mix are obvious and should be made on the basis of market, channel of distribution, and sales representative.

15. Application Engineering— Label Instructions

The aim here is to find measures of product applicability and customer understanding of product use. For standard products sold through resellers, a reliable measure would be the number of units returned for credit or exchange. For other products with a larger engineering input, the number and timing of service calls may be used. The thickness of the correspondence file accumulated between inquiry and acceptance is also used by some as a serviceable measure.

16. Customer Service

The specific possibilities for customer service are many and varied. Each function assigned will suggest its own direct measures on a per-person, per-market basis.

However, since a prime goal here is to relieve the field salespeople of the need to make nonselling customer contacts, one useful measure would be a decline in the number of sales representative's nonsales contacts. Another useful measure would be the number of direct orders closed without the participation of the outside sales force.

17. Order Entry

In contrast with customer service, the assignments for order entry are quite focused. The order editing function may be measured by calculating an error rate. The credit clearance obligation can be measured by counting the number of eventual credit turndowns or by simply aging receivables by person and market. The effectiveness with which substitutions are recommended can be measured by keeping track of complaints and returns for credit as they relate to product codes.

18. Fulfillment—Installation and Startup

The goal of fulfillment is to reduce the time between the receipt of the customers' orders and the use of their purchases. A comparison of dates is the prime measure here. However, circumstances may suggest other measures. Insurance claims for goods damaged in transit or damaged goods returned for credit would be examples. With larger purchases such as equipment and machinery, the customer signoff dates for installation, startup, and training are required.

19. Warranty and Guaranty:—Maintenance and Repair

The goal in handling warranties and guaranties is to reduce time. In this case, the time between the receipt of a claim and its resolution or the receipt of a request for service and its provision is the key measure.

The number of such requests may be a measure of product quality or of the quality of the usage instructions provided. Here, however, the concern is to reduce the customer's downtime. A secondary measure is the number of complaints about service.

20. Tracking Competition

In tracking the competition, it is vital to know as much about competitors and their activities by market, product, and territory as possible. Knowledge, here, is not subject to strictly numerical measures. This list of 25 common marketing functions provides a guide as to the kind of information needed. Although most of this information can be acquired in the course of doing business, occasionally an outside organization may be required to develop it.

21. Market Research

The market research function is carried out on two levels. Informally, it is an assemblage of surmises, hunches, and conjectures often based on observations and history developed by the sales, marketing, and other company personnel. On a more formal level, research aims at confirming or modifying such hunches and surmises.

Ultimately the quality of market research is measured by overall department performance, testing whether the actions indicated by the market research effort were or were not effective.

22. Training

Measurements of training effectiveness are simple: A continuous improvement in the performance of the functions for which training was provided. What is difficult is the ability of management to ascribe variations in individual performance to the success or failure of the training function.

23. Forecasting

Forecasting requires two kinds of measures. One answers the question: Was the forecast sufficiently accurate so that there were no surprises for manufacturing, finance, or industrial relations? This measure merely confirms that we did what we said we would do. Another necessary measure would be the market-share figures for the forecast period. When compared to these, did our forecast accurately predict total market size and our share of it?

24 & 25 Planning and Managing

The measures here are set out in Chap. 23. These are the aggregate numbers accumulated each quarter and reviewed by the CEO and the board.

The big concern here is pulling together and managing all the elements of a marketing organization in such a way as to achieve agreed-upon goals. All the measures discussed here contribute toward achieving this goal. A fractional contribution to volume and profit from each of the other 23 functional responsibilities will be a sizable improvement overall.

PART 6

Putting It All Together

*"We remain imprisoned by the past as long
as we deny its influence on the present."*
WM. J. BRENNAN

This is not going to be a *"Stars and Stripes Forever"* finale. There are a couple of new ideas to explore, and since our goal is improving the productivity and effectiveness of marketing, we are going to discuss that a bit.

On the preceeding pages we have taken a look at five areas which are critical for most businesses. We have investigated seven kinds of market and the organizations needed to exploit them. We have seen how to develop profitable new products, how to price new products, and how to reprice existing products. We have reviewed the requirements for managing a sales effort and how to measure the important aspects of sales & marketing.

What's required now is a means of putting all this together to make a business grow and prosper in markets that continually change and against competitors that are full of surprises. The conventional approach to all this is through a process of strategic planning. However, common planning processes are not sufficiently flexible to be effective in the changing competitive environment in which we bring our products to market.

The final two chapters, therefore, will review the limitations of the current planning processes, propose an alternative, and suggest ways of using this book to improve the sales & marketing operations of a business.

26
Goodbye to Planning and All That

Proposals for Improvement

It has been proposed by many, over the past decade, that the way to go about improving position in the marketplace is through a process of computerized, strategic marketing planning. That's the proposal, and it just doesn't work. Moreover, there is good reason for its not working, as we shall see.

It is a neat and tidy approach and very appealing. The larger the enterprise, the greater the appeal. The truth is, however, that a successful, healthy business in operation is kind of messy to behold. It moves according to its own logic which is quite a bit different from the Cartesian schemes of the computerized, strategic marketing planners.

Consider these things.

Computerization

There is no question that the computer in the right hands is a very powerful instrument capable of storing massive amounts of data, retrieving it all bit by bit, and manipulating it in astonishing ways. When it comes to marketing planning, however, except in a very few well regulated firms, if the computer is not a distraction—building databases and compiling mailing lists are the current vogue—it is busy churning data which is largely irrelevant to produce information which is mostly misleading. Too frequently, if a computer is involved, the focus is on technology, not on useful information. Computers have been oversold. As just one indication, the Advanced Office Systems Group of Arthur Young & Company reports this situation. Many of the firms with which it works have scores, even hundreds, of PCs in storerooms and warehouses—still in their original shipping containers. When push came to shove, they could find no cost-effective use for the equipment.

Strategy

Strategy is a military concept requiring an enemy and ultimately tested in a pitched battle from which only one victor can emerge. The notion is further complicated by the fact that even military scholars have trouble pinpointing where tactics, short-range plans, leave off and strategy, long-range plans, begins. The current situation is made more complex because, in current usage, the meaning of the word oscillates between its military meaning and the business terms *policy* or *long-term,* or *long-range,* planning.

Marketing

There are as many meanings for the term *marketing* as there are people who use the word. To some it means simply advertising & sales promotion. To others it means these things, plus the identification of markets and the development of new products. Our meaning goes quite a bit further still, covering established and new products as well as established and new markets and includes all 25 of the functions discussed so many times on earlier pages. Ultimately, of course, marketing should signify the entire posture of the organization, anything that affects the relationship of the producer to the customer or prospective customer.

Planning

Here, two words from the current sci-fi vocabulary come to mind: time warp and gridlock. We can plan only what we can do, and the doing takes time—often more time than we had imagined. Yet, planners try to circumvent what is essentially an evolutionary process, to speed up growth with, for example, mergers and acquisitions. In the process they bend time all out of shape.

People who try to acquire new products or to buy into new markets merely substitute one time-consuming process for another and at considerable cost. In most cases, not only are they out the price of the acquisition but they must watch the value of their stock decline on open exchanges and stay depressed for years. Yet, the notion that time can be warped, growth hastened, and evolution circumvented in this way continues to be part of the conventional planning process.

There is yet another part of planning that suffers from a misunderstanding of time. It is illustrated by the "make my numbers, beat my numbers" syndrome. Projects and processes are compressed or extended to fit a time and money grid. The effects are Procrustean, joints are cracked or feet are chopped off. Customers and the markets they make up, as well as the development and testing of new products have a way of not fitting into a time and money grid. They march to their own drummers, and the rhythms keep changing.

To illustrate briefly: a manufacturer of capital equipment had developed a new process for a cash-shy market. Installed, a system costs upward of a quarter of a million dollars. The firm's goal was the sale of three units during the first year the process was on the market. Yet, there was no sales force in place and no financing plan available. There had been little advertising or product public relations activity. Further, the prime prospects required from a year to a year and a half to run through their evaluation, approval, and budgeting processes once they became interested. (See Fig. 2.7: Characteristics of the Industrial Capital Equipment Market.) Nonetheless, if three units were not sold during the first year, the whole effort was to be scrapped.

Clearly there is something wrong here.

Either the planning process itself is misunderstood or the wrong things are being planned. There is, yet, another possibility. It could be that those doing the planning are not the ones who will handle the implementation and so overlook many critical considerations.

In what follows, therefore, we will take a look at the notion of strategy and see what can be adapted beneficially from it to marketing. Next, we will take a look at the planning process itself. Finally, we will review portions of the marketing process to see what portion of it lends itself to planning within a calendar, to the time-and-money grid, and what does not, thus frustrating the usual planning progress.

As for the computer, it is beside the point. It is a useful tool, or a distraction, depending upon how well the strategic marketing part of the planning process has been thought through.

The Military Notion of Strategy: Beneficial Concepts

The word *strategy* is of Greek origin and means either to be a general or to lead an army. Two things go unexpressed. One is the notion of *success*—to be a successful general or to lead an army successfully. The other is the idea of an *enemy;* occasionally, one may have to be invented.

Over the years, strategy has come to mean a plan or several plans for completely destroying the enemy's will and/or ability to resist and for achieving this goal with minimum exposure of our own resources. Over the years, too, the notion of resources has expanded to include, in addition to the armed forces, the economic, political, industrial, cultural, social, and other forces that can be applied by one nation against another. Wars may be won without a shot being fired. Japan, for example, tried military conquest and lost. The same war is now being fought on economic ground. This time, victory seems possible, even likely.

Ultimately, though, the final test of a strategy's success must be a pitched battle from which only a victor emerges. Only in this way can one know for sure if the enemy is unable and unwilling to resist.

In all of this, it is possible to see some similarity between war, military strategy, and what goes on between competitors in the commercial arena.

Business Strategy Defined

By analogy, one can arrive at a definition of business strategy as a plan or several plans for achieving long-term corporate goals, an overwhelming competitive advantage in most situations, with minimum risk and exposure of corporate resources. Conventionally, it is assumed that financial resources including, perhaps, plants and equipment are the ones to be husbanded. Other resources are often overlooked: reputation, trained manpower, established products, markets and, even, morale. These resources may be as important and, on occasion, even more important than financial resources.

Differences between Military and Business Strategy

In spite of these superficial similarities, there are significant differences between the military and the commercial. In the military arena, there are no restraints on what is an acceptable strategy. The Geneva Convention has become a bad joke. The test is simple practicability.

There are, however, real restraints in the commercial arena. While these may vary with the political climate, there are, nonetheless, real legal, social, and economic restraints and, hence, competitive restraints on what are acceptable corporate goals and acceptable means for achieving them. That's the domestic situation. Internationally, the restraints are not as clear.

To follow the analogy further, a test of corporate strategy must occur in the marketplace where the restraints just mentioned plus variable antitrust considerations prevent total victory—achieving and maintaining a 100 percent share of the served markets.

Given the limited nature of the analogy between war and strategy and commercial activities and their planning, there are still a number of important things that can be learned from comparing the two.

Dangerous Distractions

The danger of distraction is real. Military strategy is heady stuff. It is more fun to run with the big boys, talk dirty, smoke cigarettes out behind the barn, and suck beer from a bottle than it is to feed the chickens, mow the lawn, and take out the garbage.

To illustrate: Not so long ago I overheard a conversation among five high-tech MBAs. They were earnestly and seriously comparing Mark Clark's advance up the Italian peninsula from Naples to Rome with Coleco's adventures with its Adam computer and its Cabbage Patch dolls. The efforts to launch Adam were likened to crossing the Rapido under Monte Cassino and seen as a diversion from the real efforts, the launching of the Cabbage Patch dolls and the landings at Anzio. Anzio was, of course, necessary to bail out the unnecessary river crossing. The dolls were just a lucky break. So much for such comparisons. Nevertheless, there may be more to be learned from studying the works of military strategy than the stuff for sophomoric conversation.

Thus, people read Clauzewitz. And, although the experience is like eating sawdust without butter, one can see how strategies escalate. One can see the progression from simple battlefield tactics to the concept of *grand strategy* and *total war* in which all the world becomes an enemy and all of a nation's resources are applied to establishing hegemony over it. There is no cap or limit.

In the business world, hegemony over the world is not a possibility. The notion of overwhelming competitive advantage becomes the analog. Hegemony is probably an easier goal to achieve.

Since much of today's competitive activity is of smaller firms pitted against large organizations with established and entrenched positions, no doubt Vauban's work on the reduction of fortifications will be read. Further, since overseas markets and competition from overseas looms large, we can look forward to Admiral Mahan's great work on sea power being added to the list. And, since Japan seems to be the largest thorn in our corporate sides, one awaits the rediscovery of Homer Lea's the *Valor of Ignorance.*

There are two oriental works on strategy—really tactics—which have been in vogue recently: Japan's *The Five Rings of Musashi* and China's *On War* by Sun Tsu. These are short, charming works replete with the kind of folksy, practical advice that Gabby Hayes, Andy Devine, and Ward Bond used to dish out in the epic westerns of the forties and fifties.

Strategic Aphorisms

What has come from all this, besides the long-range planning process itself, are a number of precepts, which, like most aphorisms, can be adapted to almost any situation:

- To remain in ignorance of the enemy's condition because one begrudges an outlay of silver is the highest form of folly.
- Fight with the sun behind you.
- A fair-to-middling plan, executed in timely fashion, is better than waiting for a perfect plan.
- To be a good general, one must first have been a good soldier.
- The best plan is one that can be adapted to meet changing circumstances.
- Have no favorites among weapons or tactics.
- Divide and conquer.
- Never let the enemy control one's water supply.
- Never force a large engagement when a smaller will do.
- Never attack a fortified position if passing it by will do no harm.
- To defend everything is to defend nothing.
- Without harmony in the state, no military expedition can be undertaken; without harmony in the army, no battle array can be formed.

Thus we find confirmed, from far afield and after much effort, the kind of wise advice one expects and hopes would be offered by seasoned CEOs, directors, and department managers—our corporate wagon bosses, trappers, and Indian scouts:

- Keeping track of competition is critical.
- It is unwise to let the competition know what our plans are.

- Incremental advantage—one-half a percentage point of market share from 10 competitors is still a five-point gain and readily achieved—is better than an overwhelming advantage which may never be attained.
- To manage a sales force well, it helps to know what salespeople do.
- Knee-jerk responses to competitive moves are to be avoided.
- Segment markets whenever possible and profitable.
- Expand distribution or launch new products in market where competition is weak.

Strategy as Buzzword

The list goes on. This search turns up translatable slogans and aphorisms, but in the process, strategy has become a meaningless buzzword.

To illustrate: in describing the resurrection of Digital Equipment Corporation in the spring of 1986, *The Boston Globe* declared that "both Digital strategies—a unified product line and deliverable computer communications—are IBM's Achilles heel." Well, for heaven's sake! Is giving customers what they *need* a strategy?

This situation is further illustrated by comparing the current business-seminar catalogs from the American Management Association, leading universities and other purveyors of business education with similar catalogs issued 5 or 10 years ago. In them, one can find identical programs, if the outlines are to be believed, programs that differ only in title. Thus one finds that *long-range planning* has become *strategic planning; policy formulation* has become *strategy formulation; effective time planning for the salesman* has become *strategic time planning for the salesman,* and so on.

There will always be an ad man. One cannot use other tried and true slogans—new and improved, a hint of mint, or lemon-freshened—to hype courses for business executives. And so *strategic* and *strategy* will have to do.

This buzzword use of strategy is often funny and sometimes sad. Thus a captain of industry said in announcing the $1.5 billion divestiture of a recent acquisition, "The sale is in line with our strategic goals." Could he be saying that he didn't know how to run it and, more important, wasn't making any money with it?

And it is even sadder when a *Fortune* 500 firm states in its annual report that its "business strategy is to engineer into our products real value and customer benefits which will bring premium prices."

There is after all something necessarily impermanent about a strategy. The goals may not change, but the means for achieving them—hence the strategy—will change as conditions change. The implication in this annual report statement (although, since knowing the people involved as I do, it is certainly unintended) is that if circumstances change, the firm might become a *schlock* operation selling Borax and Shoddy. At one time, this idea of value and benefits would have been given permanence. It would have been stated as a company policy, more akin to a way of life (a philosophy of doing business) than to a means of making money—a strategy to fit a particular set of circumstances.

Just as the word strategy has lost its meaning and become a buzzer, the very notion of strategy itself has become a commodity. Not very long ago and in public, the managing partner of a major consulting firm and leading strategic planning boutique said, "You can't sell planning these days, strategic planning or any kind of planning. So, we now sell strategy management, the management of strategy options."

Clearly, something is amiss here. The notion of strategy has become debased.

The Limits of the Planning Process

Perhaps the most significant thing about planning is that, as formal disciplines, both short-term, job, or project planning and long-range, or strategic, planning are relatively new additions to our culture and to our managerial skills.

Requirements for Successful Short-Term Planning

To be sure, short-range, or, in military terms, tactical, planning has been with us since the beginning of time. Thus, farmers set aside seed from each fall's harvest for next spring's planting. Builders have known from the beginning what has to be done and in what order so that a structure could be completed expeditiously. Yet this kind of short-term planning in the commercial arena is only about a century old as a formal discipline. Perhaps it began with Frederick Taylor's conversion of foundry operations from a gaggle of discrete jobs, coordinated through a separate managerial effort, into a smooth flow of work in which each job automatically fed another and for which equipment was designed to optimize rather than maximize human output.

In industry, this kind of planning reached its maturity when Henry Ford combined Taylor's *Scientific Management* with the notion of interchangeable parts, developed by Connecticut watchmakers and gun-smiths, to produce the assembly line.

Since then, there have been many refinements in short-range plan-ning—PERT, CPM, and, more recently, computer modeling.

In all these short-term planning efforts, the goal has been quite clear and attainable: next spring's planting, a house ready for fall occupancy, an automobile built to sell at $500.

The cost and characteristics of the available resources, money, man-power, and materials are also known: a prime rate of 7 percent, me-chanically skilled labor at $6.50 an hour, natural gas at a dollar a therm, the setting time for cement, or the number of steps required to form steel.

The methods and procedures to be followed are known and under-stood: slab on grade, post and beam construction, regional tests and in-troductions, national rollout, etc.

The social, physical, economic, competitive, and political environ-ment in which the job is to be done is also well known: a depressed union community, modern factory space is available, the market has hardly been scratched, competition is asleep, industrial revenue bonds are available.

Experience tells us how long each part of the job takes and hence the total time from start to finish. In fact, a whole job plan modeling tech-nique, PERT, is based on the probability that a given portion of a project will be completed in a specified time. And even the *Old Farmer's Almanac* tells us about next year's growing conditions so that we can plan sowing and harvesting.

A summary of all these ingredients for successful planning is given in Fig. 26.1.

In this way, short-range planning, job planning, or project manage-ment is readily accomplished. To be sure, there is plenty of room for art, innovation, and intuition. But all the ingredients are known and summa-rized in Fig. 26.1. This kind of planning is a skill and readily taught. In fact, one of the American Management Association's most significant con-tributions to American business education was the development of a

---

1. Clear goals and objectives
2. Known resources
3. Established methods and procedures
4. Predictable environment
5. Experience with similar undertakings

Figure 26.1. Five ingredients for short-term successful planning.

nifty piece of programmed instruction which taught supervisors the basics of job planning. It is too bad that this program was not also packaged and promoted for more senior managers where the need was as great. (For a good illustration of short-term planning see sales call planning in Chap. 18.)

Now the focus is no longer on job planning but on project management. This is merely job planning in action.

So much for short-range planning.

Long-Range Planning

Long-range planning or what has come to be called strategic planning is, however, another kettle of fish entirely. If short-range planning as a formal discipline is only about a century old, the acceptance of long-range planning is less than five decades old. In fact, its introduction to our general and business culture can be dated rather exactly.

Of course, long-range social, political, and economic planning were introduced during the early and mid-thirties as part of the New Deal. However, these were thought to be socialistic notions, even foreign. Resistance was great and acceptance very limited. It took World War II to make long-range planning an acceptable idea.

To be sure, there are from the past many examples of what appears to be long-range planning, but these are merely examples of short-range, or tactical, planning extended through time a bit longer than usual. Thus, Alexander located supply depots and supply routes long before he planned his line of march. Napoleon's advance men acquired and assembled horses along a proposed route months before a campaign started. Fresh mounts were available when needed. The Rothschilds had agents in place in major European commercial centers so their banking business could start up quickly at the end of the Napoleonic Wars.

Even the growth of General Motors under Alfred P. Sloan is more the result of job simplification and delegation than of long-range planning.

The difference between short-range, or tactical, planning and long-range, or strategic, planning is very simple and straightforward.

Short-range plans are based on *certainties* or, at least, axioms while long-range plans are based on *assumptions*. The history of World War II illustrates the strengths and weaknesses of planning and the Manhattan project provides a good example of both kinds.

Building the facilities necessary to design, manufacture and test "the bomb" was, for all the massiveness of the effort, merely a series of short-term projects requiring basic short-term planning. Leslie Groves managed these planning and construction efforts very well.

The bomb itself was a different matter. The goal, the controlled reaction of fissionable material, was based on the assumption that the re-action could be controlled. A second critical assumption involved time. It was further assumed that, if at all buildable, a workable bomb would be available in time to influence the outcome of World War II. J. Robert Oppenheimer handled this part of the job under Grove's impatient supervision. The debate still goes on as to whether the second assumption proved to be correct or if, perhaps, the war was already over by the time of Trinity Flats.

A Basic Conflict

The tension that grew between the *general* and the *scientist* was to have been expected. For there is a basic and inevitable conflict between short-term planners, those who undertake plannable projects whose outcome is virtually certain, and long-range planners, those who undertake projects whose outcome is problematic. It is the conflict between management and staff; the conflict between bean counters and R&D; the conflict between action-oriented executives and those who want to "test the assumptions once more."

Figure 26.1 lists the conditions under which planning efforts succeed. In the period since World War II there have been three periods of relative economic stability. The conditions listed in Fig. 26.1 were met over long periods of time. It was possible, then, to develop successful business plans that extended for 5 years and thus qualified as long-range plans. (It is curious that 5 years seem to define the horizon for long-range planning. And it doesn't seem to matter who is doing the planning, American businessmen or the Soviet Union.)

When the economy is stable, what seems to be long-range business planning is possible, but the reality is that such long-term plans are a succession of short-term plans. Now that the economy is again uncertain, the conditions for successful planning listed in Fig. 26.1 no longer apply. Under current circumstances, long-range planning takes another form. Rather than develop just one good plan, many long-term planners are now forced to develop a set of plans—scenarios, if you will—one for each complete set of assumptions about future economic conditions. This brings us once more to the basic conflict that exists between the two kinds of planning. It is probably why so many firms are abandoning long-range planning efforts and letting planning staffs go.

Everyone Plans in Same Way

There is yet another problem with the long-term planning process. Everyone does it in the same way. No one has the advantage of a different kind of planning process. Unfortunately, the planners have all been trained to evaluate the same set of assumptions, assess the same resources, and plan toward similar, if not identical, goals.

One of the reasons that World War II turned out so well was that planning for most contributing projects was in the hands of a bunch of odd sticks of vastly differing backgrounds who reviewed their assignments fresh and without blinders. This was the beginning of Operations Research. The process has congealed into the *interdisciplinary approach* and lost its whacky effectiveness.

In recognition of this problem, the management of some firms have become "Maoists." They change their planning processes periodically, whether they need to or not.

Long-Range Planning: A New Discipline

In all this, it should be remembered that while long-range planning is only five decades old, long-range *business planning* is only about 30 years old—not much time to master such a tricky discipline. For until 1958 when Harper & Row published David W. Ewing's *Long-Range Planning for Management,* most of the discussions and writing about long-range planning or strategic planning was either military in origin or about the military applications of it. Long-range economic or social planning remained suspect.

A military plan for achieving a long-range or strategic goal is generally based on the thorough and simultaneous analysis of the considerations outlined in Fig. 26.2.

This planning process is well-established and is fairly consistently followed. Present a situation to most graduates of any command and general staff school or to most high-tech MBAs and this planning process is all they can see. They are sunflowers, and this is their sun. It is a very powerful process, but in most situations it is overkill.

Look, especially, at Fig. 26.2d—the mission statement, or definition of goal. It is in the middle of the process, not up front. And, although these items are to be considered simultaneously, they usually are taken up one at a time. This may indicate another problem with long-term planning.

The American business and political community was exposed to this kind of planning for the first time and in an acceptable way, when Lt. Col. Albert C. Wedemeyer's Victory Programme was presented to President Roosevelt. The date: September 21, 1941. It was the overall plan for the invasion of Europe and breaking the Nazi war machine.

The plan covered all the points of Fig. 26.2.

a. The current situation, the disposal and characteristics of our forces in relation to the enemy

b. The strength, condition, and disposition of the enemy forces

c. The assumptions about how things will behave and the way they will change with developing events and circumstances

d. A definition of the goal, or mission; what is to be accomplished and the time frame for doing it

e. The execution—how the plan is to be carried out with special attention to the achievement of subsidiary goals along the way

f. The requirements in manpower, materials, and equipment at various stages of execution

g. Administration and logistics—how the program is to be supervised and supported

h. Command—how decisions are to be made and responsibilities are to be assigned

Figure 26.2. Considerations involved in the long-range (military) or strategic planning process.

It proposed a date for invasion, the summer of 1943. Among other things, it discussed the shipping required to move men and materials to Europe and assumed that new technology would be developed to produce that tonnage on time. It was . . .welding ships, not riveting them together. It discussed manpower, both for the armed forces and the number of people who would be required by industry to produce the necessary equipment and materials.

It was an extraordinary piece of work by an extraordinary man greatly aided by circumstances. For in 1938 Wedemeyer had graduated from Germany's *Kriegsakadamie.* There he not only had studied Germany's techniques for warfare, including its innovative use of tanks, but had attended the lectures of Karl Haushofer on *Geopolitik* and *Realpolitik,* the natural power that flowed from any nation that controlled Europe's heartland. This detailed familiarity with the enemy made it a bit easier to keep the main chance in focus.

The timing of the invasion was off by a year—1944, not 1943; three years, not two. The lost time was caused by bickering among allies about tactics. Few long-range business plans come this close to meeting their target dates. But then, few business plans are developed by people who understand their business and their competition as well as Lt. Col. Wedemeyer understood the Germans.

Obviously a planning technique this complete and this powerful would be attractive to any organization that expects to be around for a while. And, although the *Harvard Business Review* dates industry's romance with long-range planning from the publication of the Ewing book, bits and pieces of the process were in use long before then.

By now the vocabulary of long-range planning is in the language, and it is, itself, a relative commonplace. Some people seem to understand the process and its limitations intuitively. Others adopt it and follow along. And yet others, grasshoppers forever, never seem to understand even the rudiments of planning for tomorrow.

The grab-the-money-and-run crowd, for example, let their plants and equipment atrophy, abuse their employees, and write long-term agreements that cannot be kept. Thus steel tries to make do with plants designed for World War II's heavy plate. Others expand and contract their labor force like an accordion and willingly sign labor agreements in good times that will come back to strangle them when things turn down.

Another group slavishly follows: last year, venetian blinds; this year, long-range planning; and next year, wall-to-wall carpeting.

Differences between Business and Military Planning

The lucky few understand the process, take from it what they can use, and forget about the rest. Most important, they understand the few basic but critical differences between successful long-range planning for military purposes and successful long-range planning for business purposes.

These differences are significant.

For strategic, or long-term, military planning, there is one supreme goal which provides focus for everyone involved in the effort. In contrast, a business, especially one of any size, may have several parallel or similar goals which make it very difficult to provide such focus to the planning effort.

It is not just the problem of several goals versus one goal. The conventional objective of long-range, or strategic, business planning is to achieve a dominant competitive advantage by the time one has reached the edge of the planning horizon. If there were only one served market, that might be possible. But, how does one define "competitive advantage" in several markets 5 years out? How can one be sure that the market will even be there?

A second difference involves resources. Military planners can assume that the resources of the state are available to them. Business planners cannot count on such bounty and, one would assume, need to be more careful in the commitment of resources. However, it should be noted that the resources of the state as compared to the resources of business is a relative thing. Thus, the republics of Central America had little chance against United Fruit, and it seems the United States has little chance against the automotive and microelectronics industries of Japan.

But, there is yet another and more important difference. Military planners can assume an enemy. And it is axiomatic that war is easiest to wage and surest of victory if there is a real enemy recognized as such by all the people and if the entire populace, civilian and military alike, knows what must be done to further the necessary and noble cause. The differences between World War II and Vietnam illustrate this quite well.

Statement of Corporate Purpose

This lesson is difficult to adapt to a business situation since it involves shared values, common purposes, morale, and worthwhile goals. When translated for the commercial arena, this idea might come out something like this: "A business will be easiest to manage and surest of success if everyone—clerk, machine operator, salesperson, president, and chairman—knows what the business is all about, if everyone is personally committed to the business, and if everyone understands how his or her job contributes to the success of the business."

Thus a vital ingredient in the long-range planning process and a rallying point for everyone involved is a clear statement of corporate purpose of what the business is all about. And if the organization is made up of several businesses, each of these requires its own statement of purpose. The parent or holding company must agree with these and meddles with them at its peril.

The effectiveness of a clear statement of corporate purposes is readily demonstrated. An industrial distributor, a mill supply house, was doing no better than others in its class. It continually looked for hot items to sell and generally acted as sales agent for the manufacturers whose lines it carried. Very typical.

Then came a realization that they were not sales agents for their principals but purchasing agents for their customers. This simple perception became a statement of corporate purposes. The effect on growth and profitability became apparent about 6 months later.

The alternative would be to make each business a speculator, involved in a continuous series of acquisitions and divestitures, or a compulsive gambler taking a chance on anything that comes along. Some people like to play under these circumstances; others prefer to work where there is a clear statement of corporate purpose.

For example: "We will make money for our stockholders and provide tenured employment for our employees by developing a continuing series of new products based on technologies we understand and which satisfy the real needs of our customers and others like them."

Here is the way another such statement might go: "We design and build the finest _____ in the world and if one fails in service, we will fix it or replace it within _____."

In this instance, the trick is in defining whatever it is that we design and build the finest of. Here the description ought to suggest what services it performs for the user and not merely use the common name of the thing itself. Thus "handwriting instruments" is better than listing "pencils", "pens", "felt-tipped pens" or whatever. By thus allowing for other technologies and writing instruments not yet dreamed of, one prevents the myopia Ted Levitt warned us of years ago.

Had the proverbial buggy-whip manufacturer thought about and defined his business in this way, he might have developed the self-starter, the storage battery, spark plugs, fuel injection, and electronic ignition.

This, however, is only part of the task and relatively easy to accomplish. Once done, it is easy for everyone to understand. It makes it easy for everyone to figure out how each job contributes to furthering the corporate purpose.

What is also required are a few simple statements of what's needed to make this statement of corporate purposes come true. These further requirements in one type of business might be summarized like this:

- What-ever-it-is must be designed and built to make its operation, maintenance, trouble shooting and repair simple and easy.

- Operating, maintenance, and trouble-shooting instructions must be simple, clear, and complete.

- Spare parts must be in adequate supply and conveniently available to all installed equipment.

- Enough well-trained and customer-oriented service technicians must also be available.

- Telephone or other means of easy and rapid communications must be staffed and available so owner-users can get help quickly when they need it.

- Installation and start-up procedures must include training in operations, maintenance, and trouble-shooting procedures. And

- Decent, publically available, financial statements—*D & Bs* or audited annual reports—must be available to assure prospects and customers of sufficient staying power to provide needed support for warranty and quaranty claims.

The simple statement of what a business is all about, plus the seven corollaries, will give the firm its basic direction. Minor amplifications of these points may be required here and there to make sure everyone understands just how his or her job furthers the achievement of these corporate goals. Thus there is the basis of a corporate ethic and culture. Not as convenient as a common enemy or as powerful. But as effective in reducing the planning and supervisory and communication requirements at lower echelons.

There are examples of how this works or doesn't work available to all of us. The *telephone company* provides one such. For years it was a regulated public utility, a monopoly. Its profitable income was assured by periodically negotiated rate changes with utility commissions. Its people and its management could focus on providing and maintaining a high level of service for anyone asking for a phone.

Now, the telephone company must generate income in competition with others offering the same service and comparable or even better equipment. Its management and customer contact people do not yet understand this challenge, so ingrained are they in their old culture. Customers are thought of as people who run up operating costs not as providers of revenue. It vigorously shuts off service when bills are not paid but is diffident about selling equipment and service.

The automobile industry provides another example. The typical, Detroit-trained dealer has a knee-jerk response to customer complaints. It takes two forms: the vehicle is "out of warranty" or, in any case, the customer is wrong. As for their sales efforts, its salespeople are either suede-shoed and chrome-plated, or they can't be bothered. Further, advertising is apt to *seem* deceptive (rain-check requirements do not apply to car dealers), or it *is* deceptive. I have never known a car dealer to lose a franchise because of bamboozling the public. Those car manufacturers and dealers who have bucked that old Detroit culture and take customers and prospects seriously have a growing share of the market.

Conditions for Business Success

There is one more consideration here. If one is to run a business enterprise with a clear statement of corporate purpose, not a long-range plan, then one must know the conditions that must exist for that purpose to be attainable.

If one were to run an automotive repair garage, the requirements are readily established: easily available parts and other supplies, tools, and equipment; a cadre of trained workers, working capital; suitable space for operations; and an accessible market. If any one of these is removed, there is no business.

IBM has thwarted many other businesses by changing the architecture of its computers to eliminate the plug-in compatibility of certain peripherals and by itself entering the software business.

Sometimes defining the conditions that have to exist for the business to exist is not so easy. Banks, for example, once had three quite well defined roles to play. They borrowed money from depositors and loaned it out at a profit; they transferred money for their customers; and, through their trust departments, they managed their customers' money. They performed these services under state and federal regulations.

As long as they were the sole providers of these services, they could easily establish policies as to how these product lines would be brought to market and had little trouble determining the conditions that had to exist so that they could do so. Now, the regulations under which they operate are changing continually and unregulated competitors are springing up all around including, among others, insurance companies and brokerage houses. The traditional foundation of their businesses, near-monopoly control of deposits, has been blasted.

Other businesses don't have quite such problems. If they do, they are usually of their own making.

This all boils down to a simple proposition. If top management can define its business in such a way as to keep everyone bunched up and headed in the same direction, they can forget about long-range planning and buck the planning job down to the operating management level. They will not need long-range planners. Instead, they can use a small staff—call it the "crow's nest"—to continually scan the horizon for signs and signals that the conditions which make the business possible are changing and that the statement of corporate purpose might need revision.

Top management's job, then, becomes one of allocating resources among, and coordinating the activities of, the operating groups: manufacturing, human resources, research and development, finance, and marketing. Each of these, then, has its own planning tasks and parameters are easily established to guide them.

This approach relieves top management of the very difficult task of converting long-range plans into a series of short-term plans. It leaves them with the less difficult, but possibly more demanding, task of understanding the nuts-and-bolts problems of the five functional groups: marketing, manufacturing, finance, research and development, and human resources.

27

Improving Marketing Effectiveness

As we have said elsewhere and in other ways, the marketing effort has three tasks to accomplish:

- To optimize the productivity of existing products in existing markets
- To develop profitable new products and new markets
- To provide the services necessary for these two tasks to be continued smoothly and effectively

Improving what we do in each of these areas is our constant goal.

Breakthroughs

Breakthroughs, which we all hope for, are beside the point. We would all like to see an established product take off or an existing market expand. We all look for and hope to find our own Land camera or silicon chip. We'd all like to identify a new market as physicians have discovered the walk-in emergency room.

And we would all like to find new profitable ways of supporting sales & marketing and serving customers as one particular major pharmaceutical house did in the late fifties. It simply installed a battery of telephone salespeople to sell fill-in goods to drugstores and pharmacies across the country. In doing so, it freed its "detail men" for more productive activities, increased sales, and provided significantly better service for its customers. At the time, this telephone sale effort was a breakthrough of monumental proportions.

However, such sudden, dramatic breakthroughs are rare things. They cannot be planned and they cannot be counted on to happen. Excellence, it has been said, lies in doing the little things well. We don't wait for breakthroughs, therefore, although we never stop looking for the opportunity to make one. Rather, the goal should be to achieve continuing improvements. This means finding situations to improve, creating situations to improve, and always staying with what's possible.

Sales Programs

One area where such improvements are possible is the way we develop sales programs to launch new products and services or to revitalize the sales of existing products. Too frequently, such programs are less effective than they might be. They are unfocused; important participants are often left out; and, occasionally, unfounded assumptions are made about the ability of others to follow through. Figure 27.1 lists the important characteristics of successful programs. It provides a useful checklist for making sure that all the bases are covered.

Sales programs which provide focus for everyone's efforts, however, are few and far between. While they are not as rare as breakthroughs, they are not exactly commonplace, either. We must look elsewhere to find opportunities and, for the most part, they will contribute incremental improvements.

- Is specific and focused
  - Market
  - Customers and prospects
  - Product or service
  - Goal
  - Timetable, check points, and target dates
- Covers all 25 functional responsibilities
- Stresses training
- Assumes nothing, requires the demonstration of necessary
  - Knowledge
  - Skills
  - Attitudes
- Reflects past experience, both the successes and failures of other efforts
- Is based on the real, mutually compatible needs of customer and supplier

---

Figure 27.1. Characteristics of successful sales programs.

Opportunities for Incremental Improvements

Once more, our list of 25 functional responsibilities of marketing becomes useful. It shows where to look for opportunities for improvement.

There are, unfortunately, no generally accepted measurements for many of them. We have proposed a few and urge that measures be developed for all of them. Measurement is, after all, the key to achieving the incremental improvements we seek.

This is not to say that measuring performance is not also useful in determining who gets raises, who gets promoted and who gets transferred, but measuring has another and more important function. It should not only be thought of in terms of rewards and penalties.

By measuring performance, we learn what's possible. If it is possible for one, it is possible for others. To illustrate: In 1954 Roger Bannister broke the 4-minute mile. At that time it was quite a feat. Now such performances are commonplace. The front runners in the Boston Marathon very nearly sustain Bannister's speed for miles on end.

We measure to find the best performer, the least performer, and the middle group. Whether we measure the performance of products, of markets, or of people, the goal is the same. When we find the winner, we try to account for the difference, the better performance. When we have done so, we have something to transfer to others and so expand the area of improvement.

A simple example illustrates the principle. One of the inside salespeople at a firm suddenly began to outperform significantly the others in the group, a group responsible for following up leads and inquiries and converting them into customers. Each member of the group was responsible for handling inquiries from a large geographical area. The high performer worked the factory time zone. What made the difference was coming in an hour before the start of normal business in the assigned time zone. She had found that that was the best time to talk with the typical inquirer, an engineer who came in early. When the rest of the group adopted this technique, performances went up all around.

Building from the experience of the high performers is simple technique, to be sure; but it is one that works, and there is a reason that it does. Most people and most organizations resist change. An idea or a method that is different and new to the organization will be resisted no matter what its promise may be. However, if someone from within the organization is already using it with considerable benefit, resistance will be significantly lessened. Acceptance will be that much more assured.

Obviously, time is limited. Management cannot apply these techniques indiscriminately across the board to all 25 marketing functions.

It needs some way of setting priorities, of determining where the leverage points lie. This is readily done by locating those situations where the spread between the high and middle group and between the high and lowest performer are the greatest. Where the spread is greatest, the opportunity is greatest.

The process works. It is a matter of building from successes already in-house, not continually hoping for a breakthrough or of continually trying to find something new from the outside.

There is a caution here: There are specific situations and possibilities to be aware of.

Changing the Environment

Occasionally, there will be no difference in the performance of anyone or anything. Things just go along, all in a *rut*. In situations like this, the answer is always to make a change, to shake things up, to alter the environment in which people work.

Sometimes, people are involved in the change. A new sales manager is appointed, or a new district manager, or a new advertising manager, or a new supervisor of customer service. This doesn't always mean that somebody will have to get canned; usually a transfer is better. Many firms routinely rotate people through jobs just to keep them from getting stale.

On occasion, other means work better. Faced with such a situation, one firm I know called a lot of favors and had two nearly ready-for-market new products pictured on the cover of *New Product News*. It got more than it bargained for and was swamped by RFPs, RFQs, and simple inquiries. The environment surely changed and so did the performance of everyone, even the performance of other established products. Everything improved.

Staying with the Possible

One way to measure the success of any enterprise is by comparing results with expectations. The extent by which results exceed expectations provides a measure of success. For better or for worse, management has let itself into a situation in which results are to be stated every quarter and compared with the expectations of others. More important, it permits itself to predict the outcome of plans, the generation of income and the advent of new products according to this progression of the calendar.

Not everyone and everything, however, fits conveniently into a quarterly, semiannual, or annual time-and-money grid. People—especially vendors, customers, and prospects—and tests and new products still in development will all frustrate a timetable. This is especially important to keep in mind when something new is being attempted.

If over the years 14 products have been placed on the shelves of Safeway and Jewel, it should be possible to place the fifteenth successfully. A plan can be made to accomplish this and fold it into a budget— our ever-present time-and-money grid. Even if the goal is to place an established product in a new market—say, to expand a supermarket base to include convenience stores—it should be possible to make a successful plan and fold it into a budget. After all, there are many similarities between the two kinds of reseller.

However, when it comes to placing a new product into a new market, expecting to meet a budget-based timetable is unrealistic.

To illustrate, Fig. 27.2 outlines virtually identical procedures followed by two manufacturers of industrial process equipment when they develop and introduce new products to new markets.

One firm has a fairly good record; its successes far outnumber its failures. The other's history is awful.

The effective difference between the two is a simple one. The first firm moves forward relentlessly, but it recognizes that the time required to complete certain steps cannot be predicted with any certainty. It doesn't waste time, but it doesn't take shortcuts either. Such projects are carried as a budget footnote, not as predictable generators of income.

---

*1. Conceptualization completed. Market and competitive information gathered.

*2. Design completed. Suppliers identified. Bills of materials completed. Costs and prices established. Unit prototyped, tested, and photographed.

3. Key account sales under way. Advertising and direct mail started.

4. Inquiry, RFQ, and RFP response packets completed.

5. Sales calls, demonstrations, and trade show exhibits under way.

*6. Orders in-house, edited and passed to manufacturing. Advance payments received.

*7. In-house testing of production models completed. Operating, troubleshooting, and maintenance manuals completed.

*8. Shipments, installations, and acceptances under way. Final payments received.

*The time required to complete these steps is unknown making absolute timetables impossible to prepare.

Figure 27.2. Progress benchmarks for new products.

The other firm forces the process to fit its time budget. It ensures the fit by truncating many steps in the process. Its operating philosophy seems to be: there is never enough time to do things right the first time, but always enough time to do them over.

Implementation

As a practical matter, adopting and implementing the methods and procedures presented on the preceding pages would be an enormous task. For most firms it would probably be an unnecessary one. After all, most firms in business today have been doing something right.

Therefore, rather than try a big effort which would largely be disruptive and alert competition, a better way would be to look for opportunities where a smaller effort would produce a measurable improvement. A procedure like the following would probably do it for most firms:

1. Identify those product-market combinations that generated the most profit with the least hassle and find out why. A reasonable goal, then, would be to find more business like this. Chapters 2, 4, and 20 would provide the guide.

2. The measurements used to evaluate performance in all areas of sales & marketing would next be reviewed and improved where necessary, and new measures would be installed where there were none. Here Part 5 and Chap. 4 would help.

3. The methods and procedures for developing and pricing new products presented in Parts 2 and 3 would be installed.

4. The sales force would be audited, and gaps in the procedures and controls outlined in Part 4 would be filled.

5. A cautious repricing of all products would begin starting with those products supporting the most profitable product-market combinations. Part 3, especially Chap. 13, would provide the guides.

6. Finally, with these efforts under way, it would be time to begin thinking about the nature of the business and its overhead structure. For this, Part 3 and Chap. 26 and 27 would be the guide.

Once this process is under way, it will be found to be ongoing. For, as was suggested elsewhere, running a continuous audit of operations is a major function of management. Management *may* be a science but it is *surely* an art. In the foregoing, I have tried to cover both possibilities. Perhaps I've just suggested them—that could be enough.

Index

A T & T, 10, 14, 78, 147, 216, 218, 349
Absorption accounting, 179, 192
Account potential, assessing, 250
Account records/profiles:
  information to be captured in, 245–246
  management insistence on, 250
  procedure for keeping, 245
  requirement of, 245
  sample form of, 247–249
  value of, 239–241
Acquisitions as source of new products, 146
Actifed, 14
Adams, Abigail, 1
Adams, Samuel, 1
Adaptation of existing products, 152
Added value per employee, 138
Adidas, 133
Adjustable rate mortgages (ARMs), 173
Advanced Office Systems Group, 333
Advertising Age, 96
Advertising and sales promotion:
  by agencies, 98
  allowances for, 28, 34
  for automobiles, 108
  benefits of, in consumer and industrial markets, 103–104
  for blue jeans, 14
  budgets for, sources of information about, 96–97
  buying decisions in consumer products and, 28, 105–106
  for cold remedies, 14
  conditioning customer's expectations, 101
  consumer fads in, 105
  creating a preference, 70
  effectiveness of, 71, 324
  for gasoline, 106–107
  goals of, 99–102
  hype as, 13–16

Advertising and sales promotion (*Cont.*):
  idea progression in, 108–109
  industrial, 104
  inept, 106
  management's attitude towards, 95
  media for, 102–103
  money stressed in discussions of, 98
  product differentiation and parity in, 97–99
  product PR versus, 71
  regional markets in, 101–102
  sold by those who write the rules, 96
  successful, conditions for, 70
  for women's shoes, 107–108
  for white goods, 107
Alternative solutions, cost of, 208
American Enterprise Institute Poll, 4
American Management Association, 339, 341
American Motors, 131
American Optical Company, 73
American Tobacco, 133
America's Cup, 2
Amoco, 107
Amtrack, 78
Andersen windows, 78
Aphorisms, strategic:
  commercial, 339
  military, 338
Applications engineering, 76
  measuring effectiveness of, 326
Ariane rocket, 51
Arnold's bread, 134
Around the World in Eighty Days (movie), 73
Assembly line, 340
Assets, costs and, 192–196
Assumption-based planning, 342
Attitude conditioning, 17
Attorneys, 10
Authorizations in consumer packaged goods market, 29, 30

Auditing:
  of competitive activities, 79
  of corporate operations, 212–215
  of marketing organizations, 119–122
Automotive repair business, 349
Automobiles, 2
  advertising, 108
  as commodities, 9
  corporate culture of dealers, 349
  Korean, 5
  markets for, 54–55
  overproduction of, 9
  quality of, 131
Ayer, N. W., Directory, 52

BIC pens, 150, 170
B & M beans, 134
Back orders, 13
Bankruptcy, 5
Banks, Japanese, 6
Bannister, Roger, 353
Barry, John W., 274, 283
Bear Manufacturing Company, 171
Bechtel Information Systems, 173
Beer, low-calorie, 154
Bell Labs, 140
Benefits:
  presentation of, 235–236
  summary of, 103–104
Bethesda Naval Hospital, 47
Bethlehem Steel, 8
Biograph Company, 15
Blass, Bill, 15
Blue-collar productivity, growth in,
  3
Blue jeans, advertising for, 14
Boeing Aircraft, 176
Book-of-the-Month Club, 49
Borrowed capital, cost of, 188
Boston Globe, 21, 339
Boston Marathon, 353
Bottom line, defined, 187
Botts, Alexander, 219
Brand names, generic use of, 113
Break even prices, 196
Breakthroughs, 351
Brennan, William J., 331
British Airways, 78
Broad product offerings, 132
Brokerage house analysts, 11
Brown Williamson, 133, 298
Browning, E. B., 23

Budget:
  advertising, 96–97
  as time and money grid, 335
Burberry, 15
Burden in pricing, 179
Burroughs, 67, 136
Business to Business Yellow Pages, 60
Business goal, defined, 189
Business strategy, defined, 336
Business Week, 11, 21
Business news, 11–13
Buying decisions:
  advertising and, 28, 105–106
  in consumer markets, 34
  defining markets, 25
  in industrial markets, 36, 37, 39, 41–43
Buying motivators, 104
Buying signals, 264
Buying sophistication and market
    segmentation, 53

CAD/CAM, 167
CEOs, 12
  as customer service managers, 77
  as marketing directors, 112
  role in new product launches of, 176
  and short term goals, 12
CPM (Critical Path Method), 341
Cabbage Patch Dolls, 66
Cake mixes, 151
Call frequency, formula for, 229
Call itineraries and reports:
  prcedure for making and keeping, 242
  simplified form for, 243
Call objectives, setting, 234
Campbell's Soup, 126, 132, 134
Cannibalism, 31, 170, 175
Capacity, estimated, 195, 196
Capital, cost of borrowing, 188
Capital accounts, 306
Capital goods market, 41–43
  segments of, 54, 60
Captive markets, loss of, 170, 173
Cardon & Cherry, 98
Carlson, Chester, 145
Catalogs:
  in industrial support consumables
      market, 36
  overstuffing to impress prospects, 154
  role in establishing market prices, 31
Caterpillar Tractors, 2
Challenger disaster, 51

Chambord Liqueur, 70
Cherry, John, 98
Chevrolet Beretta, 108
Chevron, 107
Chief executive officers (*see* CEOs)
Church & Dwight, 65
Cigarettes, 133
Circuit boards, 9
Clark, Mark, 337
Clausen pickles, 134
Clauzewitz, Karl von, 337
Closing sales:
　in sales call planning, 237
　in telephone selling, 264, 267
Coca-Cola, 5, 13, 170, 175, 188
Cold remedies, advertising for, 14
Coleco, 337
Colgate-Palmolive, 68, 98
Collection procedures, 202
College education as consumer durable
　good, 32
Combination of existing products, 151
Competitive audits, 79
Competitive prices:
　analysing, 197–99
　copying, 178
Competitive technologies, 78
Computers, 333–334
　components for, manufactured
　　overseas, 3
　cost reductions for super-minis, 140
　four-segment market for, 58
　maintaining account records with, 250
　ratio analysis of sales performance with,
　　319
Confessions of an Advertising Man
　(Ogilvy), 16
Consultants:
　and market research, 163–164
　and new market evaluations, 123
　and quality control, 5
Consumer markets, 25
　contrasted with industrial markets,
　　66–67
　customer benefits in, 104–106
　durable goods, 32–35, 182
　limits of growth in, 86–87
　packaged goods, 27–32, 181
Contests, 279
Converse, 133
Copying products, 146
Corning Glass, 78

Corporate culture, 349
　new product guidelines and, 142
　sales force and, 221–224
Corporate inputs to selling process, 295,
　296
Corporate operations audit, 212–215
Costs:
　and assets, directed and assigned,
　　193–196
　of capital, 188
　of sales calls, 290
Country Living, 172
Coupon promotions, 100
Creditworthiness, 77
Critical Path Method (CPM), 341
Crompton and Knowles, 153
Crossley, 148
Cuisinart, 151
Cullinet software, 170
Curtis Mathis, 35
Customer benefits, 104
　in advertising, 104
　in consumer markets, 104–106
　in industrial markets, 103–104
　in sales call planning, 235
Customer needs:
　differences between, as basis for
　　segmentation, 60
　in establishing prices, 177
　unfulfilled, as basis for market, 57
Customer requests as source of new
　products, 154
Customer service, 117
　duties of, 76–77
　as marketing responsibility, 76
　measuring effectiveness of, 327

Dalcon Shield, 95, 106
Dating, 203
Datsun, 148
Davis, Robert T., 282
Davis Cup, 2
Davis-Standard, 152
Decision screen, 165–174
Decision making (*see* Buying decisions)
Deere, John, & Company, 137, 143
Defense Department, U.S., 323
Defensive marketing, 137, 138
Del Monte, 134
Department stores, walk-in primary health
　care in, 58
Designer name products, 29, 147

Dichter, Ernest, 105
Dick, A. B., Inc., 58, 152
Digital Equipment Corporation, 339
Direct costing, 192–199
Direct response selling:
  as marketing responsibility, 74
  measuring effectiveness of, 326
Direct sales, 135
Disclosure Information Group, 172–173
Discounters:
  American style, in Japan, 6
  price advertising of, 35
Discover, 172
Distribution:
  in consumer packaged goods market,
    29
  in industrial make or buy consumables
    market, 39
  in industrial support consumables
    market, 36
  of overhead and profit in start-ups and
    mature firms, 191
  physical, goals of, 72
Dodge Reports, 304
Donnelley, R. R., 60
Double entry process, 77
Doyle, Dane & Birnback, 67
Dun & Bradstreet, 214
Du Pont Corporation, 40, 147

EPA, 8, 304
Earnings per share, 11
Earthworm Tractors, 219
Eastern Air Lines, 78
Easylink, 170
Economy:
  as news, 11–13
  transitional, 8–11
Edison, Thomas Alva, 15
Eighty-twenty rule:
  in allocating sales calls, 228
  in launching new products, 175
Elf Aquitaine, 53
Emerson, Ralph Waldo, 66
Empire State Building, 5, 53
Entrepreneurs, 142
Environment, changing, 354
Equity capital, cost of, 188
Erosion of profits, practices causing,
    201–204
Etonic, 133
European Common Market, 2

Evolution in marketplace, 148
European Space Agency, 51
Exchange policy, 203
Expectations, customer's, 101
Expected value, 252–254
Extended terms, 203
Extenders, 31
Exxon, 107, 173
Ewing, David W., 344, 346

Family Media Group, 172
Farley, James D., 5
Fashions in advertising, 15–16
Federal income from taxes on industry, 4
Federal Trade Commission, 214
Field Sales Managers (Davis), 282
Field supervision of sales force, 281
Fill-ins, 149–150
Finance, corporate, 167
Fine Woodworking magazine, 8
Fire apparatus, 57–58
First Jersey Securities, 95, 106
First National Bank of Atlanta, 188
Fisher Hi-Fi and Stereo, 2
Five Rings of Musashi, The, 338
Five year planning horizons, 343
Fixed costs, 194
Flankers, 31
Florida Citrus Commission/Florida
    Department of Citrus, 31, 247–249
Focus groups:
  in consumer packaged goods market-
    ing, 32
  in development of Polaroid's slide
    projector, 79
Following up leads (*see* Lead conversion)
Forbidden Fruit Liqueur, 70
Ford, Henry, 340
Ford, Model T:
  customer requested change and pick-up
    truck, 154
  design and price of, 178
Ford Motor Company, 131, 178
Forecasting, 250–254
  expected value in, 252, 254
  inputs for, 81
  as marketing responsibility, 80
  measuring effectiveness of, 328
  reality tests of, 252
  requirements and use of, 250
  sample form for, 251
Fortune 500, 339

Franklin Mint, 95
Freedent, 66
Freight policy, 202
Friends Beans, 134
Fulfillment, 88, 327
Functional responsibilities of marketing,
    summarized, 65

Gablinger's beer, 154
Gasoline:
    advertising, 106–107
    price wars on, 211
General Agreement on Tariffs and Trade
    (GATT), 7
General Electric, 67, 108, 169
General Foods, 113
General Mills, 175
General Motors, 5, 9, 138–139, 141,
    178–179, 342
Generating leads (*see* Lead conversion)
Geneva Conventions, 336
Gillette-Papermate, 170
Girlie magazines, 52–53
Goals of measuring performance,
    289–292
Gresham, Thomas, 13
Grid lock in planning, 334
Groves, Leslie R., 342
Growth patterns, 83–93
    in consumer durable goods market, 86
    in consumer packaged goods market,
        84
    in industrial capital goods market,
        92–93
    in industrial make-or-buy consumables
        market, 91
    in industrial process consumables
        market, 91
    in industrial support consumables
        market, 89
    in start-up businesses, 83
Guaranties (*see* Warranties and guaran-
    ties)
Guilt, advertising based on, 105

Haloid Company, 145
Hamilton Test Systems, 171
Hanes, 109
Harper & Row, 344
Harvard Business Review, 345
Hasbro, 172
Haushofer, Karl, 345

Health care, walk-in, 57–58
Hearst Corporation, 172
Harmon-Kardon, 2
Heinz, 134, 217
Helots, Japanese, 7
Hershey Chocolate Bars, 72
Hewlett-Packard, 143
Hierarchical organizations as apparent
    norm, 115
Hierarchy of needs, 105
High investment intensity, 137, 138
High quality products, 131
Hiring challenges for marketing organiza-
    tions, 116
Hitachi, 6
Honda, 95–96, 109, 141
Hoola-Hoop, 147
Hormel, 134
Houghton Mifflin Company, 152
House of Representatives, U.S., 78
Hustler magazine, 52–53
Hype, 13–16
Hyundai, 6

IBM, 59, 67, 96, 102, 104, 116, 122, 133,
    136, 148, 170, 211, 339, 350
Iacocca, Lee, 108, 219
Ideal Toys, 146
Ideas for new products, sources of,
    summarized, 146
Identifying and qualifying leads, 256
Implementation of procedures, 356
INC. Magazine, 141
Incentive compensation:
    basis of payoffs in, 284
    booby traps of, 283
    frequency of payoffs in, 285
    model plans for, 286
    sales performance and, 274
Incremental improvements, achieving,
    353–355
Individuals, importance of, in consumer
    and industrial markets, 67
Industrial markets, 25
    advertising and sales promotion in, 104
    capital goods, 41–43, 54, 60
    contrasted with consumer markets,
        66–67, 104
    consumables: make or buy, 38–41
        process, 37–38
        support, 36–37
    customer benefits in, 103–104

Industrial markets (*Cont.*):
  growth in, 88–93
Industrial Truck Association, 304
Inertia, 39
Information economy, defined, 9
Inquiries, handling, 256
Inside sales:
  as marketing responsibility, 74
  measuring effectiveness of, 325
Installation, 88, 327
Instant press market, 38
Institutional campaigns, 108
Instruction books, customer indifference
  to, 26
Interest payments, 189
Invention of new products, 145
Inventory line items, 31
Inventory liquidation, 215
Investment intensity, low, 137
ITEK, 38
Itineraries:
  procedure for keeping, 242
  simplified form for, 243
Ivory Soap, 53

Japan, 4–6, 347
  American acceptance of products from,
    135
  GM plants managed by, 138
  Ministry of International Trade and
    Industry, 6
  in satellite launching business, 57
  as supplier to Detroit, 2
Jefferson, Thomas, 1
Job enrichment, 279
Johnson & Johnson, 69, 113, 147
Johns-Manville, 147
Just-in-time delivery, 4, 5

Keds, 133
Key account management and sales:
  management's responsibility for, 75
  as marketing responsibility, 74
  measuring effectiveness of, 326
Kiam, Victor, 8, 219
Key Set phone equipment, phasing out of,
  10
Knock-offs, 147
Kodak, 69, 80, 132, 147
Koh-i-noor, 150
Kondratief waves, 126
Korea, 2, 5, 6

Kunnan Enterprises, 2
KWIK-KOPY, 152

Labor:
  cheap offshore, 6–7
  cost of, as price determinant, 179
Laboratory of Advertising Performance,
  97
Land, Edwin, 146
Lauren, Ralph, 29
Lea, Homer, 338
Lead conversion, 71–72, 255–271
  buying signals in, 264
  causes of failures in, 11, 255, 258
  levels of response: with inquirers, 256
    with qualified prospects, 258
  new customers in, 267
  sales department involvement in, 268
  signs of trouble in, 202
Lead generation:
  as marketing responsibility, 71
  measuring effectiveness of, 324
Le Funelle, 145
Lemming response to competitive pricing,
  211
LeMenu, 134
Lemon laws, 78
Lever Brothers, 68
Leverage points, 190, 191
Levitt, Theodore, 348
Licensing as source of new products, 147
Life Cereal, 31
Life cycle of industries, 125, 126
Liggett & Myers, 133, 298
Line extensions, 132
Linear organizations, 114–16
Lionel Trains, 8, 169
Liquid lawn fertilizer, packaging of, 69
Liquidation of inventory, 215
Long-range planning, 342–343
  assumption-based, 342
  difficulties of converting to short-range
    action, 350
  examples of, 342
  as new discipline, 344–346
  scenarios to match assumptions in, 343
  strategic planning equivalency in, 342
  uniformity of planning process in, 344
Long-Range Planning for Management
  (Ewing), 344
Lord, Geller, Frederico, and Einstein, 106
Lorillard, 133, 298

Lost business report:
  contents of, 268
  preparation of, 265
Low-calorie beer, 154
Lower prices, causes of, 247
Lowenstein, M., 28
Lumiere Brothers, 15

McAn, Tom, 107–108
McDonald's, 125
McGraw-Hill, 97, 241, 255, 290, 304, 315
Made in USA as buying motive, 15
Magnavox, 147
Mahan, Admiral A. T., 337
Maintenance, 78
"Make nice," 16–17
Management blunders in new product identification, 126, 168
Management by Objective (MBO), 17
Management consultants (see Consultants)
Management fads, 17
Manhattan Project, 342
Manufacturer's rebates, 34, 202
Manufacturer's reps:
  in industrial capital goods markets, 43
  service provided by, 229
Manufacturing:
  analogy with marketing, 293
  costs and product profitability, 214
  capacity: and Gross National Product, 2
    and establishing costs and prices, 195
  Japanese know-how in, 6
  role in new product selection of, 167
  subcontracting, and loss of technology, 5
Maquiladoras, 7
Margins, healthy, 134–135
Market audits, 157–159, 212
Market economy, defined, 9
Market research, 159–164
  assuring participation in, 163
  as marketing responsibility, 79
  measuring effectiveness of, 328
  questionnaire for, 161–162
  requirements for success in, 79–80
  sample size for, 160
  simplifying factors in, 161
  who should conduct, 163
Marketing:
  analogy with manufacturing, 293
  defined, 63

Marketing (Cont.):
  functions, in new or segmented markets, 119–122
  goals of, 111–112
  high-tech discipline of, 20
  measuring effectiveness of, 289
  new product development and, 167
  responsibilities of, summarized, 65
  tasks of, 351
Marketing organizations, 63–81
  dynamic, 64
  hiring challenges of, 116
  modeled by job function, 117, 118
  non-linear, 115
  problems common to, 64
  reporting relationships in, 116
  standard organization impossible for, 63–64
Markets:
  advertising and, 95
  defined, 23
  identification and development of: as marketing responsibility, 66
    measuring effectiveness of, 323
  product management versus, 113–114
  segmentation of, 49–61
    automotive market, 54–55
    capital equipment market, 54
    considerations influencing, 54
    defined, 50
    impermanent nature of, 51
    narrow, 132, 133
    needs of customer as basis of, 59–60
    requirements for successful, 61
    size, 51–53
    as source of new product ideas, 151
    vendor's needs as basis for, 60
  share of, 8, 133
  (See also Consumer markets; Industrial markets)
Marriott, J. Willard, Sr., 77
Maslow, Abraham, 105
Massachusetts, 171
Massachusetts General Hospital, 98
Materials, cost of, 179
Matrix organizations, 114–116
Maytag, 108
Measurement, 289–292
  of effectiveness of marketing functions, 321

Measurement (*Cont.*):
  of performance, 353
    manufacturing, 293–294
  of return on capital, 298, 300–303
  of sales productivity, 299
  of total marketing productivity, 297, 298
Media, advertising, 102–103
Medical centers, walk-in, 57–58
Mejors, 30
Melville Shoe Company, 108
Men's shoe market, 137
Merlin telephone systems, 10–11
Merrill-Lynch, 148
Me-too products, 97–99
Mexico, Border Industrialization Program of, 7
Middleman, elimination of, in cost control, 148, 218
Middle class, declining, 3
Military organization, 115–116
Military strategy, 336–338
Milk runs, 230
Milton-Bradley, 172
Mini-mills, steel, 8
Minimum wage, 3
Minute Maid, 150
Mission Oaks Hospital, 57
Mitsubishi, 6
Mobil Oil, 107
Models:
  functional, of marketing organization, 117
  computer, as planning tools, 341
Monitary incentives (*see* Incentive compensation)
Monopolies, 51
Monroe, Marilyn, 108
Morris, Robert, Associates, 214
Mortgages:
  adjustable rate, 173
  income required to support, 3
Motivation of sales force:
  identifying areas for performance improvement, 725
  matching motivators to individuals, 277
  monitary incentives, 282–288
  non-financial motivators, 277–282
  role of supervision in, 281
  three-dimensional problem of, 273
Motley, Arthur H., 220
Motor oil, shrinking market for, 215

Motorola, 109
Mrs. Paul's frozen fish, 134

National Aeronautics and Space Administration (NASA), 51–52
National Business Employment Weekly, 151
National Geographic, 77
Nestle's Quik, 31
New Deal, 342
New Hampshire, 135
New markets:
  developing, 124
  entry into, 122–123
  hazards of, 122
  management for, 123
  tests to identify, 123
New marketing organization, building, 119–122
New Product News, 354
New products, 129–143
  attitudes about, 165
  competitive offerings evaluated, 169
  in consumer markets, 25, 35, 175
  decision to proceed with, 173
  defined, 136
  effect on existing products of, 169
  in industrial markets, 26, 37, 38, 175
  as joint activity of many departments, 167
  launching: CEO and sales force in, 176
    competitive response to, 170, 175
    costs of, 171
    progress bench marks, 355
    successful, 173
  manufacturer's qualifications and, 168, 169
  new markets and, 112
  other options compared with, 172
  participation in evaluation of, 168, 279
  questions about, 166
  rejected, analysis of, 173
  samples versus production models, quality of, 169
  sources of ideas for, 145–155
  strategies for, 170–171
  team for, 168
  tests of, 171
New technologies, introduction of, 42
New York Stock Exchange, 106
New York Times, 21, 109
Newspaper advertising, 30

NIC's Supershops, 6
Niches, 49
Nielsen, A. C., 30
Nike, 133
Nomura Securities, 6
North American Phillips, 147
North American Rockwell, 178
Nuclear Regulatory Commission, 17

OEM market, 38–41
Objective criteria in buying decisions, 25
Objectives of sales calls, 234
Ocean Spray, 134, 217
O'Day Sloops, 6
Offset duplicator markets, 58
Offshore labor, 4
Ogilvy, David, 16
Old Farmers Almanac, 341
Operating philosophy versus strategy, 340
Operating ratios, corporate, 212–214
Operating statement, bottom line format, 189
Operations research, 344
Oppenheimer, J. Robert, 343
Optical scanners:
    acceptance and growth of market for, 135–136
    in consumer packaged goods marketing, 30
Order acceptance, 77
Order entry:
    creditworthiness verification in, 77
    double entry process, 77
    marketing and manufacturing responsibility for, 77
    in matrix organization, 115
    measuring effectiveness of, 327
    recommending substitutes in, 77
Organization charts, 114
Osborn Computer, 170
Outside sales:
    justifying use of, 72
    marketing responsibility for, 73
    measuring effectiveness of, 325
    reality versus image of, 74
Overcapacity, 215
Overhead:
    growth in, 212–215
    and profits, charged against products, 191

PERT, 341

P & G, 143
POP, 152
Packaging, 38
    controlling costs through, 217
    for ease of use, 69
    to increase consumption, 69
    to introduce product to new users, 69
    as marketing responsibility, 68
    measuring effectiveness of, 323
    more important than content, 70
    of Portland Cement, 56, 59
    segmentation and, 56
    size, price, and shelf space, 69, 177
Paperback books, pricing of, 178
Paper clips, packaging of, 69
Parade magazine, 95
Parity products, special advertising and promotional challenge of, 97–99
Parker Brothers, 146
Patriotism in advertising, 14
Peach Bottom Nuclear Plant, 17
Pella windows, 78
Pennsylvania Department of Agriculture, 162
Pension liability, 8
Penthouse magazine, 52
Pepperidge Farm, 134
Pepsi-Cola, 13, 169–170
Percent of sales ratios, 212–215
Perceived value, 177
Perdue, Frank, 219
Perdue Farms, 31, 176
Performance measures:
    goals of, 289–292
    to guide investment of corporate funds, 293
Personal selling, 33, 35
Peterson's Field Guide to the Birds, 152
Phases of the moon pricing, 178
Philadelphia Electric Company, 17
Philip Morris, 113, 133, 298
Phillips Electronics, 136
Phillips head screws and screwdrivers, 145
Phone company (see AT&T)
Physical distribution:
    goals of, 72
    as marketing responsibility, 72
    measuring effectiveness of, 325
Pick-up trucks:
    genesis of, 154
    high quality of, as passenger vehicles, 131

Piel Brothers, 154
Planning:
  failure of, 335
  limits of, 340–347
  as marketing responsibility, 81
  and new product guidelines, 143
  (See also Long-range planning;
    Short-range planning)
Playboy magazine, 52
Polaroid, 79, 146, 147, 150–151
Polk, R. L., 304
Popsicles, 72
Portland Cement, 56, 59
Positioning problems with versatile
  products, 68
Porter Cable, 8
Poverty level for family of four, 3
Predatory pricing, 216
Preferences, creation of, 30
Preferred lending rates, 188
Prego Spaghetti Sauce, 134
Prell Shampoo, 69
Price codes and optical scanners in
  consumer packaged goods marketing,
  30
Price to cost ratios, 196
Price to earnings ratios, 11
Price increases, necessary, 217–218
Price and quality continuum of product
  offerings, 149
Pricing:
  assumptions underlying, 205, 206
  customer needs and, 177
  with direct costing, 195–196
  by market: consumer durables, 33, 35,
    182
    consumer packaged goods, 28, 181
    industrial capital goods, 184
    industrial make or buy consumables,
    184
    industrial process consumables, 38,
    183
    industrial support consumables, 183
  as marketing responsibility, 70
  measuring effectiveness of, 324
  what traffic will bear in, 178, 205–209
Pride as sales force motivator, 277
Priestley, J., 289
Prime rate, 188
Primordial guilt, 105
Prince tennis rackets, 2
Procedures as sales force motivators, 278

Procter & Gamble, 68, 100, 113
Product champion, 127
Product design and development:
  as marketing responsibility, 66
  measuring effectiveness of, 322
  (See also New products)
Product differentiation, 31, 38
Product life cycles, 125
Product line growth as basis for segmenta-
  tion, 56
Product management, 113–114
Product-market audits, 212
Product mix:
  as marketing responsibility, 75, 76
  measuring effectiveness of, 326
Product profitability:
  with absorption accounting, 192
  with direct costing, 192–196
Product positioning, 18, 68
Product quality:
  advertising and, 95, 106–109
  in automotive industry, 131
  and reputation of firm, 131
Product specifications, 38, 87
Product strategy:
  as marketing responsibility, 69
  measuring effectiveness of, 323
Product versatility, 68
Production capacity, 195, 196
Production values versus benefits in
  advertising, 15
Productive assets, rate of return on, 194
Productivity:
  growth of, 3
  measurement of, 297, 298
Productless advertising, 14
Profit:
  erosion of, 201–204
  in industrial markets, 36–37
  versus ROI, 187
  (See also Product profitability)
Profit Impact of Market Strategy (PIMS),
  97, 129
Pro-Kennex tennis rackets, 2
Promotion, 31
  as marketing responsibility, 71
  measuring effectiveness of, 324
Prospects, required information about,
  258
Pruning product lines, 152–153
Puma, 133
Purchase orders, 268–270

Purchasing from third parties as source of new products, 146

Qualified prospects, 258
Quality assurance, 4
  consultants and, 5
  in service markets, 46
  as shared responsibility of marketing and manufacturing, 64
  (*See also* Product quality and differentiation)
Quality circles, 18
Questionnaire, market research, 162

RCA, 67, 169, 216
R & D, 139–141
ROI:
  as financial versus business goal, 189
  investment intensity varies inversely with, 137
  market share and, 133
  as measurement of success, 188
  new product volume and, 136
  options for achieving, 190
  pricing goals and, 189
Radio Shack, 35
Ramset device, 152
Rank, J. Arthur, 146
Rate of return on productive assets, 194
Rath & Strong, Inc., 5
Ratio analysis in controlling sales performance, 316–319
Ratios, control:
  calls per day, 310
  costs per call, 311
  sales per call, 311
  special, 309
Raytheon, 178
Rebates, 34
  as potential cause of profit erosion, 202
Reebok, 133
Records, account and territory, 241–242
Reese, Michael, Hospital and Medical Center, 98
Reengineering, 216
Regional markets, 2
  advertising in, 101–102
Rejects and failures as source of new product ideas, 153
Reliance Electric Corporation, 173
Remington Products, 8, 152, 176
Repackaging existing products, 150

Repairs, 78
Reporting relationships in marketing organizations, 115
Republican Party, 15
Reputation of producer, 67, 131
Research, market (*see* Market research)
Research and development (R & D), 139–141
Resellers:
  in consumer durable goods markets, 32–35
  in consumer packaged goods markets, 27
Responsibilities of marketing, summarized, 65
Retail clerks, training of, 35
Return on assets managed/capital employed, 305
  as measure of marketing effectiveness, 306
Return on equity, 11
Return on investment (*see* ROI)
Return policy, 203
Return on total capital, 12
Reverse engineering, 148
Reynolds, R. J., Tobacco Company, 133, 298
Richardson & Robbins, 134
Robotics industry, 139
Rockport shoes, 133
Roger & Gallet soap, 53
Roosevelt, Franklin D., 5, 344
Rothschilds, 342
Russia:
  planning in, 343
  as satellite supplier to U.S. industry, 51

S & H Green Stamps, 14
S & W, 134
SIC (Standard Industrial Classification), 26, 96, 258
Sales calls:
  as basic inputs into selling process, 296
  budget of, 226
  cost of, 290
  frequency of, formula for, 229
  number per day in various types of selling, 296
  planning of, 232
    anticipating resistance, 236
    closing, 237
    follow-up, 238

Sales calls, planning of (*Cont.*):
  organizing benefits, 235
  as short-range planning, 342
  setting objectives for, 234
Sales control ratios:
  graphic display of, 313–315
  using results of analysis, 315
  variation among territories, 312
Sales force:
  call budget for, 226
  corporate culture and, 221–224
  as disruptive force at factory, 222
  as order takers versus business builders,
    223
  priorities of, 225
  territory coverage by, 229
  tough questions for management on,
    224
Sales inputs into selling process, 295–296
Sales managers, 220
Sales programs, 352
Sales promotion:
  direct sales and, 135
  goals of, 71
  as marketing responsibility, 71
  measuring effectiveness of, 324
  (*See also* Advertising and sales promo-
    tion)
Sanborn Process, 151
Sanders Associates, 147
Sanko Steamship Company, 5
Sanyo Sewing Company, 15
Satellite launching business, 51–52, 57
Schwepp's, 101
Scientific management, 340
Scott, H. H., 2
Scripto-Wilkinson, 170
Sears Roebuck, 35, 147
Second sourcing:
  in industrial make or buy consumables
    market, 39
  in industrial process consumables
    market, 37
  as new product launch strategy, 170
Securities and Exchange Commission
  (SEC), 97, 173
Sedelmaier Production, 98
Selchow & Righter, 146
Self confidence as sales force motivator,
  277
Self scoring achievements as sales force
  motivator, 278

Selling:
  as lonely occupation, 221
  as oral tradition, 222
Selling process:
  corporate inputs into, 295
  sales department inputs into, 296
Service economy, defined, 9
Service markets, 43–47
Share of market:
  data on, 305
  and sales compensation, 275
Shelf space allocation in consumer
  packaged goods markets, 30
Shell Oil, 107
Shipping to stock:
  in consumer packaged goods markets, 5
  in Japan, 4
Shoes, markets for:
  athletic, 133
  men's, 137
  women's, 107–108
Short-range planning:
  based on certainties, 342
  as formal discipline, 340
  requirement for successful, 341
  tactical planning and, 340
Silver Pages, The, 60
Singer Sewing Machine Company, 35
Sippican Ocean Systems, 178
Sloan, Alfred P., 342
Slogans, 31
Slotting allowances in consumer packaged
  goods markets, 27
Smith, Adam, 1, 2
Sony Walkman, 140, 145
Sources of volume as indicators of
  corporate health, 13
Spartan, 178
Spaulding tennis rackets, 2
Specialist-client relationship in marketing
  organizations, 115
Specifications, product, 38, 87
Spiffing, 71
Sports Illustrated, 172
Standard Industrial Classifications (SIC),
  26, 96, 258
Stanley Cup, 2
Start-up, 88, 327
Statement of corporate purpose:
  and corporate culture, 349
  corollaries to, 348
  examples of, 347–348

Statement of corporate purpose (*Cont.*):
  missing in most planning, 347
Status, need for:
  as basis for market segmentation, 59
  in establishing prices, 177
Staying with the possible, 355–356
Steel production, 6, 8
Stereo and hi-fi, 2
Stevens, J. P., 29
Stimtech, 147
Stockouts, 30
Stokeley, 134
Strategic aphorisms:
  commercial, 339
  military, 338
Strategic planning:
  equivalent to long-range planning, 342
  as management fad, 18
Strategic Planning Institute, 97, 129–130
Strategy:
  as buzzword, 339–340
  as commodity, 340
  defined, 336
  as marketing responsibility, 67
  measuring effectiveness of, 323
  military notion of, 335, 336, 346–347
  successful, tests of, 336–337
Stratus Computer, 133
Subaru, 135
Subcontracting, 5
Subjective criteria in buying decisions,
  25
Sudafed, 12
Sunbeam bread, 134
Sun Tsu, 338
Sununu, John H., 135
Swanson foods, 134
Sweatshops, Japanese, 7

TRW, 151
Tactical and short range planning, 340
  strategy and, 334
Tanaka Memorial, 5
Tandem Computer, 133
Targeted ROI, pricing to achieve,
  195–196
Taxes, 4, 10
Taylor, Frederick, 340
Technological leaders as key accounts, 75
Technology:
  loss of, 5
  new, introduction of, 42

Teflon, 154
Telemarketing, 74
  as management fad, 18
  versus simply using the telephone to
    sell, 255
Telephone company (*see* A T & T)
Telephone selling, 74
  (*See also* Lead conversion)
Television selling, 74
Telex, 170
Tennis rackets, overseas production of, 2
Tenured work force, Japanese, 6
Terms of sale, 202
Territory coverage, 229, 230
Texas Instruments, 80, 172, 199, 211
Texas Oil and Gas, 8
Textile industry, 8
Thackeray, William Makepeace, 125
Theft as source of new product ideas,
  144
Threat to business, identification of, 350
3M Company, 67, 143, 152
Three zone pricing, 196, 197
Third party interviews in competitive
  audits, 79
Time Inc., 17, 172
Time-and-money grid, 355
Time warp in planning, 334
Todd, Mike, 73
Tooth picks, 69
Topsiders, 133
Toro, 95, 109
Total capital, return on, 12
Towne-Oller, 30
Toyota, 139
Tracking competition:
  as marketing responsibility, 78
  measuring effectiveness of, 328
Trade discounts, 204
Trade practices as cause of corporate
  failure, 201
Training:
  as marketing responsibility, 80
  measuring effectiveness of, 328
  of retail clerks, 35
Transfer orders, 30
Transitional economy from commodities
  to specialties, 9
Turnover rates, 212–215
TV-Cable Week, 17, 172
Two-way communication as sales force
  motivator, 278

Two-dimensional organization charts,
114

Underwood, 134
Underwriter's Laboratory, 162
United Fruit, 347
United States:
  as banana republic, 3
  income from taxes on industry in, 4
  national debt of, 6
  presidents concerned with image, not
    accomplishments in, 12
  as two class society, 3
U.S. Steel, 8
United Technologies, 171
Univac, 67
Universal distribution, 72
Unprobated wills, 10

V-8, 134
Valor of Ignorance (Lea), 338
Value:
  in buying decisions, 26
  expected, 252–254
  perceived, 177
Value pricing, 208
Van Camp beans, 134
Vauban, Marquis de, 337
Video games, 149, 172
Vietnam War, 347
Vlasic pickles, 134
Volkswagen, 66–67, 171
Volume:
  as basis of market segmentation, 56
  as measure of corporate health, 13, 297,
    302
Volume buyers as key accounts, 75
WD-40, 50
Walk-in medical centers, 57–58
Walkman, Sony, 140, 145
Wall Street Journal, 151

Wamsutta Supercale, 28
Wang Labs, 78, 102
Ward's bread, 134
Warehouse withdrawals, 30
Warranties and guaranties:
  in consumer durable goods marketing,
    33
  as marketing responsibility, 78
  measuring effectiveness of, 327
  support for, as potential source of
    profit erosion, 203
Wealth of Nations, The (Smith), 1
Wedemeyer, Albert C., 344–345
Welch's juice, 134
Western Electric, 140
Western Union, 170
Westinghouse, 106
Whirlpool, 108
White collar productivity, 3
White goods advertising, 108
White Letter tires, 218
Wills, unprobated, 10
Wilson tennis rackets, 2
Witchcraft in setting prices, 178
Women's shoes, advertising, 107–108
Wonder bread, 134
Woolworth, F. W., 57
Work force, percentage in sales and
  marketing, 3
World War II, 343–347
Wrigley's gum, 98, 113, 126

Xerox, 70, 92–93, 145

Yellow Pages, 60
Young, Arthur, & Company, 333
Young & Rubicam, 98
Yuppies as mythical marget segment, 50

Zenith, 109
Zippo Manufacturing Company, 136

About the Author

Stewart A. Washburn is a Certified Management Consultant whose practice focuses on making sales and marketing people more effective on the job. His clients include Fortune 500 firms, many smaller companies and a number of associations and governmental agencies. Mr. Washburn is a founding member of the Institute of Management Consultants, immediate past president of its New England Chapter, and practice development editor of the *Journal of Management Consulting*. He teaches the sales and marketing portions of the Institute's Fundamentals of Management Consulting program. Mr. Washburn is recognized internationally as an authority on sales and marketing management; his work on these subjects is published widely. In *Managing the Marketing Functions*, he shares some of the techniques and attitudes that have helped make his clients successful.